Peter FitzSimons is a journalist with the *Sydney Morning Herald* and *Sun-Herald* and a former national representative rugby union player who is passionate about sport and sportswriting. He is also a regular TV commentator, a former radio presenter (with Mike Carlton on Radio 2UE) and a best-selling author of nearly twenty books. These include *Tobruk, Kokoda, Batavia, Eureka* and biographies of Nancy Wake, Kim Beazley, Nene King, Sir Douglas Mawson, Nick Farr-Jones, Steve Waugh and John Eales.

Greg Growden worked for the *Sydney Morning Herald* for 34 years, and was chief rugby correspondent between 1987 and 2012, covering hundreds of Test matches around the world. During this time he also wrote about a multitude of sports including rugby league, cricket, AFL, and even once had the main race at a Wentworth Park greyhound meeting named after him. He is now a rugby expert for ESPN and *scrum.com*. He has written eleven books, including *A Wayward Genius*, which was described by *The Guardian's* Frank Keating as among the 100 best sporting books of the twentieth century.

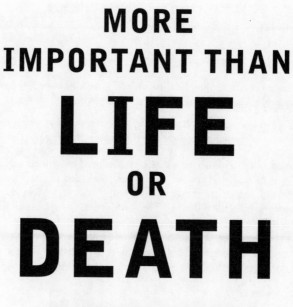

MORE
IMPORTANT THAN
LIFE
OR
DEATH

INSIDE THE BEST OF
AUSTRALIAN SPORT

EDITED BY
PETER FITZSIMONS
AND **GREG GROWDEN**

FAIRFAX BOOKS
ALLEN&UNWIN

The following articles were originally published in the
Sydney Morning Herald, *Sun-Herald*, *Sport&Style* magazine,
Good Weekend magazine and the *Age*.

Fairfax Books, an imprint of
Allen & Unwin
Sydney, Melbourne, Auckland, London

83 Alexander Street
Crows Nest NSW 2065
Australia
Phone: (61 2) 8425 0100
Email: info@allenandunwin.com
Web: www.allenandunwin.com

Cataloguing-in-Publication details are available
from the National Library of Australia
www.trove.nla.gov.au

ISBN 978 1 74331 319 0

Cover design by Darian Causby
Set in 10.5/15 pt Electra LT and Bell Gothic by Midland Typesetters, Australia
Printed and bound in Australia by Griffin Press

10 9 8 7 6 5 4 3 2 1

CONTENTS

CONTENTS

INTRODUCTION

Peter FitzSimons

Sports is in my blood, and the love of it is in my very soul. And as I have related in my memoirs, for me, just like for many Australians, it started at childhood . . .

For they say if you had a happy childhood you remember the sun shining, whereas if you had an unhappy childhood you remember wet Wednesday afternoons trudging home from school.

Me? I remember sun shining—and always on a specific scene. Waking up on the verandah of our farmhouse at Peats Ridge, just north of Sydney, I would get the cricket bat out from under the bed and walk very purposefully towards the cricket ball Dad had suspended beneath a gum tree. And as I walked, I could always hear the great ABC cricket commentator Alan McGilvray describing in his dulcet tones the final day of the deciding Ashes Test.

'And here's FitzSimons and Redpath, coming out to open the batting for Australia,' he would say as I, with studied nonchalance, adjusted my baggy green cap. 'They have a very big job in front of them indeed. Australia needs some 361 runs to win this Test match against England, and it is absolutely *crucial* that they get off to a very good start . . .'

Alas, alas, we never did. 'Redders' always let me down horribly by giving his wicket away cheaply, both Chappell brothers also threw their own wickets away by uselessly flailing away outside the off stump and in the end it was up to me and my great friend Dougie Walters to put on a double-century partnership for Australia to get the innings back on track. But even then, we were far from home. For just after we brought up our double ton, Dougie's middle stump was simply uprooted by that man Snow, to cartwheel over and over in the classic fashion. It was then that I knew that, more than ever, it was going to be up to me.

Smack!

Smack!

Smack!

'That's his third four in a row, as the ball smashes into the fence in front of the Members Stand! The SCG has never seen anything like it as FitzSimons brings up his 150 and lifts his bat in acknowledgement to the crowd!'

Thank you, thank you, thank you all!

After giving a special cheerio wave to my Dad—who I knew would be especially proud—my happiness would have been complete if only the brutes down the other end didn't continue to let me down. I was tired, but still settled, focussed on the task at hand.

And as that old gum tree still stands witness, it was a very big ask indeed, but I still thought that with Dennis Lillee helping me we could do it . . .

And so while all of Australia listened in intently through that whole unbelievable afternoon, not daring to believe we could get there, but *willing* us forward all the same, D.K Lillee and I went after the English attack. God bless Dennis, he had some pluck, I'll say that for him. He didn't know a lot about batting, but by dint of constant encouragement and tips from me that I'd originally got from my dad—'keep your left elbow up, Dennis, and keep the bat straight'—he was able to hold up one end while I simply tore them apart at the other. Single by single, four by four, the target came closer, as Alan McGilvray worked himself into a progressively higher state of excitement.

'And so ladies and gentlemen, we come to this unbelievable situation, unprecedented in cricket history. On the last ball of the day, Australia needs five runs to win, with only one wicket in hand. FitzSimons is on strike, as John Snow steams in towards him. Both sides can still achieve victory as Snow unleashes . . .'

SMMMMMMMMMMMMMMMMMAAAAAAAACK!

'Is it . . ? Has he . . ? Yes I think he's going to make it! SIX! SIX! SIX! FitzSimons has hit a six right in the middle of the Sydney Cricket Ground Hill! Australia has won the Test! They've won the Ashes . . !

They were great afternoons, the more so because quite often after winning the Ashes for Australia, I would still make time to completely annihilate Jimmy Connors on the tennis practice board in the first rubber of the Australia vs America David Cup tie. And if there was still time before Mum called me for dinner, my good friend John Newcombe and I would wrap up the whole thing by beating the Yanks in the doubles, with our good mate and team-mate Ken Rosewall watching nervously from the stands.

Such were the joys of sport for me as a young tyke, a joy that was aided and abetted by reading the pages of the *Sydney Morning Herald*. I particularly remember loving the work of Jim Webster on rugby and the Olympics, Alan Clarkson on rugby league and—most significantly, in terms of the way things would turn out—a bloke by the name of Jason Dasey, who wrote a piece about once being picked up hitchhiking by the man who was then coaching the Manly Sea-Eagles.

That particular column by Dasey gave insights into the character of Ray Ritchie and took me, the reader, well away from the usual fare of match previews, and post-match reviews and placed me in an entirely different scene. It planted for me a seed of what sports writing *could* be, and maybe . . . just maybe . . . what I might be able to attempt as a sportswriter myself.

The years passed, and though the closest I got in reality to scoring a century for Australia in an Ashes series was getting 73 not out for the Knox U/14Ds— where, I might add, I would have got a century if Hugh Sinclair hadn't insisted on setting off on a suicidal run, *not that I am bitter*. I did get into the Wallabies, whereupon I came to know the *Sydney Morning Herald* sportswriter Greg Growden, whose work I also admired.

It proved to be a very propitious friendship for in 1986 when I got it into my head to write an article for the *Herald* on Italian rugby, I made two quick calls. The first was to Greg, saying I wanted to relate what it was like to play rugby in Italy—where I had spent the previous season—with a view to the *Sydney Morning Herald* possibly publishing it. When he said, 'Go for your life' and that he would recommend my piece to the sports editor, my next call was to the landscaper friends I was working for, saying I would not be shovelling sh*t for the next two days.

And so for two days and two evenings I wrote eight hundred words, and then re-wrote, and then re-wrote some more, using a pen and endless reams of A4 paper, not to mention *gallons* of coffee. I tried to work in every funny line I could think of, every insight, every anecdote, every bit of my rugby soul.

Late Tuesday afternoon, I was finally done. I sent it to Greg Growden, who passed it on to the sports editor, Tom Hammond, and I went back to labouring the next day. At morning-tea time, I went down to get the papers, picked up the *Herald*, turned to the back page and there . . . was nothing. Stone-cold, motherless, nothing.

Bugger. *Bugger.* BUGGER!

Who had I been kidding that the *Herald* would ever publish my wretched article? Back to shovelling sh*t. BUGGER!

Then, next day, I did the same and. . . NOTHING.

On Friday, crushed, knowing it would be more of the same, I went to morning-tea, picked up the *Herald*, turned to the back page, knowing I was going to be humiliated one more time and . . . and . . . AND THERE IT WAS! At the top of the back page! All my words, completely untouched!

MY ARTICLE!

Peter FitzSimons

Game over. At that moment, I kid you not, I knew there was nothing I loved doing so much as writing, and being published, and twenty-five years later, I still have the same joy in it as I did that day. An entirely new world had opened up to me . . . and looking back upon it, I was privileged to be joining Fairfax at a time when fantastic sports writing was flowering all around me.

For that quality that I had first noticed in Jason Dasey's piece, something encompassing colour and movement and insight and humour and *everything* that took the reader beyond a mere factual account of what happened, or a prediction of what would happen, has since bloomed everywhere and the best of those blooms are in this book. What I most love about sports writing, is the sheer stunning *diversity* of it all.

Among other pearls in this collection we have Richard Hinds' yarn on the leap of Leaping Leo Barry—the whole backstory of what everyone was doing, what they were thinking—as Barry launched himself skywards for 'The Mark' that would win the Sydney Swans the 2005 Grand Final. It is a classic example of print journalism at its best, taking the reader to a place that the TV cameras can't go, actually inside the head of the sportsperson in question, juxtaposed with what his father was thinking at the same time.

'As Barry took off, in the crowd of 91,898, there was probably only one man who had no doubt what would happen next. Leo Barry snr is a big country bloke with a broad smile, a firm handshake and a nice way of making what would be one of the greatest moments in the history of grand finals seem as inconsequential as Leo jnr climbing a particularly tall tree on the family farm. "He loves a challenge, my boy," Leo snr would say later. "He just loves a challenge".

Love it!

I love the insight of Greg Growden's tight piece on the hundred things he loves about rugby union: 'The craic of Dublin. It never claims to be the greatest game of all. Nick Farr-Jones meeting Ringo Starr in Monaco (ask NFJ). Robin Williams meeting Jonah Lomu and telling onlookers: 'Quickly! Tell the other villagers we go now!"

Against that high hilarity, I defy anyone to not feel at least a little teary when reading the pathos of Jessica Halloran's profile of Jelena Dokic, of how insane her sporting life became under the tutelage of her father, Damir.

There are the illuminating reminiscences of Roy Masters about what it is to coach an iconic rugby league team like St George; the high dudgeon of the late Peter Roebuck calling on Ricky Ponting to be fired from the captaincy of the Australian cricket team, closely matched by the disgust expressed by Peter Stone on the subject of Tiger Woods' *industrial*-level adultery. And then there is the sheer love *and* understanding of cricket displayed by Malcolm Knox in every paragraph on the subject.

(I will never forget Malcolm's first column for the *Herald* as the paper's official cricket correspondent, when he referred to Shane Warne as a 'mug lair'. This man is a *legend*, I thought to myself . . . And Shane Warne can just get over it.)

In sum, sports writing has come a long way in a short time, but this collection is not just sports writing at its best, it is *writing* at its best. In no other daily round of a newspaper is there as much scope for a writer to show his or her wares, to evoke time and place, to evolve their craft with time, to take readers to places they never imagined existed.

I am honoured to have worked with most of the fine writers you will be reading in the following pages, and congratulate my first mentor in journalism, Greg Growden, on both his own writing and for his astute selection of these sporting pearls—a process I have been honoured to contribute to.

I commend the book to you.

Peter FitzSimons

THE PAIN

Moments of glory attract the biggest sporting headlines, but what is often forgotten is the pain involved in the result, or in just being part of a sporting life.

Many sportspeople endure tough moments, and some of the more excruciating are discussed in this opening chapter. One of the most revealing stories of this collection is the first, where Jessica Halloran investigates the fraught relationship between tennis player Jelena Dokic and her father, Damir. Jessica flew to Miami to interview Jelena, who revealed the extent of the physical abuse she had suffered at the hands of her father. There were ramifications after the story was published. Damir threatened to blow up the Australian embassy in Belgrade. He was later arrested and jailed. The article won the Australian Sports Commission's award for best feature in 2009.

Michael Cowley's account of how Swans captain Jarrad McVeigh and his wife Clementine coped with losing their daughter in 2011 is another poignant story.

'The Swans skipper played out the season, but not surprisingly had not been put before the media, nor spoken in public about the ordeal,' Cowley said.

'And as far as I was concerned, he didn't need to. That was beyond football, and while of course it would be a touching, good story to get, to chase it, you felt like you were crossing the line.

'But in late January 2012, the club contacted me and told me that Jarrad wanted to sit down and chat about Luella. It was thought that as captain he would have to face the media at some point, and would be asked about the matter. So the club and Jarrad felt it would be better if he just spoke to two journalists—one from Fairfax, one from News Ltd—told his story in full and hopefully that would be the end of the matter, making it much easier for him to get on with his football.

'I wasn't sure what to expect when we sat down, but by the time I walked away an hour later, I was amazed at how open and honest, brave and emotional, Jarrad had been.'

GG

JELENA DOKIC

Jessica Halloran

Pearls fall down Jelena Dokic's back where bruises once tarnished her caramel skin. She idles on a tennis court in a ball gown, diamantes decorating the nape of her neck. She's laughing now, where hours earlier she was soberly explaining how she'd escaped the physical rage of her father, Damir.

The beatings have been rumoured about for many years, but finally Dokic, 26, has chosen to speak to *Sport&Style* about the pain inflicted on her by the hands of her father. She has turned down tens of thousands of dollars to confide to this magazine about how she escaped the abuse, then fell into a private hell as she attempted to recover from those traumatic years.

Once you know and hear more about her darkest days, you realise how remarkable this young woman is. As she rests on the penthouse balcony ledge, looking out at the Biscayne Bay in Florida, it's clear she's far removed from the girl she once was.

You may remember the lonely-looking teenager who never contradicted her father's words or actions no matter how outrageous they were. In 1999, when Damir was arrested after being ejected from a tournament in Birmingham for calling tennis officials 'Nazis' during her match, she explained he was just 'cheering'. In 2000, aged just 17, a stony-faced Dokic said: 'I don't care what people say and do to my Poppa—the bond between us, my mother and [brother] Savo, no one can break.'

Two years later, in October 2002, Dokic packed her bags and ran after a tournament in Europe. She slipped a letter under the door of her mother Ljiljana's hotel room. She wrote she'd had enough and would be with her boyfriend, the Formula One driver Enrique Bernoldi. A shocked Ljiljana rang Damir in Serbia—he was outraged.

On a cloudy spring day in Miami, Dokic says she had no choice but to flee what she terms 'the situation'.

From the first moment the tennis clique noticed Dokic swinging her racquet, there were murmurs of Damir abusing his daughter. In early 1997, then just 13, Dokic was urged to take action against a man who allegedly assaulted her during a junior tournament. Victorian Police investigated, but she did not take further action.

An early coach who had a hotel room next door to Damir and Jelena heard her being slapped around. Her Fed Cup teammate Rennae Stubbs has said she saw bruises left by Damir. During the Sydney Olympics, Stubbs pleaded for Dokic to stay in the athletes village. 'Stay here, he can't get in here, he can't get to the courts,' Stubbs said. Dokic replied she was afraid for her family and couldn't leave them.

How did she survive this? Dokic lets out a tense sigh before answering, but her face remains stoic. 'I left when I was 19,' Dokic says. 'But there was nothing anyone could really do. It was up to me . . . It's the only thing you can really do.' Her dark eyes pop in surprise when her actions are described as 'courageous'. She says finding the will to leave was easy. 'There was no other way I could deal with the situation I was in . . . I decided to do it . . . The following three, four years I really struggled mentally. But if I had to do it again I'd do it—maybe sooner.'

She admits she thought life would be easy once she escaped the emotional and physical abuse of her father. But while at first Dokic felt a freedom, the following months brought long periods of depression. Months where she would sleep for up to 18 hours a day, wake up, eat excessively, then return to bed. 'I fell apart emotionally, mentally,' Dokic says, in her curt way.

'I couldn't handle life—the way it was—let alone tennis.'

Dokic didn't just leave behind an abusive father; she left a family unit. While she eventually resumed communication with Ljiljana, she did not speak to her nine-year-old brother, Savo, for two years. 'When I left, I left everything behind. 'No one was there to come with me. I was alone.

'There was a period where there was nothing that could make me happy. Nothing I could do. Nothing anyone could do. I just wanted to get out of my own skin. I wanted somebody else's life.'

While there have been traumatic days in the past where she wanted to be somebody else, at the Australian Open in January [2009] there was no doubt who Dokic wanted to be. On the eve of the Open she was a wildcard with a troubled reputation, but her intoxicating resurgence soon won the country's heart. 'The whole thing got really emotional for me after the first-round win,' Dokic says.

The Jelena wave of love started to roll in round two, when she knocked out her first seeded opponent, Anna Chakvetadze (No. 17). 'That was really huge,' Dokic says. 'It was the first time in a long time that I played on a big court, in front of a big crowd.' Then she took down Caroline Wozniacki (11) before knocking out Alisa Kleybanova (29). She had us all at fever pitch when she almost defeated world No. 3 Dinara Safina in the quarter-finals.

Dokic may not have made it through to the semi-finals that day, but she won over the Australian public after saying how unconditionally apologetic she was for the past. She entered that grand slam without a tennis uniform and exited with a $1 million sponsorship from an airline. She has also recently signed a deal with Lacoste.

Dokic's recent on-court success was how it was always supposed to be for the daughter of immigrants who moved to Australia from Serbia in 1994. Originally they lived on social-security payments. Her mother worked in a bread factory in Sydney, while Damir, a former boxer and truck driver, dreamt of coaching his daughter to tennis greatness. 'We came because life was hard [in Serbia] and the tennis was better here.'

In 1999, at 16, she burst on to the tennis scene when she thrashed world No. 1 Martina Hingis 6–2, 6–0 at Wimbledon. The Dokic family celebrated in their cheap London hotel room by eating bread and cheese. At this stage ranked 129, Dokic's career soon blossomed, and she reached a career high ranking of No. 4 in 2002, winning five tournaments on the way.

In Damir's eyes, all that hard work he had her doing as a little girl was paying off. As an 11-year-old, she would rise four days a week at 6 am to commute by train from the family's small flat in Fairfield, in Sydney's west, to the White City tennis venue in Paddington. She would always be the first at training; smashing, not hitting, the ball against the wall to while away the time.

'Her work ethic was superior to the boys,' says an early coach, Craig Miller. 'Coaches were impressed by her ability to train without stopping, turning down water breaks, because of her dedication to her game.' But her training partners noticed she never laughed. She was robotic. Her father would tell her to 'stop smiling' during training and 'not to be friendly on court'.

When asked what her memories are of being a little girl, Dokic initially says she doesn't want to talk about it. Later she does. She says she remembers it being painfully tough not being able to speak English well, and being very quiet despite having a burning desire to be loud. 'I'm an Aries,' she says. 'I'm full of energy, but because I was in a difficult situation I was closed, shy. I was not talking or smiling that much. Maybe people thought I was arrogant.'

As for that fierce face on court that we still often see, that was also a product of her childhood. 'I had to be emotionless. There were a lot of things going on; I had to deal with everything at the same time. Maybe that's why I cracked in the end. Why things went wrong.'

Those 'things' always involved her relationship with Damir. His list of offences is long. Publicly, she constantly defended her 'Poppa'. But it was Damir's performance over the price of a meal at New York's Flushing Meadows in 2000 that gives the deepest insight into his extremely volatile behaviour. 'Ten dollars for a piece of fish—it's criminal,' Damir shouted in the US Open players cafe with Dokic by his side. From there the rage grew. The half-hour torrent of abuse saw him spit the phrase 'f—king US Open' at least 20 times. He called Women's Tennis Association CEO Bart McGuire a 'gangster'. He lunged at his daughter and violently ripped her competitor accreditation from her neck. He was eventually ejected while crying out: 'Fight me, fight me.' Two hours later, a journalist called Dokic at her New York hotel room. Sobbing, she dutifully translated for her father. 'We have to fight the Jewish in New York,' Dokic quoted her father as saying. 'We're not scared to fight. I don't care if they put a bomb in the plane.'

It's a miracle Dokic is still playing after enduring such maniacal episodes. 'I've been through a lot worse than anybody on the tour,' she says, quietly sipping a soft drink. 'When you go through stuff like that, playing a tennis match is easy. Even if I lose, or don't play well, I'll be disappointed, but it's not the end of the world. When I win today, it's so much more satisfying.'

When she escaped, Dokic also left behind a fortune: career earnings in the millions. So, while her mother currently lives in a bedsit in Fairfield on a pension of $550 a week, her father lives on a million dollar property in Belgrade. Dokic says she doesn't care that his property, dotted with thousands of plum and pear trees, was bought with her money.

'When I left I wasn't as well off as I could have been, for obvious reasons,' Dokic says. 'It was just another thing I had to deal with; another thing that was taken away from me. I don't have feelings for material stuff. It doesn't bother me that much because I still have the ability to earn and to be financially stable. At times it was not easy, but that was the least of my worries.'

While Dokic may look like an ice princess, she is warm and kind-hearted. She's caring and vivacious. When she laughs, it is beautiful because it's such a rare sound. Her face lightens. The person responsible for this positive change in her life is Tin Bikic.

Dokic met Tin, a small, muscly Croatian man with a warm nature, in Monaco just three months after she left home in 2002. Her romance with Bernoldi had fizzled. She soon moved in with Tin and his brother Borna, who is now Dokic's coach, in Zagreb. She says that their relationship is the only 'good consistent thing' that she has had in her life so far. Tin has seen her 'go crazy'. He's endured the terrible mood swings; she'd be fine for a few hours, then sobbing for the next few. 'It went around in a circle like that,' Dokic says. Tin has also heard Damir's claims about him and his brother. 'I believe they drug her,' Damir once said. He also claimed that Tin and Borna had kidnapped Jelena. Yet it was Tin who researched depression and tried to find the right people to help her.

On reflection, Dokic, who at one stage ballooned to 83 kilograms, believes she should have taken a longer hiatus from the sport. 'We tried to find ways to get better,' Dokic says. 'Whether it be going to talk to somebody, or just talking between ourselves. [Tin] didn't know how to deal with the tennis part—whether I should play or take time off. Neither of us knew.

'We have a really good relationship. We fit together. He really helped me get through. He saw me at my worst and at my best.' When asked if he'd be interviewed, a smiling Bikic raises an index finger to his lips and says 'Shhh!'. 'He's very closed to outside people,' Dokic explains later.

Despite the hell Damir put his daughter through, Dokic has tried to reconcile with him. For 10 days the family reunited in October 2004 at his property in Vrdnik. Her father's thinking hadn't changed. He detested Tin. 'It's been impossible,' Dokic says. 'I've given up.'

It's this honesty and bravery that has made the Australian public love Dokic again. For years we were distracted by her father's antics. So now, by herself, what does she dream of becoming? She doesn't imagine she'll be remembered as a 'great'. It's a desperately hard slog for her: she's still carrying weight from her break.

'Just because I had the situation that I had and the four-year lay-off that I had, I don't think I can ever really have a 15-year career and be great,' Dokic says. 'I would like to win a grand slam. I would like to be No. 1. But just to be in the top 10, top five, it would be an unbelievable achievement.'

When asked about the troubling memories, she says they have become part of her. 'Whatever has happened, good or bad, will always stay there,' Dokic says. 'It makes you what you are.

'We can't pick who our parents are and what happens. When you have a situation like mine, you just deal with it.'

7 May 2009

I'M PROUD OF HER: DAD'S TRIBUTE TO LUELLA

Michael Cowley

Jarrad McVeigh leans forward on the couch, offering his phone for shared viewing. As he flicks through the photos of his daughter, Luella, you can hear the pride in his voice—punctuated by a gulp of emotion—and see the love in his face as he scrolls from one picture to the next.

Every father's photos are special, but these, and the accompanying memories—many painful—are all the Sydney co-captain and his wife, Clementine, now have of their baby girl.

Luella was born on July 25 last year with a serious heart condition. Four weeks later, on August 24, she lost her fight for life in Sydney's Westmead Hospital.

Speaking for the first time about the family's loss, McVeigh admits his emotions span the spectrum when looking at pictures of his daughter's month-long life.

'Sometimes I just find myself looking at them and maybe cry, or I'm happy,' he says of the photos. 'I think after every game I played at the end of the year, I'd go and sit in the toilet and just look at my phone.'

He says he's happy to be finally talking about his little girl, because he's so proud of her. 'She's touched a lot of people here at the club, a lot of people who never met her, even though she was here for only a short time,' he says.

'There was a little spirit in her that everyone who saw her could feel. She was a very strong little girl. She went through a lot of trauma with four operations and kept fighting back [but] it came to a point where there was nothing anyone could do.'

As the first anniversary of Luella's birth approaches, the emotions the McVeighs are feeling will be heightened by the fact that Clementine is due to give birth to another daughter in July.

She fell pregnant in Italy two months after Luella died. The couple had decided to go overseas to try to work through their grief. 'To get away from everything, to spend time together and heal together, was very important for us,' McVeigh says.

The first most people knew of McVeigh and Clementine's tragedy came on Saturday, August 27, last year, three days after Luella's death.

Wearing black armbands, the Swans stunned Geelong (who also wore black armbands in honour of Luella) by ending the Cats' 29-game winning streak. The emotion of the moment was personified by the sight of McVeigh's close friend and co-captain Adam Goodes in tears after the game.

'I think that's the first game Clementine has watched fully. That [win] put a smile on our faces,' McVeigh says.

Goodes, who, along with coach John Longmire and teammate Jude Bolton, was among a close group who had shared the McVeighs' tragic journey, recalls how 'incredibly hard' it was to get ready for the game.

Just four days earlier the trio and another mutual friend had made the sombre journey to bid farewell to, as Goodes says, 'a brave little soul'.

'We went out and saw Luella—it may have been 12 hours before she passed—and we all said our goodbyes,' Goodes recalls. 'The next couple of days you are just shaking your head saying how the hell does this happen to two fantastic people?'

The year had begun with such promise for the McVeighs. Knowing they were pregnant with their first child had brought extra joy to their Christmas and New Year celebrations at the end of 2010.

But that excitement quickly turned to anxiety when they went for the standard three-month foetal scan in January last year [2011]. The monitor showed their tiny baby had fluid around its heart. Every fortnight for the next six months, they travelled to the hospital for scans as doctors monitored their daughter's condition.

'From January to July, that was the hardest part—not knowing what the actual issue was,' McVeigh says. 'The whole pregnancy went really well. We didn't have any complications with anything else. Clementine had a natural birth and . . . [Luella] was a good size.'

But as soon as she arrived, it was clear how fragile Luella's condition was.

'One of the hardest parts for Clementine was as soon as Luella was born, she only got to hold her—every mother wants to hold their baby—for about two minutes before they took her away.'

The McVeighs moved into a flat across the road from the hospital, and spent every moment they could with their daughter.

'Horse [Longmire] was great and gave me a lot of time off,' McVeigh says. 'I could always speak to him openly and there were a few tears, but he understood, he's got children and everything comes second.'

Doctors found the left side of Luella's heart was half the size of the right and scheduled an operation. 'We walked her to the surgery area and . . . just before she went in, she opened her eyes to us, just to say "I'll be all right."'

The operation was due to start at 8 am and last for four to five hours. It went for 10 hours after doctors realised that Luella's circulation was back to front. Suddenly the McVeighs' beautiful little girl was living minute to minute. 'Slowly that got to hour by hour, then they moved her into the intensive care unit, where we could go and see her, but they had six or seven doctors beside her 24 hours a day. Her chest was still open at this point and . . . I actually couldn't look. Seeing her chest open and the heart beating, just with a bandage over it, it was too hard for me at first.'

Luella had retained large amounts of fluid in her body as a result of the surgery and doctors were unable to close her chest because it would have placed too much pressure on her heart.

'We ended up massaging her for up to 10 hours a day trying to get [the fluid] out—myself, Clementine, her mum, my mum, Clementine's sister, all rubbing her, and she seemed to respond well to that,' McVeigh says.

But Luella's condition deteriorated and she was still retaining fluid. The multiple surgeries had left her with severe brain damage. Then doctors discovered that her right lung was half the size of her left. 'We didn't know at that point [that the end was near] but I think the doctors did.'

The hospital gave the McVeighs one last night together as a family. 'They put us in a room with her and gave us a double bed. They took as many of the wires and stuff off her as they could, for us to be able to hold her and cuddle her, and that was the first time we bathed her that night. She really liked the water. She opened her eyes, she was really receptive to us and our voices.

'Then the next day that was it . . . then the whole world changes. It was us as a little family holding her, before she passed away. She opened her eyes to us, and then looked at us, before she went away, which is something we can hold with us for a long time,' McVeigh says, as his voice breaks and eyes well with tears.

McVeigh returned to the field the week after the Geelong game, and was among the Swans' best in their final outings for 2011.

But as soon as the football season was over, the couple headed off on a two-month trip to Europe and America to grieve and heal together.

McVeigh says they found comfort in realising they had done all they could for their beloved little girl. Then in Italy, Clementine discovered she was pregnant again. 'It was a really special moment for us. [But] it was a bit sad as well. We asked ourselves if we were doing the right thing. "We're not forgetting her [Luella]. Are we forgetting her?" But we realised it wasn't about that.'

Scans show the new baby is healthy. 'It's good to try and get back into normal life, and prepare for another baby, and we can put all our effort into giving her a good life,' McVeigh says.

'But it doesn't stop. Everything we do, we still think about Luella every day . . . She will always be a part of us. We treasured every moment . . . Just that look, and how she would squeeze our hands all the time, that was the best.'

5 February 2012

VETERANS OF A DIFFERENT WAR TACKLE KOKODA

Roy Masters

You know your Kokoda trek has been tough when the doctor accompanying the group—a fit 45-year-old—ends up in hospital with a 39-degree-plus temperature.

It's three weeks since our group of 16 made the final torturous ascent to Owers' Corner at the southern end of the track, with some yet to return to work, most suffering stomach ailments, a few with respiratory infections and John Quayle and myself recovering from trench foot.

Trench foot is a condition where the feet peel to expose raw flesh, caused through excessive time in wet boots, including the last day of the trek when we crossed one stream 21 times.

Quayle, the former ARL chief executive; Tom Raudonikis; past Newtown teammates Phil Sigsworth and Col Murphy; Melbourne Cup–winning jockey Larry Olsen and myself formed 'F Troop', the slower, ageing group where arthritis has reaped a delayed harvest.

The faster group, carrying heavier packs, was known as the 'Young Silvertails', although it included the very fit 64-year-old former News Ltd boss John Hartigan, who was initially and innocently addressed as 'Dave' by Tommy, who is oblivious to rank and reputation.

All of us were united via friendship with loveable larrikin John Singleton, whose annual expeditions focus on 'Ks'—Kilimanjaro, the Kimberley, Kinabalu and now, for some, Kokoda twice. 'I wouldn't do Kokoda again for a million bucks,' I whispered to Tommy as we stood, at the end of eight days, in a muddy embrace at Owers' Corner.

A keen student of a quid, he thought for some time and said: 'A million yes. Half a million, no.'

Singo's typically wicked motivation in inviting Quayle and Hartigan—protagonists in the Super League war—was to set up evening campfire debates with the possibility of insults and fists flying through the flames.

But by 8 pm most days, everyone was too tired to talk, let alone debate. In any case, the arduous demands of the 96-kilometre track, with its near-vertical heart-challenging ascents and knee-achingly treacherous descents, meant the fitter ones encouraged the strugglers and we all quickly became mates.

Our leader, former SAS major Brian Freeman, pointed out lost battle sites of the 1942 conflict between Australian and Japanese forces, and it was Hartigan who made the very telling link between mateship and the design of the foxholes.

'The Japanese ones are circular and house one soldier, while the Australian ones are rectangular and contain two—a digger and his mate,' he said.

There was also the constant reminder of the Kokoda spirit in the innocent and hopeful face of 18-year-old Joe Singleton, Singo's younger son. After all, when those young men from NSW and Victoria were shipped to PNG 70 years ago to repel the advance of the Japanese on Kokoda, many were Joe's age. Plus, they had to carry a rifle, ammunition and rations, while we had the assistance of porters.

If Joe's uncomplaining manner offers comfort that the spirit of Kokoda will endure with the next generation of Australians, the presence of the 'fuzzy wuzzy angels' guarantees it.

These guides, recruited from villages along the track, carry half their body weight in their backpacks, while some of us struggled hauling an eighth of ours.

There were times on some cruel climbs where I looked up through sweat-streaked glasses to find the outstretched hand of my guide, Gerry, offering to pull me up a dangerously high step. Because I was often placed at the lead of the slower group to ensure a steady walking rate, we dubbed our pairing 'Gerry and the Pacemaker'.

The first two days were almost idyllic: challenging, occasionally exhausting terrain . . . softened by the sight of mist-shrouded valleys and the feel of a gentle track, together with the intriguing mystery of strange trees whose roots began high in their trunks and bushes of curious red flowers. And there were the constant reminders to Tommy and myself, treading in each other's footsteps, from 'Canon' Quayle. 'Look up, look up,' he encouraged.

We spent the first three nights in single-man tents and bathed in mountain streams, but everything changed for me after day two when rain followed us like a threatening stranger on a lonely road.

Suddenly, the twisted tree roots that had offered a springboard to the next step on ascent became treacherously slippery in descent, with muddy pools of water within their threatening, gnarled matrix.

Boots slid sideways, landing us on our backs, or forcing ancient knees to double up underneath.

Every downward step became measured, and the only relief from straight up, or directly down was a 10-kilometre level section, which, perversely, was covered in ankle-sucking mud.

The rain did, however, force us into the native huts where, if any more democracy was needed, it came with ubiquitous snores, farts and the unranked power of each other's stories. Two people told their life histories each night, with revelations unlikely in any other theatre.

Apart from the footballers, we had friends of 40-year-old Jack Singleton whose careers are already worth chronicling—including Welshman Andy Palmer, a merchant banker, art salesman, university lecturer and prawn-trawler deckhand who was once officially dead for 23 minutes.

Two American friends of Singo's were quickly reminded of General MacArthur's 1942 observation that one Ohio farm boy knows more about jungle fighting than 10 Australians. But the Yanks were there at the end, as Tommy, gasping for air via the pump of a quadruple bypass heart, led us up that final 500-metre direct ascent.

Then followed photographs, the first beer in eight days, a visit to the cemetery of the war dead and liberal gifts to the porters, including a petrol-driven post-hole digger for their village.

'Larry the jockey', who lost his wife late last year, won the John Metson award for personal achievement. You'd sometimes see Larry staring off into the distance, like those paintings of the bereaved looking out to sea, but laughter and the love of mates brought him back.

Quayle won the Charlie McCallum DCM award for display of the Kokoda spirit, continually boosting the enthusiasm of F Troop, which was undermined by Tommy's and my constant moans. Afterwards, all echoed the mantra of

Kokoda trekkers: 'The hardest thing I have ever done.' Each of us was brought back to reality, some quicker than others.

Hartigan, on buying a book at Port Moresby airport, produced his credit card. The female sales assistant, an indigene, said: 'Hartigan! News Ltd!' He gently inquired where she had heard of him. 'Melbourne Storm,' she said in quick reply.

And as for me, news of my skinned feet reached my former players.

Rather than be complimented for completing Kokoda at age 70, former Wests five-eighth Terry Lamb said: 'Hear you got trench foot? Put your foot in your mouth again?'

2 June 2012

KATSIDIS: THE AGONY AND THE ECSTASY

Chris Roots

Stathi Katsidis admits he took ecstasy—he served a nine-month ban after testing positive to it in 2008. He also insists he wasn't the only sportsman to take the party drug, claiming 'about half' of jockeys and football players take it. It's a claim that will send tremors through the football and racing industries. But Katsidis is not bitter. Instead, he credits the whole episode with helping him turn around his life.

'I took it when I wasn't riding about three or four times a year,' says Katsidis, who tomorrow will steer favourite Military Rose in the $3.5m AAMI Golden Slipper. 'It goes on—footy players and jockeys [take it]. Well probably about half of them might do it. When you take things like that it was good for your weight because instead of drinking piss you drink water.

'It was a Sunday night when I did it and my manager rang on the Monday and said, "Jim Byrne has been suspended, can you ride these horses on Wednesday?" I said, "Yeah". 'Three days, it will be out of my system,' I thought—because generally it's two days and you're right. I got tested and I had a feeling. I was only just over, but I was over.'

Katsidis couldn't have known it at the time, but the suspension passed down by Queensland stewards turned out to be a blessing. His return to racing was conditional upon his attendance at a rehabilitation course, and Katsidis credits the two-week program with helping salvage his controversy-prone career.

Not only did the enforced break force him to reassess his wayward path in life, it also allowed him time to develop his relationship with Melissa Jackson, a long-time friend who would become his soulmate. While working as a breaker on a stud farm to pay the bills, Katsidis found the ballast in life that had previously eluded him. 'When I went positive for drugs, I had to do a two-week rehab course to get two months off my sentence,' he says. 'It helped with the way I think about things now. I was lucky because I was an outpatient. They said I wasn't that far gone. I had to drive there every day—six days a week—and saw where I could end up. I learned it was not really about drugs but . . . about life management. It's the major thing that makes me more dedicated now.'

The notion of Katsidis riding the 2010 Golden Slipper favourite seemed implausible two years ago. The nine-month suspension seemed a continuation of a self-destructive past. He had previously twice tested positive for a banned appetite suppressant, and been arrested for drink-driving in a matter that almost resulted in a jail term.

In 2003, Katsidis first returned a positive test for Duromine, which he used to control his weight. 'Back then I was always suspended and struggling to ride 55, 56 [kilograms],' he says. He failed a second test for the same drug after Victoria Derby day in 2007 and was banned for a month. On his return he secured a ride on Gold Edition and it seemed he was back on track. But things soon started to unravel.

After riding Gold Edition in the 2008 Lightning Stakes, in what was to be her final start, Katsidis headed back to Brisbane as usual. He decided to have a drink on the plane.

'I was just loose at the time,' he admits. 'I rode Gold Edition and drank all the way [home]. We had a lift organised [back to Toowoomba for an awards night] but the bloke couldn't make it for some reason. I said, "F— it, we'll drive". The other bloke was more pissed than me, so I said, "I'll drive." The other bloke wanted to but I said I wanted to get up there safe.'

It would have been a hair-rising journey, with Katsidis more than three times over the legal limit. The police received a call telling them a car was speeding and being driven erratically near Toowoomba. They stopped it and Katsidis was breathalysed. He failed. Worse was to follow, with a police search of the car unearthing ecstasy and a steroid.

'It was just stupid,' Katsidis says. 'The cops found the tabs in the car and the Clenbuterol, which I was taking back then. I was always looking for the easy ways out back then. Clenbuterol strips fat from your body and it worked, but once again it was a short cut. After talking to a couple of doctors I found out how bad that stuff is for you. You get shakes on it and it's bad for your heart.'

Katsidis's mate copped the rap for the ecstasy tablet but by the time the jockey was back in court in June to plead guilty to possession of Clenbuterol without a prescription, which earned him a $500 fine, he was in trouble again, this time with stewards. He tested positive to ecstasy in May. It would be the start of 18 months away from racing.

Katsidis has been riding for 18 years but he will tell you he has been doing it properly for just 18 months since he ditched the party-boy attitude to focus on becoming the best jockey in the country.

'I have always ridden the same—I have been a brilliant rider,' he says of a career in which he won his first Group 1 race as a 19-year-old apprentice. 'But I lacked the finer things. The past couple of years [I've] been more professional and just grown up.'

Katsidis knows the short cuts and knows they don't work. He has won a fortune and has also had a good time blowing it. He doesn't own a house and is determined to make the most of his second chance to set himself up for life.

'I started doing this [riding] when I was 13 or 14 and then really serious from 15 to 19,' he says. 'The dedication needed to make it then meant I didn't go out and drink. I didn't do what all the kids were doing my age. I won my first Group 1 at 19 on Show A Heart in the TJ Smith and started to do things I didn't do when 17, 18, 19. It took me another six years to win my next Group 1 because I was living my childhood. I'd ride for a few months and then take a month [off]. It took 2008 for me to stop and say, "What am I doing?"'

While he was serving his nine-month suspension for testing positive to ecstasy, Katsidis worked as a breaker on a stud farm and developed his relationship with Jackson. By Christmas, he had asked her to marry him. Maybe now his luck was turning.

But fate had other ideas and just days before he was to return to the saddle, a horse he was breaking reared and came crashing down on his leg with enough force to break it.

'I was lucky I had really good motorbike pants so I didn't see it but I had bone sticking out of both sides of my leg,' he says. 'I'd been out for seven months and was keen to get back riding. But I still didn't have my weight sorted out, so breaking my leg was probably a blessing in disguise. I was another eight months out but I got real light and was walking around 52 kilograms because I lost all my bulk and muscle definition. It was then I thought, "I am meant to be a jockey".'

When he eventually returned to the track in Brisbane, he rode winner after winner. On the track, it was the same old jockey—full of talent and flair. But off it, Katsidis had changed—no more taking the easy route, no more taking his talent for granted. 'I had realised myself that there are no short cuts—you just have to do the work,' he says. 'I'm on a low sodium diet and Melissa makes sure I stick to it. She is so important to my success.'

Katsidis has also become a mentor for apprentices. It is about as far away as he could get from the wild man of two years ago. He sets the best example by being a winner. He has won the Magic Millions with Military Rose, the Karaka Millions on Sister Havana and the Randwick Guineas with his derby ride Shoot Out in 2010. 'It helps working with the kids because I say do this and do that and then I think I should probably be doing that as well,' he says. 'I have had apprentices come to me and say, "Should I take this [drug]", and I say to them, "You can take it but it is a short-term fix".'

While Katsidis doesn't want to forget the past and the lows that started him on his path to redemption, he prefers to focus on the future. 'I'm not going to say I never did drugs or tried ecstasy or drunk as much as I did,' he says. 'But during that time I experienced a lot of things that make me the person I am today. That's my nature—I'll take gaps six inches wide and I love the thrill of it. But I had to learn you have to choose your times. I have.'

2 April 2010

THE TURBULENT DEATH AND LIFE OF A GIFTED HORSEMAN

Chris Roots

At his best, Stathi Katsidis could ride like an angel—but he had his demons, too. The troubled jockey had had a chequered past—he tested positive twice for a banned appetite suppressant, was convicted for drink-driving, only narrowly avoiding a stint behind bars, and finally copped a nine-month suspension from stewards for ecstasy use in 2008. Things got worse for Katsidis when his return to racing was further delayed by a compound fracture to his leg as he tried to break in a horse towards the end of his ban.

Then, after 18 months away from the sport, the 31-year-old from Too-woomba returned in a blaze of glory midway through last year [2009], booting home winner after winner. He won the Magic Millions on Military Rose at the start of the year and also linked with Shoot Out, the horse he was booked to ride in Saturday's Cox Plate and on which he won the AJC Australian Derby at Randwick in April.

Until his death yesterday, it had seemed as if Katsidis had turned his life around and was finally making the most of his talent.

Before riding Military Rose in the Golden Slipper in April, Katsidis had talked of his realisation that it was hard work and sacrifice that delivered results—not short-term fixes. It looked like a turning point. He was focused on the future and said he was learning to curb his risk-taking nature.

Katsidis said he wanted to be remembered not for the turbulent off-track dramas, the drugs, the booze and the parties, but for what he did as a jockey in the theatre of racing. He talked about the cultural taboo of drug use among professional sportsmen. He was a charming, confident person. People wanted to see him succeed.

The Golden Slipper ended in disappointment on the favourite but a week later Katsidis would ride Shoot Out to his biggest success, victory in the AJC Australian Derby.

Now, just days out from what promised to be another career highlight on the same horse, Katsidis is gone. He was found dead by his partner, Melissa Jackson, at his Eagle Farm home yesterday. Police have ruled out suicide, but said it was not suspicious. Melissa and her four-year-old son, Brooklyn, had played a huge role in helping Katsidis confront his dark past. They travelled the path towards the top of Australia's riding ranks with him.

Throughout his turbulent career, Katsidis had struggled with his weight. Melissa gave constant support, knowing her man was torturing his body in pursuit of making correct weight on a racehorse.

Katsidis rode more winners than anyone else in the country last season after settling down with Jackson, who he asked to marry him on Christmas Day last year. It was a long way from his 'loose' days.

Katsidis came out of Queensland in a boom time for apprentices with Michael Rodd and Zac Purton among his classmates. He claimed his first Group 1 as a 21-year-old on Show A Heart in the TJ Smith in 2000, but it would be another six years before he won another.

His problems started long before his first positive test for Duromine in 2003, a drug he would again be banned for using on Victoria Derby Day in 2007.

Katsidis's life continued to spiral out of control and he was arrested for drink-driving, more then three-times the legal limit, after driving from Brisbane to Toowoomba in early 2008. Police also found ecstasy and a steroid in the car, which resulted in the jockey being fined $500 for the steroid, while a friend took the rap for the ecstasy tab.

He would follow that by testing positive to ecstasy in May as he got near rock bottom.

Katsidis entered rehab for a two-week course as a part of that ban, which he said made him aware of how lucky he was. However, an accident just as he was ready to return to the saddle sidelined him for another nine months.

He admitted he had little to show for his 18 years in the industry, but in the past 18 months Katsidis had started to plan for the future.

A reformed man, he had a family to look after and wanted others to learn from his mistakes; he volunteered for a mentoring role with apprentices in Queensland.

It is probably how Katsidis would like to be remembered. Unfortunately, it won't be.

20 October 2010

NEW BARRIER FOR BEADMAN

Craig Young

Darren Beadman is on a walking stick and may never ride again.

For the first time revealing the true extent of the injuries he suffered in a barrier trial crash last month (February 2012), the Hall of Famer told *The Sun-Herald* the simple act of riding a racehorse again is of little concern. The 46-year-old jockey is not even allowed to drive a car. He has been inundated with well wishes from family, racing friends and strangers.

The decorated horseman has a brain injury. The man who has handled thoroughbred greats such as Saintly, Octagonal, Super Impose, Lonhro and more has entered a pale place.

'I was a highly disciplined person, now everything is grey, not black and white,' the champion jockey said from Hong Kong, where his riding career may end.

Whether this gazetted horseman rides again is not of concern, but in typical Beadman style there are people to thank. No sign of 'why me' but a 'heartfelt thank you' for a racing industry, and those outside, that have inquired about his health.

'Everyone has been really good. The support from everyone has been fantastic,' Beadman said. 'I can't fault it. I've had people ringing up from everywhere. As I've said, I'm just glad I've had my day in the sun. Whatever I get from here on is just cream. I've had a great career. Some people haven't had the opportunity to have that. That's the way I look at it.'

What a career. Melbourne Cups, Golden Slippers, a Cox Plate, Doncasters, Epsoms and a whole heap more. Enough major race trophies to earn him a place in Australian racing's Hall of Fame.

Will there be any more triumphs of the grand kind for the guy who has won races in Europe, Hong Kong and his homeland, and is regarded as one of the all-time greats? 'Just slow, steady, you know,' Beadman said. 'I'm out of hospital now, been at home about a week. It has been good. Sometimes you are good. Sometimes you are bad. I don't know what is going to happen. It [riding again] is really up in the air at the moment.

'Look at me, you'd say "nothing is wrong with the bloke", but I know what is going on in my body. It is a closed head injury.'

The brain injury was the result of a barrier trial crash on February 17. Just another set of mundane heats at Hong Kong's Sha Tin racecourse. The type jockeys turn up for in the hope of finding their next thoroughbred winner or perhaps even a champion.

'It seemed like a simple fall. I was knocked out for like two hours,' Beadman said. 'I've had race falls, been involved in them. I've been conscious all the way through. Sometimes I've been knocked out. It feels like you're going in slow motion, everything slows down. This one I don't even remember going down.

'They sent me home from hospital a couple of days later but the room at home kept spinning, I'd get up and go to the toilet and I'd fall over. They put me back in hospital straight away.'

Specialists had already picked up a fractured right cheekbone but the second time round the lights of hope were dimmed. The diagnosis was that Beadman had suffered a diffuse axonal injury, which affects balance, speech and memory.

'It is a traumatic brain injury,' Beadman said. 'What's happened is, through the fall, there is acceleration and deceleration. The inside of your brain is like gelatine and it compresses against the skull. When you have that shearing, shaking, it tears the neurons and nerves. Like telephone wires—I actually tore nerves in my brain. My balance is up to shit, I get vertigo. It is not very good, not very good at all.'

Beadman has three sessions of physiotherapy a week and sees a psychologist. Trying to concentrate 'is doing my head in', he says, and 'it feels like I'm half pissed all the time'.

'I don't want to say I'm not riding again. I don't know what I'm doing,' Beadman said. 'They don't really know how long it will take because it is nerve related. Six months, they hope for an improvement. It is a brain injury not a limb. When you're talking brain it is a whole different ball game.'

SMALL GOALS REPLACE RACING ON ROAD TO RECOVERY

The simple joy of cooking a barbecue is beyond Darren Beadman at the moment. The champion jockey—who suffered a head injury in a barrier trial fall at Sha Tin on February 17—has to learn to walk again. He has to rewire his memory, and cooking is no longer an easy task.

He can also forget about riding thoroughbreds any time soon. Steering 500-plus kilograms of thoroughbred muscle, going 50 km/h, may never be possible again.

Nonetheless, Beadman remains in good spirits. His glittering career has been stopped but the family man remains upbeat. 'I have all these goals I try to achieve,' Beadman said. 'Even something as simple as cooking a barbecue, that was funny. I really love cooking, but when I have to concentrate for a long time, I can't cook what I used to. My psychologist said, "Out of all the goals, what do you want to achieve—riding horses, walking dogs, cooking dinner?" I told her I wanted to cook a barbecue, and she said, "That's what I wanted to hear."'

Beadman said it sounded 'childish', but the only way the barbecue was going to work out was to do a bit of homework the day before.

Beadman rang up rival jockey Jeff Lloyd. The South African, who had a stint riding in Sydney before returning to Hong Kong, had been 'one of those really good supporters', Beadman said. 'I'd planned to watch him cook so I could do it the next night. He said, "What is going on here? You invite me over and I'm doing the cooking". I told him, "I've got to do things different." We had a laugh.'

25 March 2012

ON THE
FRONT FOOT

Sportswriters and sports stars often don't get on. Sports stars don't like getting criticised, and the good sports writers tell it exactly as it is. They are bound to clash.

One of the most testing of relationships was between renowned Australian football performer Harry Kewell and long-time *Sydney Morning Herald* football writer Michael Cockerill. The experienced, highly respected and always forthright Cockerill never copped too much nonsense from Kewell. It all came to a head during the 2010 World Cup. Cockerill was critical of Kewell's involvement during the tournament, and the player reacted publicly, demanding in front of the world media that our man showed his face at the press conference. Kewell's outburst led to headlines. Cockerill was elsewhere, and handed Kewell the perfect reply. Cockerill's piece, with the memorable introductory paragraph 'Here I am Harry, where I was always going to be and where I'll be for the next few weeks. Covering the World Cup' is a classic of 'up yours' journalism.

Other biting pieces in this chapter include Peter Roebuck's controversial article, which was run on page one of the *SMH*, demanding Australian captain Ricky Ponting's sacking. His piece on Michael Clarke similarly does not include any shady areas—again, straight to the point, right on the front foot. It is also clear that Australia's most respected golf writer, Peter Stone, wasn't too overwhelmed when Tiger Woods went off the rails.

Jessica Halloran, meanwhile, generated international headlines when on-the-rise Australian diver Matthew Mitcham became the first athlete to publicly 'come out' before an Olympic Games. It took some convincing for Matthew to go public about his sexuality—two interviews later he felt comfortable about it. Mitcham went on to score a perfect 10 to win Olympic Gold at the Beijing Games. Halloran's series of stories on Mitcham were nominated for a Walkley award in 2008.

GG

HERE I AM HARRY

Michael Cockerill

Two minutes on the park in the past six months. That's all we've seen of Harry Kewell, the footballer. Harry Kewell the fashionista, however, we've seen everywhere. Cover stories in magazines such as *Good Weekend*, *Sport&Style*, *Emporium*, and *InStyle*. Thousands of words written elsewhere. Front page of both dailies when the Socceroos kicked off their World Cup against Germany. Talk, talk, talk. A compliant, obsequious media lapping it all up.

One television reporter went one step further. At the end of Kewell's first round of media interviews last week, he signed off with: 'Don't worry, Harry, we love you.' True story.

And where was our Harry when Germany were systematically, surgically, dissecting the Socceroos? On the bench. Where he was always likely to start the World Cup. No sign of him on the field with the rest of the subs in the warm-up and in the end he didn't take the field.

In between he was seen warmly embracing a member of the German coaching staff at half-time, and then smiling, chatting to family and friends at the fence after the final whistle. If the catastrophe that unfolded before his eyes upset him, there were no outward signs of distress.

Pim Verbeek gambled on selecting Kewell for this tournament. Right now, the gamble hasn't paid off. Don't worry, came the message from the coach throughout the build-up, he'll be right to play the opening game. He wasn't. If he can't even complete a proper warm-up with the other players, how could he have been?

There was always going to be a point where the talk became cheap. More than that, irrelevant. Well that point has arrived. No doubt there will be plenty of headlines over the next few days about King Kewell coming to the rescue. By accident, or design, he seems to embrace the role of saviour. Well this time it's not about Harry saving Australia. It's about Harry saving what's left of his international career.

Guus Hiddink never indulged Kewell, and given his chronic injury list you can't imagine he would be playing in his second World Cup if the Dutch Master was still in charge. However, the Dutch Apprentice has obliged him at every turn. In return, Verbeek has got one influential performance out of his star man since he took over. Against Iraq, in Brisbane, where he led the line with enthusiasm, energy, and—most of all—courage. Since then, Kewell has basically been a myth.

On Saturday (midnight, AEST), in Rustenburg, he gets the chance to prove he's got something left to give. At times in his career, Kewell *has* been a genuine star. And his long, arduous battle to keep his body together remains a tribute to his bravery, and resilience. But he's never been able to accept his diminished circumstances. Instead, he's chosen to deflect the scrutiny with hype. Kewell Inc is on the way up. Kewell, football player, is on the way down. And has been for years.

Now there is nowhere left to hide. If he's got any petrol left in the tank, he's got to show it, against Ghana. Preferably by starting the game, *and* finishing it. Preferably by providing a point of difference. Preferably by giving glimpses of the Harry of old. Anything less, and there's no more excuses. None.

If the Socceroos lose to the Black Stars, they're out of contention. With a new coach coming on board, there'll be a broom swept through a squad creaking at the joints. Believe it or not, Kewell is likely to be part of the clean out. A few years ago that was unthinkable. But a few years is a long time in football. 'Our Harry' knows that better than anyone.

16 June 2010

•••

Here I am Harry, where I was always going to be and where I'll be for the next few weeks. Covering the World Cup.

Not covering you, exclusively, I must admit. I like to get around. On Wednesday afternoon, when you seemed to be rather upset that I wasn't squeezed among the press pack at Ruimsig, tape recorder in hand, I was actually in

Pretoria. Months ago I applied, and received, accreditation to report on South Africa's game against Uruguay. You can check if you like.

Perhaps if I'd known you were going to front the cameras—we're not generally told who Football Federation Australia are 'putting up' in advance—I would have changed my plans. Come to think of it, no I wouldn't have.

You see, Harry, I spent a lot of years, a lot of energy and a lot of effort chasing you for quotes around the world. I was there when it all began for you in 1996—in fact, I was there a long time before that—and I'm still here now.

Ninety per cent of that time, you've blanked me. The last time, four years ago in Yokohama, I made a decision there wasn't much point in the charade any more. Something I conveyed, quite clearly, to your manager, Bernie Mandic. So you got on with your life and I got on with mine. That's fair enough. There's plenty of athletes and plenty of journalists who don't get on. Nature of the beast and all that.

What's also true in this business is that if you dish it out, you've got to take it. I've dished it out to you in the past week and I'm happy to take it. But I stand by every word I've written. Every single one. You've had a dream run in terms of scrutiny, real scrutiny, regarding your performances. You know it, Bernie knows it. In fact, Bernie once told me—remember when you brushed me at Waverley Oval?—that as far as Team Kewell was concerned, the football media was a joke, utterly irrelevant. Give us Ray Martin over you numpties any day was Bernie's point. A message conveyed, I might add, in much more forceful language than that.

So if what is written by a football journalist means diddly-squat, I'm not quite sure why my words over the past few weeks have got under your skin. And they have because you went to the FFA last week and demanded my accreditation be revoked. The accreditation I need to cover the Socceroos. That's 23 players, by the way, not just you.

So here's the thing, Harry. You know and I know that most of the media are in your thrall. One hack even professed his love for you the other day. I happen to believe it's what you do on the pitch for Australia that counts. Not what your PR machine spins out. Not how good you look in a pair of undies. And I happen to believe, since the last World Cup, you've done bugger all. I couldn't praise you enough after the game in Brisbane against Iraq. You can get the clippings if you like. But the rest of the time, as far as I'm concerned, you've been a myth.

Now you've got the chance to show you're not. That there's still something in the tank. Go out against Ghana, when our World Cup is on the line, when your own international career is on the line, and do something. Actually DO something. Prove something. And if you do, I'll be the first to praise you. As for the rest of it, I'm still here, still writing about football, and hope to be for a long time to come.

18 June 2010

OUT, PROUD AND READY TO GO FOR GOLD

Jessica Halloran

Matthew Mitcham is brave enough to dive from a 10-metre platform for Olympic gold and courageous enough to do what no Australian athlete has done.

When Mitcham balances on the Beijing diving tower this August, like all Australian Olympians, he will be hoping the ones he loves will be there to watch him.

The gold medal hopeful's journey has not been easy. Those close to him have seen Mitcham, 20, battle depression, retire in his teenage years after physical and emotional burn-out, then nine months later resume his sport and build himself into the champion he is today.

One person who has been by his side for the entire tumultuous journey is his partner, Lachlan.

Months out from the Games, Mitcham has taken the courageous step of revealing his sexuality to the media for the first time, in an exclusive interview with the *Herald*. He has also applied for a grant through a Johnson & Johnson Athlete Family Support Program to have Lachlan near him in Beijing.

'We can't afford for Lachlan to go at the moment,' Mitcham said. 'But Johnson & Johnson offer grants to go to Beijing and I've nominated Lachlan as the support person I want to go.'

It's not only Lachlan who has helped Mitcham to Beijing. His coach, Chava Sobrino, had faith in him when no one else did and resurrected his career. Former athlete Sarina Bratton cares for him like a son and fellow diver Alex Croak is a constant sounding board and his best friend.

'That little support network has made my dream possible,' Mitcham said. 'It would have been impossible and I probably wouldn't have made it without their help.'

Those who adore him could be watching Mitcham win gold after his performance just over a week ago in Fort Lauderdale. Mitcham stood 10 metres high with the fierce wind whistling in his ears and battling trying conditions. 'When I was whizzing around, the sky is the same colour as the water. I was freaking out. It was the first time I had dived outside since I left the sport.'

His performance was astonishing. Mitcham beat two top Chinese divers who will challenge him for gold. When he saw his four perfect 10s he whooped and leaped on the pool deck. Finally, the man who had battled anxiety and depression as a teenager, taking medication and seeing psychologists, had arrived on the world stage. And it proved the time he spent away from the sport last year had been worth it. Mitcham's premature retirement had been a chaotic and unusual time when he 'partied' and lived without regimen.

'I was a free spirit,' he said. 'It was a break for me to explore myself and get familiar with who I really was and to be happy with who I really was. Just being a happier person really radiates into other areas of your life.'

To make money, among other things, he plunged from a tower 14 metres high into a pool of water for crowds at the Royal Easter Show in Sydney last year. It was a blessing in disguise.

'At the same time I was applying for the NSW Institute of Sport to try and get into the diving squad. It was a good warm-up. I was doing similar dives and getting my head around all of the movements again. It was a pretty smooth lead into intense training again.'

Mitcham thinks he would not be going to the Olympics if not for the hardship he endured.

'I probably wouldn't have as much of a fighting spirit,' he said.

'The more you have experienced, the more you have to draw off. I look at the last 20 years as a long, winding path of lessons and some hardship. I hope the rest of my life isn't straight because that could be boring.

'I hope it continues to wind, but maybe not so tumultuous. I hope I do have a long and winding path and more lessons to learn. I look forward to that.'

24 May 2008

ATHLETES DESERVE A BREAK THAT DOESN'T DISABLE

Glenn Jackson

Every so often, generally when there's debate around how much our sports stars are paid, and whether it's too much, I think of a crack I heard from the grandstand. I heard it from about 60 metres away and remember it even though it was seven years ago.

This week, I found the bloke who not only heard the crack but felt it, too. Any time I hear criticism of footballers earning the money they do, I think of Dean Byrne, who snapped his tibia early in 2005 and still feels the effects today.

Playing halfback for Balmain Ryde–Eastwood in the Premier League, he darted for the try line, was dragged back, but reached out. As he did, the weight of an opponent came down on his leg, and Byrne heard the crack. So did many others. Players from the Wests Tigers NRL side were warming up nearby and stopped when they heard the noise. Byrne's battle was just beginning.

He speaks now of complications. Back then, it was reported he almost died on the operating table after he stopped breathing. He later developed compartment syndrome, required a fasciotomy (look it up, but make sure you're not eating) and was in hospital for six weeks. He had numerous operations; he doesn't know exactly how many—'it could be anywhere from eight to 15'. He watched the NRL on a laptop while wondering if he'd ever get to play in the competition again. Ultimately, as those hopes faded, he was just happy to walk again, even with a limp.

After he was discharged, he was addicted to painkillers for about eight months. 'That was nearly worse than breaking my leg,' he said.

Byrne walks better now that the rods and screws have been taken out but still has foot drop. The muscle damage means he cannot raise his left foot with his ankle, and he has to compensate by lifting his knee higher than normal. 'I can hide it to the naked eye but the odd person will catch on,' he said.

He is largely over the fact that his NRL career ended just seven matches into it. Now 30, he might today have been nearing the end of his career, and admits that makes him more at ease. He knows that many of those he played with or against have retired, and are doing what he is doing, what many would term real work. Sort of, anyway. Not only was Byrne forced to stop doing his first choice profession, a rugby league player, he has been denied his next choice, too.

Byrne did two years at university studying landscaping but the damage to his leg means he can't landscape. He now works as a courier, which can still be taxing on his limbs. Not surprisingly, Byrne believes footballers should be compensated for what they do and the risks they take.

'They're not there for a very long period, maybe 14 years at the most,' he said. 'They are the lucky ones.'

In fact, players in the NRL competition play, on average, 43 matches. Kane Cleal played that many games and the former Bulldogs and Souths forward now addresses under-20s players and country hopefuls about how careers can end so quickly—given he is the definition of an average footballer. 'Most people would say I was below average,' he laughs now.

Cleal was forced to retire in 2010 because of a hand injury. 'I was at training one day, got hurt and never played another game,' he said. 'I don't give them a sob story but it's reality. I landed wrong; that was it.'

Michael Greenfield, the most recent example, fell five games short of the average. After 38 matches, through a career with Cronulla, Souths, St George Illawarra and Melbourne, he was forced to retire following neck surgery last month.

Before that, Brisbane, Queensland and Australian winger Jharal Yow Yeh's career was placed in doubt after a sickening ankle break in March that has resulted in more than a handful of operations. Go back a bit further and it was Wests Tigers back-rower Simon Dwyer, with nerve damage in his neck and shoulder. He is still hopeful of a return. Another former Wests Tigers player, Taniela Tuiaki, is not.

They are all extreme examples, those whose careers were clouded quite suddenly. There are countless others who will still be limping long after retirement, setting off airport metal detectors. Some might need knee replacements; others shoulder.

Byrne said his ordeal 'doesn't bother me any more. I've had a few other things to deal with [since then], family passing away, and it doesn't compare. There's a lot more than footy. At first, it was pretty hard knowing that I couldn't play any more. But you have to move on. It's in the past now. There's always someone worse off than you. I guess it's a bit of a life story. It's something to tell people.'

Over the next few months, you might hear NRL players jockeying for a share of the new broadcast deal. You might hear them ask for more money not only for the fortunate few on top dollar but those on average or minimum wages.

You might hear them ask for insurance that is proportional to the risks they take. You might still not agree. But listen to them because it doesn't take much to go from a form player to a former player.

4 August 2012

ONE MAN'S SORRY TALE

Stephen Gibbs

A block north of South Sydney Leagues Club is a pizza shop, but they do a good lamb kebab, too. Three months ago I was outside inhaling a nicotine entree when a black man walked up to me.

This bloke, who looked to be Maori, saw me reach for my pack before he spoke. He smiled and said, 'Thanks, bro' for the cigarette, walked to the corner and then turned back. Grinning now, he tried some amusing amateur psychology.

'Bet you never heard no black c— say thanks for a smoke before, eh?' he said, breaking into laughter as I shook my head.

Without me thinking in terms even remotely like that, this stranger had caught me adopting his own racial slur. There's a case for suggesting I'd just contributed to perpetuating the use of this language by letting it slide.

If we say in the wake of Bryan Fletcher calling Dean Widders a 'black c—' that such an insult is unacceptable anywhere, anytime, there's no get-out clause to make it OK sometimes. Fletcher, like Justin Jagamara Harrison before him, seems to have suffered a brain snap rather than been caught expressing a racist view he secretly held. Souths punished him for general deterrence, not rehabilitation, and we're reaching a point where public exposure is punishment enough.

By now we all know how a footballer says he feels when sprung wielding racially demeaning words as weapons. We've heard it over and over again. But is there any benefit left in punishing the guilty and would contrition be more convincing if the offender dobbed himself in?

Like drink-driving, homophobia or domestic violence, racial vilification won't be eliminated permanently but has long been an exception rather than a rule.

Arthur Beetson indicated on Monday he was sick of commenting on specific incidents: 'I'd prefer to say nothing. I've been through it all before.' Searching for where this takes us next individually, I sought Gary Foley this week.

One of the most militant of the young Kooris drawn to inner-city Sydney in the late 1960s, he's been through all this before. Born in Grafton, Foley grew up at Nambucca Heads and at 15 was expelled from school. He arrived in Redfern as a 17-year-old apprentice draftsman and was soon part of the black power movement growing there. He helped form the Redfern Legal Service and pitch the Aboriginal Tent Embassy.

About the same time, Foley was among those Aborigines who protested against the 1971 Springboks tour of Australia—a tour that divided this country on racial grounds in a way that sport never has since. Foley's website www.kooriweb.org details its impact on indigenous activism and records some of his group's audacious stunts.

One of the most successful began when former Wallaby Jim Boyce supplied South African jumpers to the group. Foley, Billy Craigie and others paraded them outside the Springboks' motel.

Believing Foley and Craigie to have stolen the jumpers, Special Branch arrested the pair. Inside the Squire Inn at Bondi Junction, police tried to find the victims of this theft. Instead they found the Springboks outraged by two proud young black men wearing the colours of their team.

Foley was just out of his teens.

Just out of my teens, during a stint in Melbourne as part of my cadetship, I called Gary Foley a black c—.

Technically, what I did was send a story tagged 'BLACKC—' to my newspaper office in Sydney on a wire that could be accessed in other capitals. You can assume it wasn't deliberate but I won't revisit all that now.

Likewise, there were sudden and lasting—but not insurmountable—consequences that I don't intend playing up or down. I was not in Melbourne the next morning and wasn't working at the same paper the next week. It was fair.

Thirteen years later, my first email to Foley requesting a chat about something personal to do with racism in 'the greatest game of all' found Foley marking papers at the University of Melbourne.

His reply stated he detested league due to its 'racist, sexist culture' and his only comment on the latest controversy was to ask why anyone would be surprised. 'I might send a more considered response later, but then again I may not,' he wrote. 'Feel free to press me if you want.'

What I felt like [doing] was throwing up.

I wrote back and told Foley I'd once called him a black c— and now wished to apologise. Nothing had ever made it so clear that those words were impossible to justify. Foley's reply was deeply moving and began: 'Dear Stephen, Thank you for your email . . . Now I understand, and appreciate your apology.'

There was an invitation, and a great closing line: 'I can also try and educate you a bit about which is really the greatest game of all, which was probably the greater faux pas that you committed.'

Until reading Foley's reasoning for accepting my apology, I don't think I properly understood how much I needed to apologise.

9 July 2005

BIG BUM RAP FOR SERENA

Stephen Gibbs

Serena Williams has a big, fat arse. You read it here first.

Others have come to this same conclusion and suggested it elsewhere, too. It is possible to reach this position independently and unassisted, but today we officially bring you the news.

Our nation's tennis writers have been too busy revealing Serena Williams is back bigger than ever, with no ifs and one very big but(t).

Serena has been beset by injury, which reduces her mobility. That, in turn, leads to her having an arse Greg Ritchie would be too shy to have worn. It also allows newspapers to wrap snickering remarks on Serena's shape within a cloak of comment on her fitness, or ability to perform.

The rare times I'm found watching tennis, I'll be watching those players I would most like to take to five sets. Serena Williams ain't one of them, but neither was Pat Rafter.

Writing about tennis and tennis players is hard work. After two minutes, I'm worn out. Real tennis writers practise year-round so they can comment with authority on changes in Serena's arse form. Many have career-threatening wrist injuries.

That is probably unfair. So are the best scenes in *Black Hawk Down*. The world's cruel. Anna Kournikova couldn't win a singles title. I've got a head like a prison informant, and Freya Stafford has hardly been on the tele since they axed *White Collar Blue*.

And still, Serena Williams has this great big arse. Some tennis commentators seem able to ignore the urge to record that for posterity and instead have concentrated on her career. Some have chronicled every step in this extraordinary journey and are still there courtside, searching for a new angle to look up Maria Sharapova's skirt.

Righto. This is the spot for a sentence that starts: 'Before the letters of complaint come flooding in from the hairy-armpit brigade . . .' This may or may not be interesting, but in fact they never do. Those sentences are written for female colleagues and partners rather than letter-writing lesbians.

Back to Sharapova, who is a Russian glamour girl and can apparently play a bit, too. She is tanned, teenaged, firm of bottom and pert of breast. She has for some time been ranked No.1 by the tennis world as the female player heterosexual males most want to up-end.

But that is not how they put it in the media, just as we don't say Serena Williams has a big arse.

The closest I could find published anywhere were three instances of 'Serena Williams has a fat ass' on the web. One came from a message board on ESPN's college basketball site. That thread was begun with a link to a pic of Serena's huge arse.

'Serena is a real nicely built woman,' one visitor commented on the sight tennis writers feel they have to excuse. 'I never thought she had the body that she has. Always thought she was too athletic. Now I know better. She is Fine.'

Most are direct, many crude, but every one of 160—regardless of language—says much the same: 'Simply the best that an ass can get.' Apparently not everyone attracted to women gets off on looking up the skirts of slim Caucasian teens. Some of the messages are enigmatic: 'I told myself i wasnt gonna Cry'. Some are sassy: 'Put yo booty back in yo panties yo girl.' Some silly: 'Each cheek is like a bowling ball! Awesome!!!!' And some overawed: 'Wow! man, this is the best ass in the whole world . . . Damn.'

Sometimes they go over the top: 'Serena is DOMINANT POWERFUL BRAVE and is our new leader. Her ASS controls all inferior men's minds.' And then there's this: 'If Sara Lee could get the recipe to those buns; it surely would be a garrantied trip to the top of the FORTUNE FIVE HUNDRED list.'

Some contributors are unwell. There is the childlike, 'U R REALLY SEXY I LIKE U'. The unsettling: 'That ass is icredible is perfect y will like to tuch it.'

And then there can be found what is clearly dangerous: 'i need more pictures on this.'

Some see a heavenly hand in this work of arse: GOOD GOD ALMIGHTY In the beauty of this woman, God reached the top of his creations. Thanks to the lord. Some give thanks straight to her: Man!!! Serena, let me tell you, you has the best body that i ever seen in my life! perfetc for me! I just love you! Serena I aint eva seen a ASS LIKE THAT! yo serina you really sexy baby i love ya and that a fine ass girl you sexy baby.

Some are simple: ha, Ulala! Oh! La Serenade . . . Many become lost for words: Shit! she is so . . . I AM SPEECHLESS. lost for words.

After that, me too.

21 January 2006

JOHNS REVELATION NO SURPRISE

Greg Prichard

The fact that Andrew Johns took drugs throughout his career won't surprise anyone in league circles, now he has made the admission.

The rumours, the stories—they've been around for years. The shocking thing is he never got caught.

How did that happen? Can anyone really be that lucky? The NRL prides itself on its drug-testing system, but here is a player who tried his luck on a regular basis for more than a decade and never tested positive. It really is amazing.

Different drugs stay in your system for different lengths of time. Players know that. But drug testers don't only arrive to take urine samples from players after games. The surprise visit is supposed to be their greatest weapon. Johns was a magician on the field and—it appears—a magician off it, as well.

If you've had anything to do with Johns, it isn't hard to buy his explanation that he needed to take drugs to cope with the pressure of being a famous football player. In an interview with the *Sydney Morning Herald* last year, he referred to his dislike for the spotlight by saying: 'I've just got a natural aversion to it.'

His admission that he battles depression doesn't come as any surprise, either. Johns has always had ups that go through the roof and downs that go through the floor. A genius in any field is different to the rest of us, but Johns is different again.

He could be the face of joy in the dressing-room after a win or drowning in sorrow after a loss. It was always extremes with Johns.

A person like him doesn't enjoy being interviewed regularly by reporters he knows. Add to that being constantly stopped in the street by people he doesn't know.

Johns would have preferred to have come off the field when the game was over and have that be the end of it.

'All the attention is a bit too much, but you learn to deal with it as you get older,' Johns said in a previous interview. 'I'm two different people: Andrew Johns out of football, with my close mates and family, and Joey Johns the footballer. That helps me cope with it.'

Johns, ever the superstar, has now been the subject of the two biggest league stories this year: one, his retirement, and now this. The drugs revelation is the biggest league story since the Bulldogs cheated the salary cap in 2002 and the biggest story about a league individual in memory.

Even with his playing days behind him, Johns has the ability to still rock the league world.

The question now is: where does he go from here? Yesterday, he probably felt surrounded, but from today he should be able to start feeling a weight disappearing from his shoulders. He has made public admissions that must have been very hard, and if he needs help in taking further steps forward, then he should get it.

Johns has a strong relationship with Cathrine Mahoney, and he has a son, Samuel, 7, by a previous relationship. He has a strong family around him, including a brother, Matthew, who was the voice of reason for him yesterday.

The greatest player of our time has admitted to making a huge mistake. He has been stupid, and he's been incredibly lucky to get away with it. His career could have easily been ruined. How it didn't come to that is astonishing.

But it takes a lot of guts to spill your guts the way Johns has. You have to hand it to him for that.

31 August 2007

ARROGANT PONTING MUST BE FIRED

Peter Roebuck

Ricky Ponting must be sacked as captain of the Australian cricket team. If Cricket Australia cares a fig for the tattered reputation of our national team in our national sport, it will not for a moment longer tolerate the sort of arrogant and abrasive conduct seen from the captain and his senior players over the past few days [January 2008]. Beyond comparison, it was the ugliest performance put up by an Australian side for 20 years. The only surprising part of it is that the Indians have not packed their bags and gone home. There is no justice for them in this country, nor any manners.

That the senior players in the Australian team are oblivious to the fury they raised among many followers of the game in this country and beyond merely confirms their own narrow and self-obsessed viewpoint. Doubtless they were not exposed to the messages that poured in from distressed enthusiasts aghast to see the scenes of bad sportsmanship and triumphalism presented at the SCG during and after the Test. Pained past players rang to express their disgust. It was a wretched and ill-mannered display and not to be endured from any side, let alone an international outfit representing a proud sporting nation.

Make no mistake, it is not only the reputation of these cricketers that has suffered. Australia itself has been embarrassed. The notion that Ponting can hereafter take the Australian team to India is preposterous. He has shown not the slightest interest in the well-being of the game, not the slightest sign of diplomatic skills, not a single mark of respect for his accomplished and widely admired opponents.

Harbhajan Singh can be an irritating young man but he is head of a family and responsible for raising nine people. And all the Australian elders want to do is to hunt him from the game. Australian fieldsmen fire insults from the corners of their mouths, an intemperate Sikh warrior overreacts and his rudeness is seized upon. It might impress barrack room lawyers.

In the past few days Ponting has presided over a performance that dragged the game into the pits. He turned a group of professional cricketers into a pack of wild dogs. As much can be told from the conduct of his closest allies in the team. As usual, Matthew Hayden crossed himself upon reaching three figures in his commanding second innings, a gesture he does not perform while wearing the colours of his state. Exactly how he combines his faith with throwing his weight around on the field has long bemused opposing sides, whose fondness for him ran out a long time ago. Hayden has much better in him.

Michael Clarke also had a dreadful match but he is a young man and has time to rethink his outlook. That his mind was in disarray could be told from his batting. In the first innings he offered no shot to a straight ball and in the second he remained at the crease after giving an easy catch to slip. On this evidence Clarke cannot be promoted to the vice-captaincy of his country. It is a captain's primary task to rear his younger players and to prepare his successor for the ordeals of office. Nothing need be said about the catch Clarke took in the second innings except that in the prevailing circumstances the umpires were ill-advised to take anyone's word for anything.

The Indians were convinced Ponting grounded a catch he claimed on the final afternoon at the SCG. Throughout those heated hours, the Australian remained hostile, kicking the ground, demanding decisions, pressuring the umpires. So much for the corporate smile that has been produced these last few years.

Probably the worst aspect of the Australians' performance was their conduct at the end. When the last catch was taken they formed into a huddle and started jumping up and down like teenagers at a rave. It was not euphoria. It was ecstasy. They had swallowed a dangerous pill called vengeance. Not one player so much as thought about shaking hands with the defeated and departing. So much for Andrew Flintoff consoling a stricken opponent in his hour of defeat.

Nor could Ponting and Gilchrist stop themselves publicly chiding Tony Greig for daring to criticise the timing of the declaration. They should have been thanking their lucky stars that three wickets had fallen in five balls, one of them in dubious circumstances. Australia had 150 runs and five minutes to spare. It was unfitting conduct from an Australian captain or vice-captain. By all accounts Ponting was later rude towards Indian reporters at his news conference.

Ponting has not provided the leadership expected from an Australian cricket captain and so must be sacked. On this evidence the time has also come to thank Hayden and Gilchrist for their services. None of them are bad fellows. All will look back on this match not as their finest hour but their worst. Obviously a new captain and side is required. But that is a task for another day. It is possible to love a country and not its cricket team.

8 January 2008

TIME FOR CLARKE TO DECIDE ON HIS CAREER PATH

Peter Roebuck

Michael Clarke needs to choose between a fraught personal life and his career in cricket. All the evidence indicates that the current position is untenable. As Mark Antony could testify, obsession can be a man's undoing. If Clarke is unwilling to make the call then cricket will make it for him. In the nick of time, Ricky Ponting sorted himself out. Now it is Clarke's turn.

Ordinarily, journos are the last people on earth entitled to speak about anyone else's affairs. Most adopt the approach advocated by the great Bill O'Reilly, namely that players are fair game on the park and otherwise off limits. Now and then black eyes and publicised text messages force reporters to don the clean skin but it is an uncomfortable guise reluctantly undertaken.

However, it is no longer possible to turn the other ear and ignore the gossip. Clarke's hasty trip home from New Zealand denies him the luxury of privacy. It is no small thing for a vice-captain to walk out on a team at any stage, let alone on the eve of a big match. A few days ago he was leading these same men, and doing a good job by all accounts. Make no mistake, a lot is at stake, for a fine player and Australian cricket.

Ordinarily a player rushes home upon hearing some dreadful news of a family loss, impending or completed. Or else he has been informed of a devastating sickness. Now and then a player is allowed to attend a birth in the modern way. Occasionally depression strikes a player down, a curse that afflicted Marcus Trescothick. On these occasions all and sundry conduct themselves with due sensitivity.

Clarke's case is different. His responsibilities do not permit withdrawal in any except the most desperate circumstances. None of the evidence indicates that any such conditions prevailed. Certainly he heard some bad news about his partner, but it pertained to disarray as opposed to crisis.

Clarke's problem is easy to state and hard to resolve. He is locked into a love affair with a beautiful young woman. Whatever the reality of her life, supposing reality makes an appearance now and then, Lara Bingle stumbles from public relations disaster to public relations calamity. Restaurateurs complain about her manners and the poor company she keeps. Fashionistas talk of her headstrong ways and dubious customs. Moreover, she seems intent on boosting the sales of all those magazines purchased by the female of the species. In short, she craves attention and courts controversy. Yet Michael, the class act of the pairing, seems besotted. Beauty and danger have always been a potent combination.

As far as Australian cricket is concerned, the problem is the instability caused by this turbulent relationship. Let us get away from all the talk about sportsmen being role models. Precious few of the younger brigade spend enough time away from their computers and iPods to give a hoot about anything else. In any case, it is time to stop expecting sportsmen to conduct themselves like novitiates. Let them inspire on the field and otherwise be granted the same leeway as everyone else.

Maturity is the issue. From a distance the romance has all the traits of a schoolboy crush. Clarke has scored a stack of runs for his country, has travelled to many places, has seen and done a lot, has become accomplished. By now gilded youth ought to have given way to adult sensibility. Perhaps it has. Perhaps the problem is that Bingle remains the same waif-like figure supposedly in need of protection.

On this occasion, it is true, Bingle has been grievously wronged. Apparently some dickhead thought it amusing to pass around pictures of her emerging from a shower. Her chivalrous partner rode to her rescue. Nothing in her life, though, suggests that she has ever emerged from the chrysalis of youthful beauty. It's a dilemma. Clarke yearns to fulfil himself yet remains in thrall to a lass living in a celebrity time warp.

By and large top-class sportsmen marry young. Among cricketers, Viv Richards, Ian Botham, Steve Waugh, and Sachin Tendulkar walked the aisle at an early age. All of these marriages survived the ensuing years. In each case the wife had the maturity and adaptability needed to survive the demands of the distant life. They understood their role, did not make any extra demands. They were the counterpoint that ambition required. Accordingly their partners were able to focus on their cricket.

Clarke has no such settlement in his life. Until it is obtained, Cricket Australia will be reluctant to put the national team completely in his hands. He has always come across as an essentially likeable young fellow currently a little off track but bound sooner or later to emerge as a sincere and big-hearted man. Now might be a good time to take that step.

3 March 2010

WHY I AM DISGUSTED WITH TIGER WOODS

Peter Stone

How long ago was it that Tiger Woods, in a speech he must have rehearsed so many times in company with a Hollywood director (pause for dramatic effect, a choking of the voice and, most of all, look sincere) said: 'I do plan to return to golf one day. I just don't know when that day will be.'

It was February 20, to be exact. So, just over three weeks later, he announces the Masters as his return to golf, which just about sums up the insincerity of his statement in front of the chosen few at PGA Tour headquarters in Ponte Vedra Beach, Florida.

No questions were allowed on his sexual exploits, which must have had legendary Tasmanian pants man Errol Flynn turning in his grave in admiration.

Shortly after news broke in November that Woods had a trophy cabinet full of cocktail waitresses, porn stars, etc, I wrote a column not so much defending Woods as observing that golfing history was full of philanderers who hadn't been exposed because the media were far less intrusive than in these times of the internet and a rabid tabloid press. It was also before every blonde Jungers, Grubbs and Jolie stepped forward.

Now I am as disgusted with Woods and his secret life as I have always been about his on-course behaviour, which runs the gamut of foul language, ugly fist pumps, the throwing of clubs (nearly decapitating a spectator at our Masters at Kingston Heath last November) and spitting. He was untouched by a fawning media that has since become increasingly feral.

About the only comments we should believe from his statement are that he has been 'selfish and foolish'. And, more tellingly, 'I thought I could get away with whatever I wanted to. I felt that I had worked hard my entire life and deserved to enjoy all the temptations around me. I felt I was entitled.'

How very true that is: 'I felt I was entitled.' 'Selfish.' It sums up everything about Woods. He feels he is not only bigger than the game he has dominated but also beyond the bounds of all moral and social behaviour.

His colleagues, good unionists that they are, have all said they welcome him back. Of course they do. When Woods turned professional in 1996, the total prizemoney for the PGA Tour was $US70 million. This year it is around $US270 million ($295 million). In 1997, Woods's first full year as a professional, 18 players won more than $US1 million. Last year, 87 players earned $US1 million-plus. They've filled their pockets on the back of Woods.

Give me Ernie Els any time. He is everything that is great about the game of golf and the most engaging bloke to have a chat with over a cold one. He was world No. 1 for a week in 1997 and for eight weeks, in brackets of four weeks, in 1998, but then Woods began his mesmerising march into the history books with very little left to achieve, save Jack Nicklaus's mark of 18 majors.

Yet the spectre of Woods surely haunts Els. He admitted it once, back around the turn of the century, when he sought help from a Dutch shrink, Josh Vanstiphout, to give him the mental fibre to tackle Woods.

Els has just three majors to his credit but six runner-up finishes. In 2000, he was second in the Masters to Vijay Singh and second to Woods in both the US and British opens.

The timing of Woods's statement, with the compliance of PGA Tour commissioner Tim Finchem, on the Friday of the WGC World Matchplay Championship (sponsored by Accenture, one of the companies which dropped Woods from its books), really riled the man who is known as The Big Easy for all the best of reasons. 'It's selfish,' he said. 'It takes a lot away from the tournament.'

Then, just last weekend, Els won the WGC-CA Championship at Doral to break a PGA Tour drought dating back to March 1998, when he won the Honda Classic.

His victory should have had the world of golf pondering his chances of winning at Augusta for a first time but the ink on the newsprint heralding his win was barely dry when Woods announced his return to golf at the Masters. Fade to the background Ernie Els.

The positive for Els is that he is back to the winner's circle in style. In 2007 he said it was the start of a three-year plan in which he would totally rededicate himself to the game. His three years was up and he'd delivered.

It would be great for Els to win among the magnolias and pine trees, but if he does, regrettably the headlines would be that Woods failed because he still has other issues on his mind.

21 March 2010

THE TEAM IT'S HARD TO FALL IN LOVE WITH

David Sygall

The Australian cricket team has an image problem.

It's one the players and Cricket Australia find hard to understand. It's an issue that extends beyond on-field controversies, polarising leadership and perceptions of arrogance. It's not just about poor scheduling, advertising overload, high ticket prices or confusion about the game's future. It won't be fixed by a stage-managed makeover, nor by the team winning match after match. The players are only part of the cause. But, as the faces of the juggernaut, they bear the brunt of public frustration. They are winners but they are not as loved as they should, could or want to be.

CA's research says the team's image is sound. Yet something is going wrong. And even experts are challenged to define the problem. It suggests there are many factors. The first stop must be the team itself.

There is a perception that they have a streak of arrogance and a lack of grace about the way they behave,' says the ABC's Jim Maxwell, who has covered cricket for 30 years.

'It's not universal but it's hard to ignore. [Captain Ricky Ponting] with his look of chewing the gum, unshaven, spitting in the hands, his dishevelled cap . . . it's not perceived well by everyone.

'My 15-year-old son was on the fence getting autographs [at the Sydney Test] and, with a few exceptions, he thought the Pakistanis were far more accommodating and friendly. They come across as more relaxed and not so caught up with their celebrity.

'I don't think there's any doubt that the senior Australian players recently have been so caught up in the cricket and their business deals that there's not much left over.

'It's not to say they're unlikeable. There's just a different agenda these days. You'd just hate to think it would lead to them losing the common touch. They should always be grateful to the people who support them. You can run the risk sometimes of losing touch with that reality.'

The common touch with a dash of class was among Steve Waugh's strengths. He was heavily criticised at times for a gruff leadership style yet, on an ABC radio poll recently, was voted overwhelmingly the most popular captain of the modern era.

Former CA and CNSW board member Brian Freedman—a long-time associate of the Waugh brothers Steve and Mark through his role as president of grade club Bankstown—says Steve 'didn't win that poll on personality. It was because he was tough and uncompromising. People like that. So there's no simple answer to why the team's less popular than it should be. On one hand, the public wants them to be tough, but if they go a touch too far, everyone gets into them. Many fans want their cake and to eat it, too.'

Freedman describes the team's sportsmanship as 'reasonable' although, 'We are probably lacking some of the gracious personalities we used to have.' The big problem, in his view, is that the players are physically and symbolically distanced from the public.

'They are certainly more aloof these days,' he says. 'Steve and Mark used to play grade cricket at least a couple of times every season. We had a rule at our club that everyone had to bring a plate of afternoon tea. The last time Steve played for us he was Australian captain, and he turned up with a child under one arm and a plate of caramel slice in the other. There's none of that any more.

'The players move in more rarefied air these days. There's all the physios who make them rest, pull them out of the state games and so on. It has had a negative effect, I believe. It's moved the players further away from the people.

'Money is the king now. Managers get their 20 per cent . . . and push the players into more and more money-making opportunities. It makes the players less accessible and "relatable". Those sorts of issues weren't around as much even 10 years ago.'

Other factors, Freedman suggests, are less complex. 'I was talking to [CA chief executive] James Sutherland about why Shane Watson's not as liked as he should be,' he says.

'I've known Shane since he was a kid, and he's a lovely fellow. We thought it might be as simple as him not smiling enough.'

Perhaps the players take themselves too seriously and are losing touch with average people. But cricket icon Len Pascoe puts the blame for the mixed feelings squarely on administrators.

He is deeply troubled with cricket's direction, and is convinced the players have become scapegoats.

'Cricket's always been a working man's game, and when it becomes too expensive for many people to go to, alarm bells ring,' he says. 'The crowds were small in Sydney. "Thommo" [Jeff Thomson] and I were just talking about it. We're very concerned.'

Television coverage and the stadiums have become loaded with advertising, he says. Match scheduling is out of control. 'Who wants to go to a game of cricket when it's a menagerie of advertising on billboards, scoreboards, sightboards, everywhere you turn?' Pascoe asks. 'It's intrusive.'

'Same with the commentators. There's too many of them, and it's become a boys' club. They're over-talking in their description of the game and living in their own pasts. Give it a rest and just call the game, like [Henry] Blofeld, [John] Arlott, [Richie] Benaud and [Alan] McGilvray did. Kerry Packer had a wonderful ability to gauge the mood of the viewers. He knew when enough was enough. That's all been lost.

'All these bits of the jigsaw puzzle are changing the way the team is perceived. There is no more mystique. The game has been denuded. It needs to breathe. And because the players are the public face, they are copping the brunt of people's frustration.'

Pascoe believes the players are being pushed to meet the 'insatiable demand of the marketing machine' and the perception of the national team is suffering as a result.

Backroom deals filter through to affect the team's public image. Huge money and responsibility have led to CA being increasingly vigilant in protecting its brand. It has been challenged recently to reassess its approach because of two factors: the retirements of famous players such as Shane Warne, Glenn McGrath, Adam Gilchrist and Waugh, and the emergence of Twenty20.

'The value of CA's brand suffered in the eyes of potential sponsors when they lost those individuals,' says Associate Professor Jane Summers, a sports marketing expert at the University of Southern Queensland. 'Those players' image and value was bigger than the team brand. CA's response has been to place more focus on the team, rather than individuals within it. It needs a product that can withstand the loss of big names so they still have something valuable to sell to their sponsors.'

Under pressure to protect the team's brand, players cannot risk exposure that contravenes a unified image. This leads to a perception of one-dimensional commentary from the players in the media.

'CA is very cognisant of the fact that the team has to have an almost neutral persona,' Summers says.

The individuality—even the beloved eccentricities—of past players could return through Twenty20. A discussion is brewing about how differently the players might be viewed across the game's different forms. 'They are completely different products with different expectations of their representatives,' Summers says. 'We've seen it already with Andrew Symonds. His personal brand and the Test team's brand didn't mesh.'

Whatever CA's research says, there is clearly a need for consideration and action if the national team is to regain the public affection it once enjoyed.

'For a team that has been devoid of the types of scandals associated with the NRL and AFL, the public's perception of them isn't nearly as good as it should be,' says Gordon Coulter, a corporate and sports public relations partner with Wrights PR.

If asked to help improve the team's image, what would be his advice?

'I would encourage them . . . to be themselves a lot more, to show more of their true personalities. The team today lacks the star power and class of some of the previous teams but it would help their image if they were more natural and related better to average people.

'In the past, you had teams of champions with distinct and often pleasant or classy personalities. They were allowed, and had the time, to express themselves. They played very competitively but people didn't find it offensive. I think the team today just doesn't identify with the public the way it used to.'

17 January 2010

AN OPEN LETTER TO GINA RINEHART

Kathryn Wicks

Dear Mrs Rinehart,

How good were the Socceroos! It was fantastic to watch them against Japan in their World Cup qualifier this week. Real fighting spirit.

Anyway, forget the blokes. While that was all happening, FIFA, that's the mob that runs world football, decided that Asia should have five places, not three, at the next Women's World Cup.

This means Australia can't miss out unless something goes disastrously wrong in the next three years—like the W-League collapses or half the girls retire and get jobs that actually pay enough money for them to eat.

Did you know most of the men get paid more in a week than a women's player gets in a year?

Well, have I got a deal for you. You know your fellow billionaires Clive Palmer and Nathan Tinkler like to deposit their spare change—maybe a million or three—in football.

So why not you? There's this terrific team, the Matildas. They've got just as much fighting spirit in them as the Socceroos but they're ranked higher—No. 10 in the world—and they'll go into the next Women's World Cup in 2015 ranked No. 2 in Asia. North Korea aren't allowed to compete because six of them took steroids at last year's World Cup. Japan are the world champions and No. 1 team in Asia and I'm a bit worried they're getting away from us.

People who know more than me about these things reckon the Matildas have got every chance of winning one of the next two World Cups. They've got a group of young women aged 17–23 that the experts are calling the golden generation.

Anyway, it's not just the young ones. There's Lisa De Vanna—she's a West Australian, you know, and probably the best player in the team. She's 27 and she wants to win a World Cup so much she recently got in trouble with her bosses for applauding a move that will bring more professionalism to women's football. I know there are plenty more players who want to train fulltime—in fact it is a source of unnecessary stress around this team.

Now imagine if the top 25 players could make minimum wage—like maybe what they would get if they stacked shelves at Woollies. They could train six days a week, have more camps and just maybe spend enough time together in the next three years to have a red-hot go at that Women's World Cup.

So how about it? If you want to check out your potential investment, some of them are playing a friendly against New Zealand next Sunday, June 24, in Wollongong. It's a bit of a shame the superstars won't be playing—they're in Europe and the US bettering themselves and making a few bucks. But still, plenty of good young ones will be on the pitch—and it's always fun flogging the Kiwis regardless of the sport.

And it's also a bit of a shame Australia aren't going to the Olympics and New Zealand are—but I think the Matildas are looking at this as an opportunity to show those old dudes at FIFA that Asia should really have more spots at the Olympics—or at least play off with the Oceania champions for a place. Maybe next time.

I can't promise you a great financial return on your investment but I am sure if you can spare some change you'll change women's football in this country forever.

Yours in football

Kath

15 June 2012

THIS
SPORTING LIFE

For many, supporting a football team or an individual athlete can turn into an obsession. It provides relief, a purpose, hope that someone else can enrich them. However, those in the sporting pursuit can be overwhelmed by the experience.

In this chapter are examples of how people can inspire others, how sporting teams can be all-encompassing and how individuals can be driven by the sporting experience.

How rugby league can overwhelm you is clear in Steve Mascord's piece on John Dorahy, which was part of an *SMH* series about Sporting Heroes. Mascord is one of rugby league's biggest tragics, having travelled around the world for years on end watching the game in the most bizarre spots. If there is a league game being played in the deepest Congo or the Sahara Desert, more than likely Mascord will be there. Friends are accustomed to him sending Facebook messages saying that one day he is in Manchester, the next Houston in search of either a league game or a Kiss concert.

Roy Masters provides enlightening articles on what it means to be part of the South Sydney and St George rugby league machine, and how it can enrich your life. Masters, one of Australia's most respected journalists and who knows rugby league backwards through his long first-grade coaching stints with Western Suburbs and St George, is renowned for his anecdotes. One of the best in the book is in his piece on the 'People's Team'—the South Sydney Rabbitohs. Jersey Flegg's speech is the clue, and a gnarly Rabbitohs supporter provides the perfect answer back.

Then there is Craig Young's masterful piece on how important his father was in his development. And for telling stories, none beats Myer Rosenblum providing details to Spiro Zavos about his trip to New Zealand, and an encounter with a Wellington waitress.

GG

MY SPORTING HERO

Steve Mascord

This writer finally secured John Dorahy's autograph in November 1981. It was the Illawarra Steelers' first training session for their debut season in what was then the Sydney premiership.

My sister and I were the only spectators, and my sister was there somewhat reluctantly.

At one stage, I remember Barry Jensen, a hooker from Newtown who played for the State that year, returning from a long road run and pressing a finger to one nostril while discharging a generous quantity of snot from the other. Spotting my 11-year-old sister watching intently, he graciously apologised.

But back to John Dorahy. I was a pimply 12-year-old schoolboy and he was a 27-year-old former Test fullback who had returned to his home town after seven years with Western Suburbs and Manly.

After he silently signed my 1978 Amco Rugby League Autograph Book, which featured him in Magpie colours, I was approached by a man who looked like Bob Millward, the Illawarra secretary (they hadn't started calling them chief executives in those days), whose picture was always in the *Illawarra Mercury*.

'That signature cost me $40,000,' he said. I smiled weakly, not sure if he was making a joke. It now ranks as the funniest thing Bob ever said to me.

For the next few months, John Dorahy—the Steelers captain—and I saw a lot of each other. Myself and Scott Dunn, a childhood friend who is now a part-time rugby league and basketball writer for Australian Associated Press, went to just about every training session. And John was at them all, too, by sheer coincidence.

Not long before this, I hadn't known too much about football. Many people say this is still the case. It was something to do with Rex Mossop and those crumpled up old magazines my uncle pretended to read (no, not those sorts of magazines).

Then I went to a few games. St George and Cronulla, two successive annual Saints–Dapto trial matches and that modern classic, the 1981 KB Cup round-one tie between Penrith and NSW Country at Dapto Showground.

But in 1982, I attended just about every game the Steelers played. And I soon discovered that John Dorahy was a bit of a legend.

He was a wonderful runner of the ball, with a jink and sidestep and a sudden burst of pace. He tackled opposing centres head-on and up-ended them, and he could chip, grubber, punt and convert with the best of them.

My favourite thing about him was the way he carried the ball, in the middle of his body with both palms spread out, so those hapless defenders didn't know if he was going to pass left, pass right or kick.

Mind you, it wasn't always the opposition that was hapless in that first year.

Canberra were hapless when we beat them 45–0 at Wollongong Show-ground, when it still had a dogtrack around it. We, on the other hand, were six points more hapless when we were beaten 51–0 just seven days later by Newtown, when they still had a team.

It's the biggest form reversal in modern football I know of, and will stay that way until none of the Balmain cheergirls can get a date.

But my favourite windswept memory from 1982 (all winter memories in Wollongong are windswept) was of a drizzly July 25. The Steelers were playing the much-maligned Manly at Wollongong, just as they are tomorrow.

We were behind 17–2 at half-time, from memory, but for some reason there was confidence in the air among the locals. Maybe they were just stupid.

But fullback John Sparks proceded to blitz the Sea Eagles in the second half, and with seconds (it may have been minutes, but it seems like seconds now) remaining, former Eagle Dorahy took the ball about 22.75 m out, side-stepped the charging Les Boyd, and potted a field goal. Fulltime: Illawarra 26, Manly 25.

They used to call Dorahy 'Joe Cool'. For years I thought they made the name up specially for him, and wondered why it wasn't 'John Cool'.

Another memory is of Dorahy's stint with British club Hull Kingston Rovers, which began in the 1983–84 season. Being 14, and therefore not having been to Hull, I thought this unthinkably glamorous.

One night I sat up until all hours and watched Dorahy play in the premiership final for Hull KR against Castleford at Headingley. The very next Tuesday I made an effort to catch a bus into the showground and—low and behold, there he was, white legs and all, at training.

I greeted his transformation from Satellite God to flesh and blood in much the same way as the Israelites must have marvelled at their dry socks, having crossed the Red Sea. I spent the night standing between the goalposts while he practised his kicking and concentrating hard as I booted the ball back to him, not wanting him to know I was hopelessly unco-ordinated.

This night was perhaps the beginning of my mind's inability to draw any distinction between the words 'travel' and 'rugby league', a disorder which reached a sad nadir in late 1995 when I spent four hours on several trains from sullen St Helens to chilly Northampton for the exulted honour of watching the second half of a game between Moldova and Morocco.

It is also probably the night I began to think of British league as being far better than it really is, a misconception I am proudly still afflicted by.

Now for the most salacious revelation of all: Dorahy started me off on something else which has stayed with me for life. He is responsible for the first time I got drunk.

He was opening a gymnasium, John Dorahy's RGE Nautilus Fitness Centre, in central Wollongong and had advertised a gala launch. It was the mid-'80s and Scott Dunn and I, having no life, went along.

We were out of place. Most of the people there were not football fans, but rather older teens and early 20-somethings who wanted to pump iron and pick up. Lord Mayor Frank Arkell was there, too.

Anyway, the RGE stood for Randall, Gartner and Eadie: John's former Manly teammates Terry Randall, Russel Gartner and Graham Eadie, who ran an ill-fated chain of gymnasiums.

Then they started serving orange juice. But it wasn't normal orange juice, it tasted funny. After about, oh, nine of them, I felt dizzy. I found myself strangely fixated by someone's leotards and had to go outside. And I remember seeing the ER&S smokestack at Port Kembla in a whole new light on the bus ride home.

About a year later, I actually managed to get a girlfriend, and because I resembled a matchstick with zits, I went to John's fitness centre at her insistence. It was my first active visit to a gym.

But of the two habits, I must say that drinking has had the most lasting effect.

Since those days John and I have grown apart. I briefly had some meaningful contact with him again in 1994, when we had several conversations—me as reporter, he as Wigan coach—with him about to get sacked despite having won everything on offer.

When you're a sports reporter, so many heroes become tainted when you deal with them as people. Champions can turn out to be insecure or arrogant or not very smart.

But Dorahy has always been helpful and humble. In recent seasons he has split with the Perth Reds, where he was a development officer, and just a few weeks ago he was cut loose by Warrington, where he was coach.

By following a sportsperson closely, regardless of his or her ability or level of competition, you learn about the nature of sport and—without wanting to sound pompous—about human nature.

Football ain't war, it's life.

Dorahy missed a goal at Wembley which would have won Hull KR the Challenge Cup final in 1986. For a normal person, such misfortune would have been crushing.

But hardened by incessant competition and well-justified self-belief, he returned to Australia and made the Country Origin side in 1988—16 years after his representative debut. He was still playing at Halifax a decade after being written off.

And alongside being a leaguie for life, an expansionist, an Anglophile, a patriotic product of the Gong and an occasional drunk, I'd like to think persistence is a quality I learnt from watching John Dorahy.

Another lesson learnt, this time for budding journalists: Never use the word 'I' in your copy. It makes you look like a prat.

2 May 1997

SOUTHS EMBODY REDEMPTION, RESILIENCE AND THE GREAT GAME

Roy Masters

'The People's Team' proclaimed a banner carried by one of the 80,000 in the march to Sydney Town Hall on an oppressively hot day in November 2000, protesting the sacking of South Sydney from the NRL.

It's a tag that neatly summarises what the Rabbitohs mean to rugby league and the city which gave birth to the game in Australia.

The foundation club is an antidote to the occasions when the code suffers from lack of a looking-glass self: when it cannot see itself as others do.

I'm not referring to the sneering of rugby union purists, or Melbourne's AFL worshippers who see none of the rhythm and all of the bruise of rugby league.

Rather, Souths is a reminder in times when the code strays from its virtues: stoic bravery, flint-eyed honesty, social justice and above all, resilience.

South Sydney won more premierships than any other club because it relied on local juniors from the working-class tenements of Redfern, Botany and Mascot, recruited wisely and contracted all players fairly.

Unlike some of today's football clubs that feign interest in indigenous talent in order to win government grants, discrimination against the youth of La Perouse and 'the Block' was always less than elsewhere.

What Aboriginal kid wouldn't want to come to Redfern when stories of Kevin Longbottom kicking goals barefooted from over half way spread to the bush?

Or John Sattler captaining the club to a premiership while suffering a broken jaw?

Or George Piggins's unstoppable try at Lidcombe in 1976?

The Rabbitohs' mascot is the only one of the NRL's Australian clubs' emblems that means anything human. The others are named after birds, animals, mythical beasts, the weather or American/English folklore.

The turn of the 19th century rabbitoh was a man who earned his living selling dead rabbits for food.

Significantly, Souths' resilience is reflected in the fact it is the only rugby league club to be kicked from the competition and subsequently readmitted.

Even News Ltd submitted to the Rabbitohs' hold on the people when perhaps half of those who marched behind president Piggins to Town Hall were followers of other clubs.

News Ltd, then half-owners of the NRL, challenged the Federal Court decision to reinstate the Rabbitohs, subsequently won the High Court verdict but then declined to exercise their newly established power to boot them from the league once more.

'The Pride of the League', declared sportswriter Claude Corbett in the 1920s when Souths won seven premierships in eight years. Another sportswriter, George Crawford, created the dictum, 'When Souths are going well, rugby league is going well.'

South Sydney supporters have cut down the league's lofty figures when they commit the code's biggest crime—'big headedness'.

Jersey Flegg, the Eastern Suburbs stalwart who headed the NSWRL, once addressed a public meeting at a time he was under siege. Anxious to demonstrate the senior position he held on the Metropolitan Water, Drainage and Sewerage Board, Flegg proclaimed to the rowdy mob, 'I'll have you know I have been connected to the water board for 30 years.'

A Souths' supporter at the back yelled out, 'So's my shithouse.'

Souths stars such as Gary Stevens, Ron Coote, John O'Neill and Piggins worked as garbos, brewery truck drivers, brickies and carpenters.

Even when they retired, they were up at daybreak with hammer and nails, unlike heroes from neighbouring teams who sought sinecures and soft positions, such as 'account manager'.

Souths' last premiership was 1971 but they had already begun to leak players to other clubs. It's not hard to figure out why.

Rich clubs think the most important thing is spirit. Poor clubs know it's money.

When a South Sydney official was observed carrying a plastic bucket of 20c pieces from the leagues club to his car parked at Redfern Oval, the players understood why they were being paid less than what was offered elsewhere.

The official milked the poker machine trays, covered the coins with ice on the pretext of taking it over to the Rabbitohs dressing room, but the handle of the bucket pulled though the plastic holes, showering Chalmers Street with two bob coins.

Since then, money has always been the problem, as it is to vast numbers of rugby league supporters. During the Super League war, Souths used some of the Optus funding to keep their leagues club afloat, rather than buy players.

Even today, despite the club being owned by a Hollywood superstar (Russell Crowe) and the scion of one of Australia's wealthiest families (Peter Holmes à Court), it is in debt.

According to the 2011 financial report, Souths forecast a loss of $204,318 and has sold all its real estate assets, including the four-level Chalmers Street building, 198-space car park and 10 home units.

The development is in administration, the football club now leases office space and the small leagues club struggles.

I can't see Souths beating the resourceful Bulldogs, brilliant Storm or experienced Sea Eagles in the finals, but a near sell-out of available grand final tickets strongly hints that Rabbitohs supporters believe their team will be there.

Or perhaps supporters of other clubs, like the ones who marched with Piggins in 1999, have rationalised that if their team fails to make the semis, they can cheer for Souths.

After all, we recognise the old Souths in the skill and grit of Englishman Sam Burgess, the courageous Michael Crocker, the local junior halfback, Adam Reynolds, the loyal indigenous winger, Nathan Merritt, and the breath-taking power of Greg Inglis.

Souths part-own grand final day via the award of the Clive Churchill Medal to the best player, and should any of these five be so honoured, it would say much for redemption and resilience and all that is good in our great game.

18 August 2012

DRAGONS FIRED WITH RELIGIOUS FERVOUR TO END LONG WAIT

Roy Masters

If you are disillusioned by the cold, corporate hand of business on sport, or appalled at reports of match fixing in cricket, journey to Kogarah on Sunday and join a crowd of 18,000 fans and inhale the spring air, ripe with the sweet smell of possibility. Witness the pre-game sideline antics, the innocent pageantry that still exists in sport. The grand old ground will shake and rattle like a 1960s Valiant if St George Illawarra prevail over the Sea Eagles, initiating a wild ride which fans pray won't end until grand final day, October 3.

Hope will be highest in the hearts on the Kogarah hill, those aged 30 and under who have not seen a captain in a red and white jumper lift the premiership trophy.

Former players will assemble on 'Stoney's Slab' at WIN Jubilee Oval, a square of concrete named after premiership prop forward, Robert Stone, who succumbed to brain cancer a few years ago.

Afterwards, 'the Skinny Coach', Wayne Bennett, or 'Old Man Winner' as I prefer to call him, may allow himself a slight smile at his decision to leave Queensland and take another title ride into the sunset.

Then he will stroll to a media conference, temper expectations and create the impression he loves the experience about as much as a tax audit.

The fans—probably the most knowledgeable in the NRL—will flood across to the Leagues Club, or stream up to the Royal Hotel, Carlton, and bathe in the after-glow of the match.

Well, the truth is you won't be able to join them at Jubilee Oval unless you snapped up a ticket Tuesday after Red V members were given first opportunity.

The home club chooses the venue for the first semi final match while the NRL retains the revenue. That's a 'no-brainer' for the Dragons who opted to reward its tribe, meaning many can walk to the match, as their grandparents once did.

Last year, St George Illawarra rejected a $250,000 offer from the NRL to move the same match to ANZ Stadium, Homebush.

Across all sports there is a growing gap between the fan and the athlete, as ticket prices rise to pay the salaries of sportspeople who resent being role models and loathe the scrutiny of an increasingly intrusive media.

St George Illawarra has always been highly sensitive to the expectations of its fans, and while playing at their citadel gives the players more unity and energy, it's also a thank-you to the club's support base.

They are principally middle-class, the AB demographic which editors of broadsheet newspapers and glossy magazines lust after.

Professor George Foster, the chair of Business at Stanford University, was raised in Kogarah where his father was the principal of James Cook High School.

Foster, who has not missed a rugby league grand final in 20 years, has been asked to deliver the oration at the October 1 memorial to a US Ambassador to Australia. If the Dragons make the season decider, he plans to be there by kick off.

When the Swans—also red and white—came to Sydney in 1982, many of them settled in the St George district.

They have subsequently moved to the eastern suburbs, nearer their Centennial Park home and a view of the sea.

Nor will the players of the AFL's GWS expansion team live at Blacktown.

The AFL is being deceitful in promoting the image it wants to convert Sydney's working class west. It covets an upper middle class corridor along Pennant Hills, Castle Hill and Baulkham Hills within easy access of its new NSW Government funded home of the Showground at Homebush.

The sweep of red roofed houses along the Princes Highway to Tom Ugly's Bridge is a bulwark against other codes. Rugby league is the main religion and St George the principal denomination.

Rugby league's origin and ethos is working class but this image is a 21st century myth. The code has never made much of its upwardly mobile climb to the so called superior suburbs over the past 30 years.

The Dragons' opponents on Sunday enjoy being called 'Silvertails' and Liberal leader Tony Abbott's final photo opportunity on the day before he faced the people in the polls was to drop in at Brookvale Oval in his electorate and pull on a Sea Eagles jumper and run some drills.

Sure, Abbott prefers rugby union, as do some of the inhabitants of Blakehurst and Kyle Bay, who will pay $500 for a ticket to the Bledisloe Cup match between the Wallabies and All Blacks at ANZ Stadium on Saturday night. Some of their neighbours will fly to Melbourne to watch the Swans play the Western Bulldogs. But south of Tempe is Dragons land and it turns red and white once again, after you pass Cronulla and head to Wollongong.

The older St George fans like their players to be a decent, respectful reflection of themselves.

This is why the club would rather lose a premiership than risk a major scandal, like the NRL Hiroshima which struck the Storm.

The need to nurture the image began with the first of their 11 premierships in 1956.

The mid twentieth century was the pivot on which sport turned, leaving noble amateurs, such as Dr Roger Bannister, the first man to break the four minute mile, and Sir Edmund Hillary, the first to climb Mt Everest, as rearguards to the past.

Amateurism was in retreat. The tradition of paying athletes and swimmers in trinkets and trophies, as if their glory was somehow devalued by something as base as money, was disappearing.

Golf, tennis and rugby union were the bastions against a fast-fading amateurism, replaced by a hypocritical shamateurism, which embraced boot money for the rugby lads.

Rugby league has never made any pretence its players were paid. Nor have the Dragons denied it retained star players on the poker machine revenue of its 'Taj Mahal,' although many have stayed for a contract two thirds the value of what they could receive elsewhere.

Two of the original four 'Immortals' came from St George—John Raper and Reg Gasnier—and another, Graeme Langlands, was soon added.

All completed their careers as one-club men.

The best adjective I have heard applied to rugby league came from former Prime Minister Paul Keating, who described it to me as 'earthy'.

He didn't mean dirty, although that was a label applied in the 1970s when punch-ups were common and the 'phantom biter' lurked.

Nor did he mean soiled, although cases of sexual assault and salary cap rorts stained the code.

He wasn't referring to the two mud caked captains, St George's Norm Provan and Wests Arthur Summons, who left the saturated SCG in 1963, arm in arm. A photograph taken by Fairfax's John O'Gready is the model for the premiership trophy.

No, Keating used the word in reference to its honest toil. The players most regarded in the code are those who perform the self-sacrificial tasks of diving on a loose ball, charging down a kick, backing up on every play with little prospect of receiving the ball.

Bennett has instilled these skills in the Dragons after they lost their way for a while.

He has also varied the attack, meaning the team is less reliant on tries from kicks.

He also recruited the New Zealand hooker, Nathan Fien, midway through last year. Fien broke his leg in the opening round this year but has returned to provide much needed variety around the rucks. All clubs need an X factor in the play offs. Fien is the Dragons' X factor.

Watching a Bennett coached team click is akin to hearing music played right for the first time, or studying a flight of birds in perfect formation.

His best teams hum.

Remember the swift passage of the ball to Steve Renouf when the Bennett coached Broncos won two premierships against the Dragons in 1992 and 1993?

It didn't help that a former St George junior, Chris Johns, fed Renouf the ball and Bennett manufactured a game plan which itemised the Broncos weaknesses and then told his players it was prepared by Dragons' coach, Brian Smith.

But if the Dragons claim the premiership, he will be forgiven. After all, it's been a long wait. Thirteen premierships in 24 years, then none in the next 30 years, with five losing grand finals in between.

St George football is like a drink that makes you laugh then weep, then gibber. Hope springs eternal at Kogarah. It sometimes springs insane.

Watch the crowd in the top deck of the grandstand on Sunday if the TV cameras take you there.

If anxiety has a sound, you will detect its groaning rumble before kickoff.

If the Dragons fire ahead—which they should against the injury depleted Sea Eagles—listen to the shivering roar. Watch the season ticket holders chatter and cheer.

Their exhilaration, camaraderie will be inspiring, transporting.

The joy they share will be akin to sneaking a blanket over your head when you were a child. The troubled world goes away and nothing outside that delicious, sacred space seems to matter.

9 September 2010

MY SPORTING HERO

Craig Young

When we played in the graveyard, it was Edson. Across the road from the girls' school, just near the primary school, down the road from our high school, the graveyard was heaven.

The church made of brick had a back door from which brick steps descended with an iron rail.

Perched on top of those stairs you overlooked a green pitch. Enough of a pitch for us to play the round ball game. And to dream.

Headstones were always in great heart. It was as if they were there for us. It was as if they hummed and they sung to our every kick.

In the graveyard we played soccer. In the graveyard, Edson Arantes dos Nascimento was my hero. Maybe you know him as Pele.

The great Brazilian soccer player. Maybe the greatest soccer player of all time. Feted by kings and queens, the Pope.

Edson was my hero. But it was strange. Surely my hero should have been a goalkeeper? For I was a goalkeeping rugby league player.

When my best mate, Con Triandafilou, dreamed of conquering the soccer world, I was there and dreamed his dream.

When Con dribbled, weaved and then laid boot to ball, it was me who sailed to the right . . . maybe it was the left.

Con scored more goals in the graveyard than any man could have saved.

But that was the graveyard.

Across the road from 'Biv's' place, just down a steep road from our high school—a road we enjoyed watching 'Skak' fly down on a skateboard—was another pitch.

We enjoyed the sight and laughed loud when Skak came a cropper. We rolled around and laughed even louder when our mate returned to show us a grazed thigh, oozing blood.

It didn't stop our mate from fielding in the outer, for the pitch across the road from Biv's place was made for cricket.

We all made hundreds on the pitch wedged between two barbwire fences.

You batted at the power station end. A snick behind which hit the fence labelled 'High Voltage. Keep Out' and the batter walked.

Only 10 paces mind you, and it was your turn to bowl. Down hill and only spin. Like all youngsters growing up, we had our arguments and it was then that one bowled a bit faster.

When I took the ball or the bat, my hero was Viv, as in Richards. The gum-chewing, arrogant West Indian. The most confident cricketer I've seen.

And when Viv wasn't making hundreds he was putting on a show.

Like the time Dad took us to the first day-nighter at the hallowed Sydney Cricket Ground. Australia v the West Indians, Viv's team.

And what a place the SCG was. It will remain so, forever.

You'd finish playing junior league, 7s to 10s, if memory serves me correct, and it was off to the ground where legends were made.

The rugby league match of the day was always on a Saturday. If only it was the same now.

Dad and the boys would meet at the Carrington Hotel. While they downed schooners and debated sport, the lads and I had a sand pebble–based playground to enjoy.

The swings made things difficult but tip turned to tackle many times. The pebbles were extracted from wounds later that night by caring mums who would abuse fathers for allowing their sons to play such games.

The games ended when Dad and the boys hastily exited the old hotel and passed the playground. The walk across Moore Park was brisk and as always we'd arrive at half-time in reserve grade.

The boys stood on the concourse at the Brewongle end. We kids hugged the stairs which lead to the stand. Legs draped over the stairs, heads sticking between the rails. Best seats in the house.

And Ron Coote was my hero. Souths or Easts it mattered little. No-one covered the ground and made the tackles Ron Coote did. Coote left the ground to make tackles. Even as an aged player the lanky man with tiring sticks left

the ground to make tackles. Little wonder my Souths jumper had No 8 on it.

But back to Viv. Dad was delivering bread for the long gone Mother's Choice in those days. Got a mate from Tip Top bakeries to ferry the team assembled at the Carrington to the SCG on this history-making night.

We piled into the back of the bread truck and made for the famous ground. Our man from Tip Top went straight into the Members' Stand, for the privileged had run short of bread—or so he told the gateman—on the night the pyjama game was born.

But it wasn't bread being delivered. No, it was Dad and me, and the boys from the pub.

The green coat was no match for grown men with a belly of beer and one young child when the back door on the baker's truck swung open. We settled into seats some seven rows from the fence.

And what a night it was. Australia won. My hero got a duck. It only served to instil in this young lad that we are all mortal. Thanks, Viv.

But anyway, down the road from the real pitch, across the road from Biv's place was a claycourt, several in fact.

My mates played tennis. When I played, McEnroe was my hero. But I could never beat Biv, Skak or Digger—they were Bjorn Borgs.

Across the road from the tennis courts was a monstrous pitch. A racecourse, in fact. 'Canterbury' read the sign out the front.

Dad always provided pocket money but reckoned if I left the family flat and went down to the track after a day's racing I could earn a little more.

Of course he was right. Emus are barred from race courses nowadays and it's a pity. For when I was a lad, sporting my way through high school, picking up discarded betting tickets and cashing in winners ensured I could have a bet.

Dad never cared about me betting but Mum did.

And it was at the racetrack that I found a hero. A black horse named Kingston Town.

Champion is a word that racing folk use loosely nowadays. I say Kingston Town was a 'freak'.

And I remember telling Dad the 'black horse' would become one of the greats.

No doubt it was after I'd caught the bus to Ashfield station and jumped on the rattler bound for Rosehill. I'd climb onto a big wooden box that afforded the opportunity of seeing only the final 200m of any race but it was always the best.

Kingston Town made sure of that. When Malcolm Johnston let this equine athlete down nothing went any quicker or looked so fluent. Nothing at all.

But anyway, my sporting hero?

All of the above. Add Mark Spitz. At the Olympic Games in Munich in 1972 the bloke swam like a fish, won seven gold medals and broke seven world records. How wouldn't he be a hero?

Ali, the greatest. What about Turkish weightlifter Naim Suleymanoglu? Lifts three times his body weight and wins gold medals at three consecutive Olympic Games. And the pocket Hercules smokes.

And there are more.

But none to match my sporting hero.

Bob Young played wing for Bathurst Railway. He could barefoot on water. He played golf, squash and touch football. He even jogged. He could do anything. He was the greatest card player I've ever seen. And he encouraged me to play sport and was there when I did.

Bob Young is my father. He is my sporting hero.

14 June 1997

THE RENAISSANCE MAN

Spiro Zavos

His eye is as glittering still as that of the Ancient Mariner. His handshake is firm. Despite his great age, his shoulders are square and he retains the ranginess of the lively flanker he once was. Myer Rosenblum was born in Pretoria on January 10, 1907. He is the oldest living Wallaby. With his mind brimming with memories and opinions, he is the epitome of the Wallaby in winter.

He remembers the Tests he played in New Zealand in 1928, three against the All Blacks and one against the New Zealand Maori, as if he were still back on the mud of Athletic Park more than 70 years ago.

'I scored two tries, you know, in the first Test,' he said. 'Even though I was marked by the great wing forward, Cliff Porter. We later became great friends. The New Zealanders were big and tough but they weren't dirty. Not like the game now, which is full of biff and bang.'

The Australians lost the Test series. But New Zealand journalists were full of praise for the tourists, who were described: 'A picturesque, fleet-footed, mobile force, which tossed the ball with gay abandon and at times exhibited such dazzling speed and combination as to make the New Zealanders look sluggish.'

Rosenblum's first Test try came, according to a press report, after 'the ball swung across the breadth of the field and back, passing from hand to hand, before the harassed defence finally yielded'.

His second try came after an Australian attack of more than 50 m before the ball rolled clear of the ruck for Rosenblum to seize it and dive across the line.

'I'll tell you my secret,' he said. 'I kept close to Cyril Towers every time he had the ball. Cyril was a wonderful player with a great change of pace. He could always beat a man. But no great speed. I'd follow Cyril and finish off his breaks.'

Rosenblum was so elated at the way he played in the Test that he decided it was an appropriate time to lose his virginity.

'We were staying at the Waterloo Hotel, down by the Wellington Railway Station,' he said with a wry smile on his face. 'I had a room to myself. So I made a proposition to one of the waitresses. "You'll be number 13 in line," she told me. "I can't wait that long," I told her.'

In Dunedin, after the second Test, he and Towers spoke with Vic Cavanagh snr, the coaching guru who developed the famous Otago rucking game.

'The trouble with you Australians,' Cavanagh told them, 'is that you deprecate kicking too much. Your forwards are much smaller than ours. You should kick more to take the strain off them.'

When the Australian Rugby Union reinstated the limited kick-into-touch law in 1934, Rosenblum wrote a vigorous letter of objection: 'I have played and watched games under both rules, and consider that the old rule makes for better football. Under the proposed new rule, which of course is adopted from the league game, play will become more scrappy and disjointed. When the game starts from a set position of a scrum or a lineout much better rugby is seen, for it is then a case of forwards against forwards and backs against backs.'

He put this theory into practice when he coached Scots College to a GPS championship in 1960. His team had the Boyce twins on the wings to score tries and his son Rupert to kick for position.

The Rosenblums are one of the few father-and-son families to play for the Wallabies.

'The thing about Rupert is that he just didn't kick the ball anywhere, like they do nowadays,' Myer Rosenblum said. 'He could put the ball exactly where he wanted it to land. People forget that his kicking game helped to destroy Scotland in 1970 at the SCG when the Wallabies won 23–3 and ran in six tries.'

I asked Myer why he didn't play for Australia again after that 1928 tour. He said he was too busy getting his law degree and educating himself. 'I was avid for life, you know.'

A profile of him published 10 years ago in the Australian Jewish Times was headed: 'The Renaissance Man'. An apt description. His life is a classic example of a successful first-generation Australian who over-achieves to assimilate into the mainstream of law, music and sport, and over-compensates for his Russian-Jewish background with a multitude of good works in Sydney's Jewish community.

Living, for Myer Rosenblum, meant teaching himself French and German so he could become an expert in comparative literature. He also understands Yiddish and Latin. He won a scholarship to the Sydney Conservatorium of Music in the 1920s, where he became an excellent bassoon player. Alfred Hill, the famous New Zealand composer, was his tutor.

'I got first in the class for composition one year and then finished last the next year,' he said. 'When Hill asked me what happened, I told him, "There was rugby."'

He was an Australian record holder in the hammer throw and competed in the 1938 Empire Games, thus becoming that rare breed of sportsman, a double Australian representative.

How did he get on? 'No good. Wasn't up to it.'

It was his practice as a solicitor to only accept articled clerks who played rugby or who competed in athletics. There was one exception. His firm acted for a local garage owner. The owner's wife came to see him about her son, who had passed his law exams but couldn't get placed in a legal firm to do his articles. As a favour, she asked, could he take the young man on? And this is how John Howard, now the Prime Minister, became an articled clerk to Myer Rosenblum.

Rosenblum established a company called Australian Concerts and Artists, which organised visits by overseas musical celebrities. These celebrities often stayed with Myer and his New Zealand-born wife, Lyla, who entertained them with lieder and piano duets. One of the celebrities, the New Zealand bass Oscar Natzka, drank a bottle of whisky after each performance. 'We lost money on his tour,' Myer conceded.

As well, he was the first secretary of Sydney Musica Viva, winner of the White City tennis doubles competition, president of the NSW Athletic Amateur Association, treasurer of the Sydney Rugby Union, and a member and later secretary of the Great Synagogue choir.

The game of the 'muddied oafs' has remained a constant passion, however.

Early on a Sunday morning, in his large house with its fine view of the Sydney Harbour, Rosenblum will rise to watch the Test. No replays for him.

He was two years old when Dr Moran's Australian rugby team (the first side to carry the name of Wallabies) made its pioneering tour of Britain.

As the pictures flicker in front of the old man, therefore, there will be only one degree of separation between the Wallabies at the end of the 20th century and those wonderful first Wallabies, Olympic gold medallists, who defeated England at Blackheath 9–3.

14 November 1998

HEADLINES

Fairfax sportswriters have broken several of the most crucial sports stories of the past few decades—including the Bulldogs and Melbourne Storm rugby league scandals. Through sheer persistence and hard work, Fairfax scribes exposed sporting wrongs which had major ramifications. Their pursuit of these stories often involved weeks of telephone calls, meetings, endless dead ends and overcoming countless officials refusing to provide any information, or deliberately trying to get the journalists off the trail.

Chasing a major story often involves a lot of heartache. But the end result makes all the pain and exasperation worthwhile. The journalist has made a difference.

Some of the best headlines just involved good old-fashioned sleuthing. One of the most entertaining stories in recent years revolved around Greg Prichard tracking down one of the characters involved in a confusing rugby league betting fix saga. It became known as the Pool Man story, and was run across the front page of the *Sydney Morning Herald*. Prichard tracked down the man virtually in his own backyard.

Prichard recalls: 'The pool man had a face you couldn't miss. In the CCTV footage of him placing a bet on the Cowboys–Bulldogs match, he looked like the American actor Ted Danson. In the flesh, it was his "thick brush of grey hair and prominent chin" that stood out, as I wrote in the story.

'I was looking for clues as to the identity of punters, and was tipped off by a regular bather at the Victoria Park Pool, at Camperdown, in inner Sydney, that Tony Grech was one of those pictured and that he worked at the pool.

'"He's got quite a distinctive face," the bather told me, and he was right. As soon as I got out of my car, 100 metres away from the pool, I spotted him. Tony, who was described by the bather as being "very helpful at the pool", was approachable, but wasn't making any on-the-record comments.

'That didn't stop the *Herald* editors and sub-editors from having fun with their headlines, though. The pictures were enough. "I've come to clean up the pool." "Pool man surfaces in betting investigation." "Popular pool attendant caught in murky water."

'Funny buggers.'

GG

I SAID TO MYSELF, 'THIS COULD BE IT FOR ME'

Glenn Jackson

Rhys Wesser was rushed to hospital in Fiji in the early hours of his birthday on Saturday, wondering if he was about to die, but it would not be the closest that a group of retired NRL players came to death during their trip to the island paradise.

As Wesser, the former Penrith and South Sydney fullback, lay on a bed surrounded by domestic violence victims waiting for treatment, Adam MacDougall went outside the dilapidated Colonial War Memorial Hospital for air. A white taxi pulled up with two passengers inside, only one of whom was alive. A distressed woman motioned for MacDougall to help her, so the former Newcastle premiership winner leaned in to pull the man—who at that stage he thought was alive—out of the back seat of the cab. The man was stiff like cardboard, wrapped in a sarong to his neck, and his eyes were open. 'He's no good,' the taxi driver said.

'I picked him up to lift him out,' MacDougall said. 'When I realised he was [deceased], it's human instinct, I sort of freaked out a bit.'

MacDougall and Wesser had been in Fiji, along with former Melbourne and Manly prop Matt Cross, as part of a visit through the NRL's Ambassador Program. They encountered floods, hurricane and cyclone warnings, and airport chaos as they became stranded in the country, along with hundreds of other Australian tourists.

It was not the junket some might have expected but it would be rewarding nonetheless.

Wesser had started to feel unwell early on Friday, the day after the group's arrival, but the pain worsened during a dinner that night. His stomach felt bloated, but when he returned to his room he had throbbing pains. At 10 pm, he spent 20 minutes on the treadmill and rode about 10 kilometres on the stationary bike, hoping that would ease the pain. It didn't.

He said he felt like he was being stabbed in the stomach. He showered and tried to sleep but the pain became more intense. He lay there for an hour, curled up on a bed in his hotel room in Suva, wondering whether he should risk a hospital visit in a country he did not know. 'I was thinking, is it appendicitis, is my stomach bleeding?' Wesser said.

Eventually, he phoned MacDougall in his room just after midnight. MacDougall went to Wesser's room, thinking it was his idea of a joke, and was confronted by the Queenslander doubling over with pain, grabbing the right side of his body and saying he couldn't breathe.

MacDougall called reception and ordered a taxi, then phoned Cross, who had been joined by his wife Jodie, the NRL's community relations manager and the liaison for the trip.

'He said it was the worst pain he'd ever been in,' MacDougall said. 'Whilst I was trying to remain upbeat, part of me was panicking, thinking: "This is bad."' MacDougall and Cross took Wesser to the foyer. Wesser, a player renowned for his speed, was in so much pain that it took him five minutes to walk 200 metres. MacDougall asked the driver to take them to the nearest hospital, and the driver responded: 'He's f—ed.'

The frantic nature of the situation caused MacDougall to even seek advice from the makeshift ambulance driver. 'His organ's stuffed,' the driver said. 'Operation.' The taxi driver was good for something, though. He sped through red lights, flashed his lights and overtook cars illegally, and got the trio to the hospital in about half the usual time.

'I was terrified,' Wesser said. 'I didn't know what was going to happen, whether they were going to cut me open. When the taxi driver pulled up, and we saw this random building, I've said to myself: "This could be it for me." I could walk in here and I won't be walking out.'

MacDougall offered the taxi driver a tip to help them communicate with the local medical authorities. Fortunately, there were rugby league fans among them, and Wesser was taken to the front of a long queue. Wesser was given morphine for the pain.

Quite early, doctors spoke of cutting him open; they said they would ready theatre. MacDougall had to convince them not to rush to take Wesser's appendix out.

Outside the room where Wesser lay, bashing victims—including many women—lay on yellow blood-stained mattresses. Nearby, a man with one leg moaned and hunched forward while suffering stomach pains himself. Four dead bodies came into the hospital in the five hours or so that MacDougall and Cross stayed with their friend. 'It was just surreal,' Cross said.

As part of the Ambassadors Program, through the NRL's One Community, the players had been in Fiji to spend time in schools, teaching local children the basics of football and staying healthy. There were unexpected turns, yet they spread the message even amid the death and destruction. They posed for photographs with police, security, doctors and nurses, and other tourists stranded with them—on April Fool's Day—at Nadi International Airport.

After Wesser was discharged—diagnosed with a stomach ulcer—and when they saw the flood-ravaged country from the plane which ultimately took the group from Suva to Nadi, they knew that the pain and suffering was being repeated everywhere.

When they returned to Sydney yesterday, via Auckland, they were exhausted and rattled, but amid all the dramas of the group's three days in Fiji, not one of the ex-players regretted going.

'When Jodie called me and said I was going to Fiji, I said, "great",' Wesser said. 'I was thinking palm trees and maybe a cocktail. I wasn't thinking hospital, hurricanes, floods.

'I don't think anyone will understand what we went through.'

3 April 2012

FRANTIC SCENES AT AIRPORT

At Nadi Airport, frantic people crowded around equally frantic staff. Others lay on makeshift mattresses. Many had been stranded for several days.

Ann Wilson and her three grandchildren had to be flown by helicopter from a golf course after being stranded with hundreds of other tourists, including many Australians.

They were forced to move from the Westin hotel to the Sheraton as a result of the flooding, then she scrambled with other tourists to be selected for the helicopter, waiting 3½ hours before flying out of one of many danger zones.

'People were getting mad, saying they were elderly or they had a baby,' Ms Wilson said. 'It felt like the Titanic.'

She said she tried to explain to her daughter-in-law what conditions were like, but she would not listen.

'She said to me "I wish I could be stranded in Fiji", said Ms Wilson, who had been staying in Denarau. 'She doesn't understand. She could have been wading in sewage.'

An NRL delegation in Fiji to promote rugby league was also affected. The retired stars Adam MacDougall, Rhys Wesser and Matt Cross had been due to leave Suva yesterday, but because flights were affected they spent hours at the airport signing autographs and posing for photos.

DFAT advised Australians to reconsider their travel to the Western Division of Viti Levu, including Nadi and the Coral Coast.

2 April 2012

'DON'T WORRY, NO PROBLEM'

Pat Lavin, 69, an American tourist stranded at the Shangri-La Hotel on Yanuca Island, told her daughter Karen Kieffer there was no electricity or water at the hotel and some ill guests were waiting for a doctor.

Ms Lavin, who is in the region for a 'trip of a lifetime' with two friends, said hotel staff planned to get them to their flight tomorrow night by walking them to the edge of the resort's compound.

The tourists would then walk over wooden planks with their luggage to a bus that would bring them to the airport, she said.

'It's like the Bridge over the River Kwai,' she told her daughter in an email.

'Our spirits are good. The favourite Fijian saying is "Don't worry, no problem".'

2 April 2012

JOHNS GUILTY OF STUPIDITY, NOT ABUSE

Jacquelin Magnay

He sat with his hand on his wife's knee, his career and reputation in shreds. 'I did not commit an act of abuse to that woman,' said the rugby league identity Matthew Johns. 'I am guilty of infidelity to my wife and absolute stupidity.'

Trish Johns, his wife, was angry when she arrived at Channel Nine studios in Willoughby yesterday morning. By the end of the day she was in tears, so emotional she could barely make it into the studio to support her husband in the face of robust questioning from A *Current Affair* host Tracy Grimshaw.

But if anyone doubted her position on the question of infidelity, Mrs Johns left no one in doubt. Back off.

She said the past few days had been a living hell but emphasised: 'We did the rebuilding in the past seven years; if anything this recent event has brought us closer.'

After the interview, Mrs Johns walked off the set to be sick. Her husband slumped in his seat, head hung in his shaking hands. When Johns eventually left he had to be supported by the commentator Phil Gould and his manager, John Fordham. Then he collapsed into his wife's arms.

Earlier in the day Johns had been stood down without pay indefinitely from *The Footy Show* and coaching duties at the Melbourne Storm.

In a gruelling hour-long meeting with the Channel Nine boss, David Gyngell, Johns had been physically ill. Amazingly, at the time he still hadn't seen the *Four Corners* show that told in distressing detail of the 2002 group sex incident involving a 19-year-old Christchurch waitress and members of the Cronulla Sharks.

The woman claimed she went back to a hotel with Johns and another footballer, but other players climbed into the room through a bathroom window and watched her have sex.

Johns denied allegations he was in the room the whole time, that he was the instigator and that the woman had been ignored after the incident.

'That is totally untrue,' he said. But he apologised to her for her hurt.

'On the night when she came back to the room she was a willing participant in everything that occurred. I am very sorry for the subsequent pain, but she was a willing participant,' he said.

'At the time we went back I was totally unaware of others coming in the room. At the point they did, I stopped and backed from it.'

Johns recounted the next moment. 'She encouraged the players to come forward, she actually says "Someone come forward and have sex with me." One player said he would, she said "No, no, anyone but you," and pointed to me, at which point I declined.'

But the denial of the woman's version came too late for Channel Nine.

'The fact is, whatever the arguments about the details of the New Zealand incident involving Cronulla players in 2002, the conduct and its aftermath was simply unacceptable, full stop,' Mr Gyngell said.

4 May 2009

THE SHANE WARNE DRUGS CASE

Jacquelin Magnay and Roy Masters

It took 11 tense smoke breaks before Shane Warne would finally look to his left for the public and the cameras, a slight smirk crossing his face.

On the big plasma screen above the Australian Cricket Board's reception area in downtown Melbourne, a TV was showing the highlights of the World Cup cricket in South Africa and, bizarrely, updates about the progression of the Warne saga unfolding just metres away. But where was the key witness, Warnie's mother, Brigitte, the woman central to the cricketing future of the world's best leg spinner?

She left her beach-side Black Rock home in Melbourne's south-east yesterday morning with husband Keith in their yellow Porsche, joining their sons Shane and Jason, and Shane's wife Simone, at the plush new offices of the ACB in the city. But for the rest of the day, the blonde-coiffured Mrs Warne, who allegedly was on blood pressure medication but reportedly popped diuretic tablets on occasion to look slim on a big night, remained out of sight.

She was said by her son to have handed over the diuretic tablet in order for him to look nice for the cameras when he announced his retirement from one-day cricket on January 22. The drug testers from the Australian Sports Drug Agency arrived and tested Warne soon after.

But we won't know the intimate details of the day because her evidence given to the ACB drugs hearing was suppressed, as was even the actual list of witnesses. Indeed, a veil of secrecy surrounded the drugs hearing all day.

The ACB's public affairs manager, Peter Young, said he could not reveal the names of witnesses until the chairman of the panel, Justice Glen Williams, gave his approval. And he said even after the judgement had been delivered, no further explanation would be offered until the seven-day appeal period had elapsed. The arguments presented and the reasoning underpinning the drug panel's decision would remain confidential, he added.

A black-suited Warne, head bowed and chain-smoking at regular intervals in the smoking area of the underground carpark, passed by the huge montage of the ACB's favourite sons, Dennis Lillee and Don Bradman.

The counsel assisting the drugs tribunal, Elizabeth Brimer, called five witnesses to give two hours of evidence about the scientific analysis of Warne's drug sample. It was not until after lunch that Warne's highly priced legal team, sources claim yesterday's fees tallied more than $20,000, swung into action.

Victorian barrister Jeff Sher presented a sheaf of documentation to be tabled before he called the leg spinner's witnesses. As this was happening, just 20 metres down the road a lithe Cathy Freeman was training largely unnoticed up a hill alongside the railway track, her leg injury still a concern for her world championship comeback.

Sher had been her legal counsel, too, when she was involved in litigation with her former boyfriend and manager, Nick Bideau.

As crosses were being bounced off satellites to Europe, the US and the UK through ESPN, Sky Europe and Sky News, one correspondent Jim fended off tough questions from his studio inquisitor. 'The first question is pretty much "will the penalty reflect Australia's tough anti-doping stance",' boomed the reporter.

Meanwhile Australia's most senior doping official, the former swimmer Susan O'Neill, said she didn't have too much sympathy for Warne.

O'Neill, the International Olympic Committee athletes representative to the World Anti-Doping Agency said Warne's case would be the one to break the camel's back.

'It happens all too often with Australian athletes,' she told the *Herald* in a phone interview during the long wait. 'Warne is another one with an excuse but he has got to get a strong penalty so we can continue our fight against doping in sport.'

'I actually feel sorry for him. It sounds like he made a mistake, but everyone says that and it is hard to decipher who is really telling the truth or making excuses.'

O'Neill said the Warne case should have been held by a more independent tribunal, far removed from Warne and from cricket. 'I think it would have been much better if an independent tribunal heard it—the ACB is too close,' she said.

Then it was time to wrap things up. What was scheduled as a one-dayer has become a two-day test for Warne. After all evidence had been submitted by 3.30 pm, final submissions took a further two hours. At 6 pm, just in time for the evening television news, it was announced the three-person panel would be deliberating into the evening, but the verdict on Warne would not be delivered before 11 am today.

Whatever did happen to Warnie's mum? She was cocooned between daughter-in-law Simone and husband Keith in the back seat of Shane's silver BMW, with Shane at the wheel, and whisked away at 6.15 pm.

With the waiting media scrum broken up, the drugs panel of three left soon after, led by Dr Susan White, with her two male colleagues, former Test cricketer Peter Taylor and Justice Williams departing 10 minutes later.

Whatever the outcome of the hearing, Warne has already had one dose of fortune: the WADA released a document which would have allowed its outspoken chairman, Dick Pound, to chain the ACB and Warne together and march them back to a tribunal if it deemed the penalty inadequate.

Warne's case is likely to be the last before the WADA regulations are codified at a conference in Copenhagen on March 3–5. Pound has been critical of Australia's hypocrisy in sanctions given its elite athletes, claiming Warne's excuse of being 'poisoned by his mother is the equivalent of "I got it off the toilet seat".'

While WADA will allow each sport to select its own tribunal, it has given itself the power to order a sporting tribunal's decision to be reviewed by the Court of Arbitration in Sport.

In other words, if the Warne case had been heard post-Copenhagen and the result was too lenient, the ACB and Warne would have been ordered back for a re-hearing.

22 February 2003

ANGRY SHANE QUERIES UMP

Shane Warne was told by his lawyers not to talk, not even in his sleep, but he still managed to have a few words with his sporting mates while waiting for the verdict on his cricketing future.

Those conversations on Friday night went along the lines that he thought the hearing had gone OK but that he was facing at worst a ban of perhaps six months.

So when Warne filed into the Australian Cricket Board conference room on Saturday at 11 am sharp, flanked by his brother Jason, mother Brigitte, father Keith and wife Simone, to hear the decision of the three-member anti-doping tribunal, he was shocked when he heard the penalty was a year's suspension.

His mother, who had told the panel it was her idea and insistence that Warne take the tablet which contained the banned diuretics, was apparently devastated.

It took a while for the news to sink in to a slumped Warne.

Any thoughts of getting on a plane back to South Africa evaporated. And so did more than $1 million in earnings and his longer-term cricketing plans. In abeyance were one year of his lucrative deal with English county club Hampshire (which was going to be even more of a money spinner with the launch of his wine label in the UK), the tour of the West Indies, the matches against Bangladesh in Cairns and Darwin, a great opportunity to add to his record wicket-taking tally and the games next summer against India, Sri Lanka and Zimbabwe.

Warne, 33, probably hasn't thought too much about it but his selection for the 2004 touring side will also be tough, he won't have played the domestic season and the selectors are supposed to pick the side on form, not sympathy for an ageing spin bowler.

But as quickly as Warne's disbelief subsided, the anger emerged. Warne has said forcefully that he will appeal against the decision but he has to find a point of law on which to do so.

Judging by his comments on Saturday that he was a victim of anti-doping hysteria, he may feel the hearing had been prejudiced by the comments of others, namely high-profile peers such as Kieren Perkins, Susan O'Neill and Samantha Riley, published in the *Herald* on Friday and Saturday.

But he is more likely to be peeved by the remarks of the World Anti-Doping Agency chairman Dick Pound, who told the *Herald* last Wednesday that he believed anything less than a two-year ban would be going soft on Warne, saying: 'Poisoned by his mother? It's good, very good. It ranks up there with "I got it from the toilet seat".'

As a result, Warne and his lawyers may try to argue that he was denied natural justice.

But Warne, who thought this latest controversy could be overcome like his previous sex and betting scandals, doesn't comprehend how lucky he is to be a cricketer.

In Olympic sports there is no provision for an anti-drugs panel to downgrade a mandatory sanction on the evidence of a drugs adviser, and Olympic athletes transgressing as he has done would have received a minimum two-year ban.

On Saturday, Warne was indignant rather than grateful and an unusually uncomfortable Australian Cricket Board chief executive officer James Sutherland appeared sympathetic rather than satisfied.

'It is an unfortunate episode for everyone concerned,' said Sutherland, deflecting a question about the credibility of Australian cricket.

The ACB panel of Justice Glen Williams, Dr Susan White and former Test bowler Peter Taylor heard from ACB medical adviser Dr Peter Harcourt that there was no evidence of anabolic steroids in Warne's urine sample and cited this as a consideration in handing down their judgement.

Harcourt told the panel there was no benefit in Warne's taking steroids 'in the circumstances' and that taking the diuretic might have disadvantaged his performance.

However, the panel found there were no exceptional circumstances which would justify dismissal of the charge and that the mere presence of diuretics in the sample constituted a 'prohibited method' under the ACB anti-doping policy.

Warne's personal physician, Dr Greg Hoy, gave evidence, believed to be an explanation of how Warne had recovered from shoulder surgery in such a remarkable time.

The leg spinner and his mother also gave evidence.

Other witnesses to give testimony were ACB medical officer Dr Trefor James, the director of the drug testing laboratory, Dr Ray Kazlauskas, and Australian Sports Drug Agency education officer Tim Burke.

The panel also received statements from Australian team physiotherapist Errol Alcott, team fitness adviser Jock Campbell and the ACB general manager legal and business affairs Andrew Thwaits.

There was debate about whether diuretics were still useful in masking use of drugs such as steroids, given the advanced technology of drug-testing equipment. However, the drug testing experts argued this was nonsense, saying diuretics are still a very effective masking drug.

Warne had submitted that he should be exonerated because he had 'an honest and reasonable belief' that he had not committed a doping offence.

Should Warne's appeal proceed, it will be heard by the National Sports Disputes Centre, run by the Australia New Zealand Sports Law Association and the Australian Sports Commission.

The ANZLA board would appoint the members of the appeal committee, all of whom would have extensive experience in anti-doping, having sat on high-profile cases in the Court of Arbitration for Sport.

The 20-member Oceania division of CAS includes Trish Kavanagh, a former deputy chair of the Australian Sports Drug Agency; Bob Ellicott, a former attorney general; Sir Laurence Street, a former lieutenant governor of NSW; Alan Sullivan QC, deputy senior commissioner of the Australian Cricket Board's code of behaviour, and Henry Jolson, a Melbourne barrister.

The NSDC is chaired by Tim Frampton, a Melbourne lawyer, while outspoken Sydney lawyer Simon Rofe is the president of ANZLA.

Rofe was critical of the ACB's extenuating-circumstances loophole that allowed Warne to plead he had an honest and reasonable belief he was not taking a banned substance, and as such is not expected to volunteer to sit on the case.

ASDA chief executive John Mendoza yesterday defended the ACB's role in anti-doping, pointing out that the first meeting to achieve consistency in action against drugs in sport was held at ACB headquarters in Melbourne in early July.

'The first national consultation process where all national sporting organisations including the Olympic sports and the non Olympic sports sought to adopt the World Anti Doping Association code was chaired and convened by the ACB at their headquarters,' he said.

'If we are successful in getting agreement in Copenhagen next month on the WADA code, we'll end up with a framework of anti-doping that is light years ahead of where we are now.'

Justice Williams said the committee had also imposed sanctions under the ACB code, which meant Warne couldn't play cricket in Australia or overseas and made him ineligible to receive direct or indirect funding or assistance from the ACB for the 12-month suspension, effective from February 10.

24 February 2003

BULLDOGS BROUHAHA

Anne Davies and Kate McClymont

Just as so many Canterbury Bulldogs fans are in it for life, so it is with the Bulldogs' board, with only one or two new faces joining the board over the past 20 years. While the annual reports show that the directors receive only a nominal stipend, there are other perks, such as the all-expenses paid first-class trips to check out other sporting venues, as well as side trips to Las Vegas.

This week the directors fell to earth. The state's most successful football club—it was at the top of the table—will collect the 2002 wooden spoon, having had most of its points stripped. It has been caught in a scandal that has embroiled the National Rugby League, overpaid players and club supporters.

In the scrum with the club is the Liverpool Council, which is the co-developer of a $900 million leisure complex right next door to a planned new Bulldogs club that would not look out of place on the neon strip of Las Vegas. But the Oasis, with its whopping stadium, residential units, water park and ice-skating venue, is proving to be anything but a cool retreat from the hot reality of life for the Liverpool mayor, George Paciullo. The affair has been a potent mix of sport, famous names, property development and gambling that has captured the city, monopolising front pages, radio and television.

By week's end the *Herald* had uncovered information about million-dollar breaches of a $3.25 million salary cap. Despite promising full disclosure, the club compounded its problems by concealing vital documents from NRL officials.

On another front it was revealed that Liverpool ratepayers appeared to be providing the extra money for one of the players. And from the same fund the Bulldogs accessed about $900,000, but whether they were entitled to take the money when they did is in dispute.

In the background is a cast of characters fiercely loyal to the club and determined to protect its culture. The football club enjoys the support of patrons from both sides of politics: former prime minister Paul Keating, NSW Right numbers man Leo McLeay, former Liberal premier John Fahey and radio host John Laws.

The club's patriarch is suburban solicitor Gary McIntyre, who is president of the Leagues Club and solicitor for the football club.

The two boards work like this: the football club runs the team, pays the players and the like. The leagues club is the financial powerhouse, with its revenue coming from hospitality and gaming. In theory it is the football club which controls the leagues club, with four of the leagues club's seven directors drawn from the football club.

But in reality over the last few years McIntyre has exercised an iron-like grip over both boards.

On the football club board is chairman Barry 'Punchy' Nelson, OAM, a big, brash ex-police officer whose past arrests include notorious criminal Edward 'Jockey' Smith and a youthful Ivan Milat. Nelson received adverse mentions during the Wood royal commission, namely that Louis Bayeh had bribed him, a claim Nelson has continued to deny. He is still friendly with mates from the old days and counts disgraced cop Roger Rogerson among his friends.

Rogerson, incidentally, is facing six counts of giving false evidence to the Police Integrity Commission over his dealings with former Liverpool Council employee Sam Masri. Known as 'Mr 10 per cent', Masri, a purchasing officer, was alleged to have taken kickbacks from contractors.

McIntyre, a short, squat man who sweats profusely, has devoted much of his life to the leagues club.

Also on the board is Arthur Coorey, who despite owning Stewarts menswear shop in the CBD, only ever wears a black shirt, black pants and a black tie, when necessary.

Coorey, who has a close connection to radio host Alan Jones as well as the ALP, has been a key negotiator with players and is believed to be the man responsible for introducing controversial businessman Al (Achilles) Constantinidis to the Bulldogs. Another director of the football club is Coorey's brother George, who is also employed to run the Bulldogs Home Loan scheme.

Apart from the recently departed CEO Bob Hagan, two other football club directors Roger Harborne and Peter Lander are also former policemen. Lander is now a barrister.

The other three directors of the football club are Roger Nicely, Jim O'Brien and Alan Schwebel.

Former Canterbury star Gary Hughes, who for 24 hours this week was the CEO, has returned as the team manager.

Heading up the leagues club is McIntyre, with Nelson as his No 2. The pair have not always seen eye to eye, especially after McIntyre ousted the club hero, the late Peter 'Bullfrog' Moore.

Of the seven directors of the leagues club, the most important and influential are on the finance committee, which controls the flow of money back to the football club. Apart from the ubiquitous McIntyre, the others on this committee are Hagan, who despite falling on his sword as CEO of the football club earlier this week remains a director of the leagues club.

Also on the committee is retired printer Keith Lotty, a close associate of McIntyre's, as well as Nelson.

A central figure who is now on the outer is Constantinidis, best known for his involvement in Paul Keating's piggery. The souring of their business relationship led to the airing of much dirty linen between the pair.

It was Constantinidis's vision, along with former partner James Hanna who now finds himself in the bankruptcy courts, that began the grand Oasis plan.

The numbers sound enormous but Oasis is intended to be built over the next 10 years. Sales of the 2500 residential and commercial units will fund the development, and eventually the council will end up with the public facilities. Of course, it needed seed capital. Canterbury Bulldogs League Club promised $11 million initially and to underwrite the stadium to the tune of $50 million.

The council contributed the land, the 34-hectare Woodward Park, plus three council car parks, and it has contributed $22.25 million to fund the first stage, the basketball arena.

Announcing the approval of Oasis a year ago, Mayor Paciullo said: 'Never again will our citizens have to travel outside their own city to enjoy the best in sports, leisure and entertainment.'

But his opponents, the other clubs and the two Independents on council argue the development is just a figleaf for the real agenda, 1000 poker machines for the Bulldogs. For the football club, it is seen as central to its financial survival.

The current club at Belmore is impressive thanks to extensions done by builder and team sponsor Adco. At night the waterfalls change colour and fire periodically runs across the surface of the cascades. The sumptuous Chinese restaurant is a vision of gold leaf and plush vermilion velvet. Soon, the day patrons will be able to dine in a huge outdoor garden. And, of course, there are the poker machines, which generated three-quarters of the club's $60 million in revenue in the 12 months to last October.

But it has not been all plain sailing for the Bulldogs. Like all licensed clubs their lifeblood gaming is under attack from hotels and the Sydney casino.

Earnings before interest tax and depreciation have fallen from $14 million in 1999 to $10.7 million last year. Rather than wither slowly, McIntyre's plan is for a whole new club at Liverpool with all the glitz and the glamour of Star City Casino. The planned club was to have 1000 poker machines, although the Carr Government's freeze on poker machines means a limit of 450 at this stage.

But the rewards could be great. When the 10-year moratorium on a second casino licence expires, the Bulldogs would be sitting pretty. It's no coincidence that the Liverpool site is just outside the geographic boundary of territory reserved for the present casino.

Plans for the Oasis were going smoothly until mid last year. The council had approved the development. The partners had established the Bulldogs Sport and Community Foundation, a non-profit body with tax-exempt status as the joint venture vehicle and a second company, the Oasis Development Corporation, to handle day-to-day business. But somewhere, things began to go wrong. According to one version, it was on the way home from a fact-finding trip by council and league officials to Amsterdam that cracks began to appear.

The club split with its intended banker, Macquarie Bank, which is suing over fees. Then in June, McIntyre gave Constantinidis his marching orders, which, the *Herald* understands, was the result of political pressure from the State Government, which, incidentally, controlled a vital piece of Crown land for the project. Replacing Constantinidis as director of the Oasis development corporation was McIntyre's lawyer son, David. Meanwhile at the football club, relations were souring as well.

Even with things going badly, Alan Jones adhered to his famous boast that he is a man to 'pick and stick'. Jones continued to publicly support the project as he has done through this week's tumult.

Jones has regularly described Oasis as 'magnificent' and accused the NSW Government of endangering the project with its freeze on poker machine numbers.

Jones, a close friend of McIntyre, invited him on air to explain the story. Jones didn't share with his listeners the dinner party conversations he enjoyed with several senior executives from the Bulldogs, including McIntyre.

Jones was also instrumental in the Bulldogs signing Darrell Trindall, and he played a role in repairing relations when Trindall had an altercation with then-captain Darren Britt at a training camp at Lennox Head last year. The team wanted to oust Trindall, who was still on a trial period. But soon after, Trindall was re-signed on $165,000 a year.

A spokesman for Jones said yesterday that the announcer did not renegotiate Trindall's contract. Jones also said through his spokesman that he has never received any payment for his strong support of the $900 million Oasis project, both on and off air.

'Mr Jones has been a longstanding supporter of the Oasis development because he believes that the people of western Sydney deserve facilities of this quality,' the spokesman said.

At the end of the worst week in the club's history, the Bulldogs have been punished with fines and their odds-on premiership chances have vaporised.

Now with the ICAC announcing an inquiry into the council's relationship with the Bulldogs, the action will move to a new arena. Already questions have arisen concerning Paciullo's overseas trips with Bulldogs officials as well as interstate flights to attend the Razorbacks' basketball away games.

A spokesman for Paciullo said he had paid for airfares and accommodation himself for a trip in 1999 to Amsterdam, which was to look at a stadium. He continued to Rome at his own expense.

As to the Razorbacks trips, he says he is still awaiting invoices to enable him to pay his own way.

Much to its consternation, the council might have occasion to reflect on the old adage: if you lie down with dogs, you get fleas.

24 August 2002

I'VE COME TO CLEAN UP THE POOL

Greg Prichard

Now the pool man has joined the bar owner, the leading player agent and the controversial former player who has done jail time in the eclectic mix of identities touched by the NRL betting scandal.

The *Herald* can publicly identify another of the punters shown in CCTV images placing a wager on the NRL game under investigation by police for suspicious betting activity as pool attendant Tony Grech.

Images of Mr Grech, who works at the inner-city Victoria Park pool at Camperdown, and three other punters were released by police last Friday. Police identified all four pretty quickly, and now the identity of all but one of them has become publicly known.

There is no suggestion from police that Mr Grech, Townsville bar owner Joel Solinas, Sydney's Anthony Serratore and the fourth punter, from Townsville, have been involved in anything illegal, but it is thought they may be able to help police with their inquiries.

Player agent Sam Ayoub and former player John Elias have been charged with attempting to obtain financial advantage by deception as a result of the investigation into the plunge on novelty betting on the Cowboys–Bulldogs game last August.

The Bulldogs prop Ryan Tandy faces four charges of having provided false and misleading evidence to a NSW Crime Commission hearing, a spin-off from the investigation by the Casino and Racing Investigation unit.

The *Herald* spoke to Mr Grech at the pool where he works yesterday. He was cordial when approached and happy to talk off the record, but all he would say publicly was: 'I've got no comment to make.'

Grech works the morning shift, and one of the swimmers who uses the facility recognised him from his distinctive features in the photos and video released by police, who told the *Herald* he could be found there. That Grech was the man in the footage was obvious from 100 metres when the *Herald* went to the pool yesterday because of his thick brush of grey hair and prominent chin. He was cordial when approached, and was happy to talk off the record for several minutes but was not prepared to say anything on the record at this stage.

Mr Grech, like each of the other three punters pictured in the images released last Friday, is acting on the advice of a lawyer. The *Herald* reported yesterday that police from the Casino and Racing Investigation unit were still negotiating to formally interview the four men.

Each of them backed a Cowboys penalty goal to be the first scoring play in the game, but the plunge did not come off. The Cowboys had the opportunity to open the scoring, after Tandy was penalised for lying on the tackled player in the second minute, but the Cowboys went for a quick tap instead and scored a try.

The first scoring play is generally regarded as a novelty option, and usually attracts little interest, but on this occasion there was a huge plunge on a Cowboys penalty goal. It was backed to win more than $300,000 with various TABs and corporate bookmakers, but the plunge did not come off.

The pool where Grech works is nestled low and in the centre of the spacious Victora Park. It is a long-established facility, and regulars say the day to day clientele who swim laps include a mix of veteran inner city types and some younger men and women from Sydney University next door.

'Tony's always been very pleasant, and easy to talk to,' one of the regulars at the pool told the *Herald*.

'There is a real community feeling about the pool here. Everyone knows each other, so it was no surprise that some of the people who swim here and work here recognised Tony from the photos. He's got quite a distinctive face.

'He's had a bet on the football, but no one's going to hold that against him unless there's a good reason to. Plenty of people who come here like a bet, and are loyal to their footy teams when it comes to having a bet.'

10 March 2011

THE INSIDE STORY OF EXPOSING CAP CHEATS

Adrian Proszenko

Sitting on Brian Waldron's bookshelf is the unpublished manuscript of what really happened.

All the revelations—the dodgy deals, the cover-ups, the multifaceted roles of News Ltd in the saga and, the most important one of all, *who knew*. When he said in April 2010, in his only public interview since the rorting was exposed, that 'I am . . . prepared to give the entire background to Rupert Murdoch so that he has a full understanding of how his company has managed . . . the Melbourne Storm', those fearing they would be named and shamed assumed the foetal position.

Those close to the man fingered as 'the chief rat', having witnessed his professional life unravel, believe he reconsidered for fear of inflicting the same professional and personal pain on the culpable. Call it honour among thieves, if you will. But, while he wouldn't comment when contacted by *The Sun–Herald* during the week, it's understood there will be a day when his story is laid bare.

The fact that the story, of a News-owned club rorting the system in a competition half-owned by the media company, came to light at all is extraordinary in itself. On Monday, January 18, 2010, Fairfax received an anonymous email titled 'Melbourne Storm exclusive' from an insider promising to deliver the scoop on financial irregularities, issues regarding Waldron's tenure and, of most interest, claims of 'salary cap rorting'.

Given that journalists receive bogus tip-offs semi-regularly, usually agenda-driven campaigns from rival clubs, this was not out of the ordinary.

However, it soon became apparent the information, while difficult to prove, was credible.

Another source provided a vital clue that something was amiss, which led to headlines almost two months later—that salary cap auditor Ian Schubert was concerned about several Storm contracts, including one struck between Fox Sports and star player Cameron Smith. Although it was the back-page lead of this paper [*Sydney Morning Herald*] on March 28, few knew how the story would snowball.

Waldron continually denied anything was amiss and most of the media attention at the time was on the Gold Coast Titans and claims their co-captain Scott Prince had a house built by a former sponsor for free. Those allegations were denied and subsequently disproved. As one insider said: 'If the NRL want to find a salary cap cheat, they're looking in the wrong place.'

Of course, everything—well, at least most of the story—came out on April 22. Waldron, having initially denied any wrongdoing to myself and countless others, finally came clean as the walls closed in.

That date could well have sounded the death knell of the club. Years of toil by the players, coaching staff and officials proved literally pointless as premierships minor and major were stripped away. There were fears that rugby league's Victorian experiment would be abandoned altogether.

'The Emperor', former Parramatta chief executive Denis Fitzgerald, had long railed against the Storm and already called for the club to fold. He almost got his wish.

The NRL was strongly condemned for allowing News to commission the final investigation and then only releasing some of the detail publicly. *The Sun-Herald* published the names of seven of the players who had received illegal payments, based on information from the initial source, well before Deloitte handed down its findings.

The former *Herald Sun* editor Bruce Guthrie, who famously took News to court and won, described the cap scandal as a direct result of the media company's win-at-all-costs culture.

The NRL's then chief executive, David Gallop, was in an impossible position. His hard-line punishments erased fears the game's conflicted interests would result in a light punishment. The penalties were swift and brutal—those involved in Melbourne claim overly so.

'It's been well documented, we have,' forward Ryan Hoffman said, when asked if the players felt they were still the premiers of the 2007 and 2009 seasons. 'We feel that way and we're allowed to feel that way.'

The cost paid by some is far greater than many know. The pregnant partner of one of the sacked officials lost their unborn child as a result of the stress. Others who have never spoken about their involvement are considering telling their side of the story.

Sacked independent director Peter Maher, a radio host in Melbourne, believes public perceptions will change when the full details come to light.

'At some point or other the way those decisions were determined will be made public,' he said. 'Some of the people involved are starting to talk quite openly about how those decisions were made and how wrong those decisions were. That will all come to the forefront. When that occurs, it wouldn't surprise me in the least if those decisions were reversed. Due process was not adhered to.'

Whether they are now the beneficiaries or the victims of being over the cap for so many years is still a point of debate. In his brilliant 'Stormland' column last week, the *Sun-Herald*'s Malcolm Knox described the Storm as 'cap clean now as an athlete who uses drugs to build his strength but is clean on competition day'. However, due credit must be given to the club's ability to rebuild. Their Fab Four have become the Big Three, with a team of discards and journeymen assembled to fit alongside Smith, Cooper Cronk and Billy Slater.

Other vital cogs in the Storm machine have taken considerably less money to remain under the tutelage of Craig Bellamy. There is no better example than Ryan Hinchcliffe. Parramatta offered the Storm forward, who was on $180,000 at the time, a starting spot and a four-year contract that would have netted him about $1.6 million with third-party payments. The Storm's revised deal didn't come close, but he took it anyway.

'I haven't heard of a player stopping for the amount of money he could have earned elsewhere,' Bellamy said when Hinchcliffe recommitted in June. 'It shows the character of Hinch.'

When asked whether today's grand final appearance vindicated his decision to stay put, Hinchcliffe replied: 'When I think about that decision now I know I've made the right decision. It's something I looked very seriously at. It was very tempting but in my heart of hearts I knew I wanted to be a Melbourne Stormer. I have a great love for this club and this team.'

That love also extends to Bellamy. One of his closest confidants, football manager Frank Ponissi, spoke about the coach's disappointment after being bundled out of last year's competition by the Warriors. There were even concerns the crushing defeat could send the club backwards.

'They were my immediate thoughts last year,' he said. 'He was shattered. We went on a trip, myself and a few other staff, to the US in October. That's when he got his spring back. Talking about different ideas we were going to bring back to the club. I saw quickly how that fire came back in the belly.'

Petra Fawcett, another of the sacked independent directors, also spoke of 'Bellyache' when asked for her reflection on the club's journey to ANZ Stadium today.

'I think the big story is in the coach,' she said. 'He's inspirational in my eyes. He is fundamentally the reason they are where they are today.

'They have a strong leadership group within the team and they have moved on.'

30 September 2012

THE ORIGINAL BREAKING STORM STORY

THE NRL is investigating Melbourne over alleged salary-cap breaches that occurred during their premiership triumph last year.

The Sun-Herald can reveal that salary cap auditor Ian Schubert has raised concerns over several issues pertaining to payments to Storm players, including a third-party deal between skipper Cameron Smith and Fox Sports.

But the man who brokered the arrangement, Super League architect John Ribot, denied it was an enticement to keep the Australian hooker at the Storm and that the NRL was 'up to their eyeballs' in the details of the deal when it was struck last year. NRL chief executive David Gallop confirmed his salary-cap team would fly to Melbourne this week to examine the Storm's books.

'This is the time of the year when the salary-cap audits are being completed,' Gallop said yesterday. 'It's not unusual for a number of matters to be under investigation. It's fair to say that there are some issues at the Melbourne Storm that are being looked at carefully. Those investigations are ongoing. I understand that the salary-cap team will be going to Melbourne in the next week or so.'

Fox Sports paid Smith $45,000 a year over three years as part of a third-party arrangement that Ribot helped to arrange. The deal was struck when Smith was coming off contract in late 2008 and considering a massive offer to join the Gold Coast.

Ribot, Fox Sports and the Storm have denied that the third-party arrangement was used as an enticement to keep Smith at the Storm and that it would have remained in place regardless of which club employed him. Fox Sports penned a letter to all parties backing up the assertion.

'It's certainly not a salary-cap breach,' Smith's manager, Isaac Moses, said yesterday. 'The NRL has been informed about this all along.'

Smith also addressed the issue following the Storm's 16–10 win over the Panthers last night.

'I heard there was a bit of an issue today, just before we got to the ground actually, I don't know what the detail is or what the problem is, mate. It was the first I heard of it,' he said. 'I heard someone broke a story there was a problem with my contract and the best thing to do is speak to our CEO. I have no information for you.'

Former Storm chief Brian Waldron, now the chief executive of the new Melbourne Rebels rugby union franchise, declined to comment.

Acting chief executive Matt Hanson confirmed he met Gallop and Schubert a fortnight ago in an attempt to resolve the matter.

'Basically the NRL are wanting to include a portion of that deal in the salary cap and we believe it is not in the salary cap,' Hanson said.

'Cameron didn't have a manager at the time and John Ribot helped him to negotiate that deal. It's our belief that it shouldn't be in the cap and Ian believes that a portion of it should be. It's ongoing, it's nothing new, and they need to make a determination.'

Asked if Ribot's involvement in the deal could be viewed as a bid to keep Smith at Melbourne, Hanson said: 'That's the way [Schubert] is viewing it, that it was brokered to keep Cameron at the Storm. But Cameron has a deal with Fox irrespective of which NRL club he plays for.'

The salary cap has been hailed as the great leveller of playing talent, with the days of dynasties said to be over. The Storm, however, gunning for their fifth straight grand final, have bucked the trend. The club has retained some of its best players on long-term contracts, including Australian stars Greg Inglis, Billy Slater and Smith. To do so, the Storm have reluctantly parted with a number of club favourites and last year shed Steve Turner, Dallas Johnson, Joseph Tomane, Matt Cross, Aidan Guerra and Will Chambers.

It is understood Schubert is investigating a number of other possible anomalies at the club. Hanson said Schubert had raised the issue of Johnson's termination pay, with a query over which year it should be included in the cap.

Ribot said that his involvement with Smith was only as a 'supporter'.

'I have no official position with Melbourne but I just helped as a friend,' Ribot said.

'I'm a huge supporter of Cameron's and I thought he was good for the game. I spoke to David Gallop about that. When we did that deal it was in conjunction with all parties and the NRL were up to their eyeballs in it. His manager [Isaac Moses] did the deal and I wasn't involved in the last part of the deal. I was more of a facilitator to bring all the parties together.'

Asked why he thought the NRL was reopening its investigation into the matter more than a year on, Ribot said: 'I wouldn't have a clue.

'If they have some questions they are fully entitled to investigate those things. We were fully transparent . . . no one was hiding anything.'

This is the second salary-cap drama in as many days following reports that Gold Coast captain Scott Prince was involved in a plan to have a $400,000 house built for him as part of an alleged cap rort. Prince and the Titans have denied the allegations and are considering defamation proceedings against News Limited.

28 March 2010

A FRESH VIEW

Some memorable sporting articles take weeks, months to formulate. Others sometimes are straight off the top of the head, as Fairfax sports editor Ian Fuge explains.

'I was the sports night editor at the time and Alex Brown was the chief cricket reporter. We were sitting in the pub across the road from the office after another day's hard slog covering what was, as always, an eventful Ashes tour when Brown's mobile phone beeped at about 10.20 pm—it was a message that Marcus Trescothick had just caught the late plane home to England, having quit the tour due to stress.

'Alex and I ran back to the office—we had about an hour to get the back page redrawn and the story in. Alex hit the phones to get the yarn up and suggested I call Peter Roebuck, who had known Marcus at Somerset.

'With some trepidation, I telephoned Peter, knowing his reputation as a man who went to bed extremely early. Unusually for Peter, he answered the phone—but it was clear he'd been fast asleep.

'I rattled through the situation and asked him for a few words. With little more than a trace of irritation in his voice, he said in that brisk, slightly haughty manner of his: "Very well, do you have a pencil?"

'I replied: "No, don't worry, Peter, I'll type it straight in."'

'He then went on to dictate 700 words of pure gold off the top of his head about Trescothick's travails as a cricketer, from the young greenhorn who turned up at Somerset with the world at his feet to the troubled Test batsman with the weight of the world on his shoulders.

'Only occasionally did he punctuate what was almost a stream of consciousness with the odd "um" and "where was I?" before he asked: "Is that enough? Is that OK?". All the while my jaw was dropping to the floor, it was just so impressive hearing him rattle off this stuff.

'I told him it was brilliant, to which he replied, "OK, thank you, I'm going back to bed!"

'When we went back to the pub after sending the back page, Alex and I read over the column again, both gobsmacked that he'd done it all with no notice and off the top of his head. It wasn't the first or the last time that Peter left me stunned by his mastery of language and his ability to dictate words off the top of his head, but it's the one that sticks in my mind. Pure genius.'

GG

ORIGIN: PACE AND SKILL BUT STILL AN AIR OF BOREDOM

Stuart Barnes

The writer, a former England Rugby Test representative and columnist for *The Sunday Times*, attended the second State of Origin match in Sydney in 2011, Origin II. Here's his verdict.

Origin: Australia's equivalent to Rome's Colosseum. Instead of bread and circus to amuse the masses, rugby league delivers Origin, the game's ultimate spectacle. Instead of clowns and foolery to open the festivities, we are treated to NSW under-18s beating their Queensland counterparts. Amidst the promise are some poor errors but here is a harbinger of things to come.

Outside the ground, the food stalls are sucking supporters into their some-times malodorous tents, but who cares: the quality is awaiting us inside the stadium. Forget the impending union strike action (that's not rugby union) and the state of the world's economy, this is Origin and that's all that counts.

A lady in tasteless maroon cools herself on the overheating train from Central Station. The laminated card that acts as her fan reads, 'It is official— New South Wales sucks.' The NSW supporters stand politely aside as the train doors open. The concourse is filling up, and all the manners I see are better than the sausage I eat, which is described as gourmet and is close enough to the mark to see me contentedly around the stadium to entrance K for the media.

So, to the action and the gladiators with their grand entrance the fore-ground to the bolts of flame; nearly 82,000 are hooked, hollering, howling—in the main for maroon blood. It is everything I expect—until the kick-off. At which point I am curiously bored. The first 30 minutes is deja vu. It is the stuff I have seen in England's undoubtedly inferior leagues; heck, it is nigh identical to the kids' warm-up game.

The problem has nothing to do with the combatants. They are fabulous. Paul Gallen is bringing down the bigger Queensland beasts as Sam Thaiday rampages around. Michael Ennis swings an arm dangerously high, and we all love it. Best of all are the constant collisions as Queensland's vaunted pack run straight at the Blues, pounding the defences but getting nowhere—well at least no more than eight points away.

But the game's shape is so predictable. In the getting-to-know-you bash-up period, the ball is almost exclusively played between the two 15-metre lines with the backs accessories to requirements. The pace is unrelenting, much quicker than nearly all union games, and the error count is astonishingly low. Queensland do not drop a ball in the first half, and only one pass fails to find its target.

These men are in fantastic shape and highly skilled. I imagine most union forwards playing at this pace and with this skill but my imagination fails me. And yet for 30 minutes of high-octane, low-error rugby I am bored. There might be hardly any dead time but nor is there much in the way of thinking time.

Watching the back three run back kicks is a snore-fest. Sure, Akuila Uate is dynamite but there is never a need to weigh options and make any important decisions. Pick an angle and go for it. If you are tackled, fall to the ground and start again. No risk of being isolated and turned over, no chance of the opposition stealing away for the score. Union requires players to think through every step of the way; league, even at this level of skill, does not, and that is why elite union eclipses the best league.

However, the best union is admittedly a rarity, and more often than not when players are not capable of making good decisions the laws of unintended consequence produces a match where wingers think and kick and think and kick ad infinitum. The men and women who like their bread circus are not going to abide much of that passionless stuff, and by full-time I cannot say I blame them.

If the sheer predictability of the first half hour is tedious in a punishing sort of way that seems to satisfy the crowd, the last 50 minutes flowers into something quite marvellous. Ricky Stuart and his radical reassessment of the front row works wonders.

Once the Blues get hold of the ball and their kicking game, they run the bigger Queensland side off their feet. Queensland looked comfortable while Jamie Soward kicked straight into the waiting arms of Billy Slater, whose reading of the game is quite brilliant. When Mitchell Pearce's wonderfully weighted high kick results in a try for Luke Lewis, the pendulum swings.

Growing in confidence, Soward grows an identity other than the faint shadow of the Emperor's favourite, the great Darren Lockyer. The Queensland five-eighth might have been forced into a quiet game but still showed enough flashes to make me wish he had spent a few years gracing the other code. But tonight the game slips from him.

Balls kicked hit the grass, no longer zeroing into waiting Queensland arms. Escape from deep positions becomes so much more difficult. The foundations of a league team can clearly be undermined by a great kick-and-chase game. In the last 50 minutes, the transformation in the fortunes of NSW's kicking game pulls the rug from under the feet of galloping monsters such as Dave Taylor.

Now the ball moves in all directions. Occasionally the lack of giant carriers gives the Blues' attack the look of a demented pinball machine, but with such high individual skill levels they are able to extricate themselves in the way most union players cannot. The crowd roar their pleasure as the Blues pull clear. The masses have been given their show and a NSW win.

In the press box, the atmosphere muted by the glass, and with a dose of bronchitis from the SFS last Saturday, I am not quite up for a Damascene moment. I still think union is more varied and superior but league's players sure can play; some circus.

6 June 2011

HOW LEAGUE GOT ITS MOJO BACK

Richard Hinds

The most exciting thing about this NRL grand final is the excitement itself. If the city is not gripped by the game, then it is at least having its coat firmly tugged. And why not? St George Illawarra and Sydney Roosters. Two traditional, well-supported heartland clubs. One looking to atone for lost opportunity, the other riding a euphoric wave that has lifted it from the bottom of the table to near the top.

A compelling contrast in styles. Wayne Bennett's methodical, reliable, defensive Dragons. Brian Smith's more expansive, adventurous Roosters. This is not only the way the clubs play, but the way they are facing the world.

Burnt by the 'choker' jibes, St George Illawarra seem pinched and suspicious. Us against them. The Great Wall of Kogarah defence does not just go up on match days.

Sydney Roosters, in contrast, have quite literally thrown their doors open. Total access. Nothing to hide. Their week will be enjoyed, not merely endured.

Some experts lament the grand final will almost certainly be low-scoring and defensive. But, equally, it should be taut, riveting and up for grabs in the last 20 minutes. The type of game that provides a searching examination of temperament and technique. One that can make centimetres seem like kilometres and transform mistakes into lifelong regrets.

It is a grand final that has people talking rugby league around coffee urns and in supermarket aisles. Although, I suspect, that is not just because it features two local giants. It is also because Sydney has, in the past few years, rekindled its love affair with the game.

Or, to be fair to the very large viewing audience that never strayed, those fans who were disillusioned, or who flirted with other distractions, have accepted the very good reasons now given to celebrate rugby league. They no longer feel awkward or even mildly embarrassed about their first love.

Not like many people seemed when I lived in Sydney in the late 1990s. Back when the Super League war had divided, but failed to conquer. When there was a sudden and violent dislocation between league, clubs and fans. When, in 'polite circles', the mention of rugby league was like the proverbial fart at the Buckingham Palace tea party.

Even if rugby league needed to be dragged from its Byzantine roots, it chose a poor time to tear itself apart. Just as the Sydney Olympics allowed sporting aesthetes to declare their 'internationalism', the Wallabies won a World Cup, 'Plugger' Lockett's Swans dragged Bob Carr, the cast of *Home and Away* and thousands of others to the SCG, and the Socceroos began to benefit from a rare crop of stars.

To the recently arrived Sydneysider—one with NSW heritage and an appreciation of rugby league's traditional dominance—the change in the city's sporting zeitgeist at that time was palpable. It was not merely the lingering recriminations from the Super League war that diminished the passion for league. A sport once intrinsic to the city's identity allowed itself to become a mere commodity to be weighed in value against enticing imported goods.

An enduring memory is of colleagues returning to the *Herald* office after the vote that secured the Balmain merger with Western Suburbs, a historic deal decided, to my surprise, by a paltry handful of votes measured in the hundreds. Whatever the merits of the deal, the lack of strong participation by the fans seemed typical of the game's malaise. Even the initial South Sydney protest was in defiance of the game and the direction it had taken, not purely in support of the club itself. All this, at the time, was more evident to the interloper than the blinkered die-hards. With their game crumbling around them, many seemed to lurch from one crisis to the next like Corporal Jones in *Dad's Army* yelling: 'Don't panic! Don't panic!'

So, more than a decade later, what has changed? Rugby league's regeneration is partly a consequence of the improvement in the game itself.

The most startling and, beyond its parochial borders, under-appreciated feature of rugby league is that it is now played by a group of athletes unprecedented in the game's history. The Polynesian influence is profound, producing as it has the multi-dimensional star whose combination of size, power, speed and skill can astonish.

The most instructive moments I've had about modern rugby league have not come from games, but from standing near the in-goal area as the Melbourne Storm performed kicking drills. You first imagine trying to chase and catch the towering kick. Then you imagine doing so with canon-ball forward Jeff Lima running at you full tilt. Then you watch Israel Folau perform the imagined task with a balletic grace that leaves you slack-jawed. Folau's defection is a terrible blow, but also the most sincere compliment.

If it can be said in the week Tigers half-back Robert Lui faces domestic assault charges, the NRL's earnest attempt to address behavioural issues has helped its cause—if not among diehards who continued to support the game in record numbers last year, then among those likely to be turned off by the stigma. As a result, it was at least possible for one newspaper to claim, without statistical evidence, that rugby league's behavioural record this season bettered that of the AFL's without provoking raucous laughter south of the Murray.

The manner in which the NRL is reported by the media has also changed over the past decade. Once, coverage centred almost entirely on confrontation and dispute. The eight games seemed to produce—in every sense—only losers. More recently, there has been a greater emphasis on the uplifting and, in the remarkable case of Dally M Medal winner Todd Carney, the redemptive features of the game. More talk about what holds the game together and less about what pulls it apart—even at a time when the Storm salary cap scandal exposed obvious weaknesses in the game's administrative structure. Watching Phil Gould and Ray Hadley chatting warmly, even excitedly about Sunday's game on Nine's *Mad Monday* this week was a welcome alternative to the hectoring and faux confrontation that has predominated.

Importantly, rugby league seems to be regaining a sense of its heritage and tradition. Not the retrograde culture of violence that alienated, particularly, females, and threatened to keep the game in the dark ages; the enduring link between past and present that reminds you why the game was played in the first place.

Two of my most enjoyable afternoons this year were spent watching St George Illawarra and Sydney Roosters at the SCG, and Wests Tigers and Melbourne Storm at Leichhardt. Big crowds, exceptional players, raw passion, exciting games. Perhaps atypical of the week-to-week atmosphere, but the very best of the old and the new. Eddie Perfect, the Melbourne writer who composed and starred in *Shane Warne: The Musical* believes the production failed in Sydney because the city's cultural elites 'didn't like laughing at the same jokes as the bogan down the aisle'.

Perhaps so. But as much as some have been eager to hide it, there is a place for rugby league in the hearts of most true Sydneysiders—theatre-goers or monster truck enthusiasts. This week, as some retrieve the Roosters scarf or the Dragons cap from the bottom drawer, the heart of the city's biggest game is beating proudly.

2 October 2010

CRICKET: WHAT DOES IT ALL MEAN?

Malcolm Knox

If you want to slow down the passage of time, Albert Camus once said, go and listen to a university lecture in a language you cannot understand.

To many, the foreign language of cricket is the time-retarding soundtrack to summer. Stand still in Australia, open your ears, and from a hazily distant radio or television will waft the sound of cricket: summer's white noise.

Learning the language of cricket is often judged more difficult than it is. Cricket's eccentric vocabulary, of short legs, silly mid-offs and glorious cover drives, is a barrier. But if you listen hard, and go beyond the words, you can hear the language speak. A game of cricket is like a book. It has its own units of narrative: its own words, sentences, paragraphs and chapters. You don't need to know cricket's jargon to understand the stories evolving at each given moment.

THE BALL

The ball is the basic unit of the cricket narrative. The single ball has a hermetic, simple beauty. For the 10 seconds or so from the start of the bowler's run-up to the moment the ball hits the fence or the wicketkeeper's gloves, the ball is alive. Everything else is, according to the lingo, 'dead ball'.

While it is fair to say that the bowler's basic aim each ball is to get the batsman out and the batsman's is to score runs, this is not always so. On the first ball of a match, for instance, Australia's opening bowler Glenn McGrath is more likely to bowl a 'loosener', to build confidence in his rhythm and footing. The opening batsman, likewise, is not going to try to score runs until he is relaxed enough to take the necessary risks.

Once he has warmed up, the initial onus is on McGrath to attack, and take wickets, and on the batsman to survive. The tone of recent Australia–England Test matches has often been set by McGrath's confrontation with England's tough opening batsman, Michael Atherton. If McGrath can take Atherton's wicket with the new ball, England are on the defensive. If Atherton can 'see McGrath off', or repel his attack, England hold an advantage. McGrath will be anxious not to waste a ball on Atherton; hence he must try to 'make the batsman play'. A new batsman likes nothing better than to watch the ball fly harmlessly past, so he can adjust his eyes to the light and the pace and bounce in the turf.

The other actors in each ball are the 10 fielders. McGrath and Mark Taylor 'set a field' for each batsman, hoping to capitalise on his weaknesses or constrain his strengths. Early in a batsman's innings, the fieldsmen will be placed in the aggressive 'catching positions', near the bat, to exert pressure on the nervous batsman.

McGrath attacks Atherton with the 'bouncer', or the ball that bounces up towards Atherton's face. Atherton has often been caught attempting the 'hook shot' against the bouncer—a difficult shot which he has often skied over his shoulder to the fielder on the boundary at 'deep fine leg'. But if Atherton can survive this early period and then flourish, the fielders will spread, their primary purpose gradually changing from getting him out to stopping him scoring.

THE OVER

If a ball is a single word, an over is a sentence. An over consists of six consecutive balls, bowled by one man from one end. The next over must be bowled from the other end of the pitch. In Test cricket, 90 overs must be bowled in a day.

Batsmen will try to concentrate on one ball at a time and 'play each ball on its merits'. That seems simple enough, but the fact that the world's toughest and most focused batsman, Steve Waugh, repeats it as a mantra indicates its difficulty. All sorts of distractions crowd into a batsman's mind—his score, his team's situation, the bowler, the 'sledging' (or distracting commentary) from the fielders, and so on.

At the other end of the pitch, a bowler will construct each over as a project. His aim is to keep one batsman 'on strike', so that he can build a plan through a number of balls. Immature or over-aggressive bowlers make the mistake of 'trying to take a wicket with every ball', whereas the best bowlers 'work on' a batsman throughout an over.

Shane Warne is a master of this art. Warne might bowl deliberately wide, tempting the batsman to slash, and then send a tight ball across the batsman's legs. Warne usually spins the ball away from the right-handed batsman ('leg spin'), so he might land a few leg-spinners in one spot, and then bowl the surprise ball that spins the other way ('wrong 'un').

The fascination of watching Warne is in his ability to construct a wicket with several balls, setting the batsman up before going in for the kill. After a long period of pressure, Warne often bowls an intentionally loose ball, allowing the batsman to hit him to the boundary. This seems to break the batsman's concentration—he thinks he has finally mastered Warne, and his adrenaline runs too high. Warne has taken an amazing number of wickets immediately after being hit for a four.

THE PARTNERSHIP

The 'paragraphs' around which good Test cricket is built are partnerships, either batting or bowling. Both teams are trying continually to establish a partnership which will place pressure on the opposition.

For the batting team, the opening partnership is crucial. The best teams in history have formed around great opening partnerships. The great West Indian teams of the 1970s and 1980s, for all their frightening fast bowlers and flamboyant hitters, rested on the foundation laid by their opening batsmen, Gordon Greenidge and Desmond Haynes. Australia's dominance in the 1990s has owed much to the partnership of Mark Taylor and Michael Slater—Australia's overall scores declined markedly when either Taylor or Slater fell out of form.

The reason is straightforward. At the start of an innings, the bowling side is full of fire. It has a new ball, fresh bowlers, an attacking field, and high hopes. If this momentum can be punctured, the bowling team is like a racer who has missed the start: the batting team now has the initiative.

Throughout an innings, each new pair of batsmen will try to stay together. The psychological value of a good partnership is immeasurable, for once the bowling team starts to lose the feeling of taking wickets, it can slide towards panic or dejection.

Some bowlers, for mysterious reasons, are famed as 'partnership breakers'.

They are not necessarily great bowlers—Doug Walters and Steve Waugh, two proven Australian partnership breakers, are only part-time bowlers—but they have an uncanny knack of taking comfortable batsmen by surprise.

Another important thing about batting partnerships is that once they are broken, wickets tend to cascade. Two batsmen can be together for hours, making batting look easy, but once the partnership is broken, the surviving partner often gets out too, and the bowlers suddenly have new life.

Bowlers, too, work best in partnership. The great fast bowlers tend to hunt in pairs: Lillee and Thomson, Trueman and Statham, Ambrose and Walsh, Wasim Akram and Waqar Younis. Often, one bowler is a 'foil' for the other. Dennis Lillee, steady and smart, was a perfect yin to Jeff Thomson's unpredictable, explosive yang.

Shane Warne's career has been notable for two successful partnerships. In his early years, he bowled in tandem with Tim May, an innocuous-looking spin bowler who rarely took wickets but applied just the right amount of pressure to soften batsmen up for Warne. More recently, Warne has bowled in partnership with fast bowler Glenn McGrath, whose mean, nagging pace counterweighs Warne's subtleties.

Just as batting partnerships build pressure on the bowlers, bowling partnerships intimidate batsmen. When Warne and McGrath bowl together, the batsmen's sole aim is often to 'see them off' and wait until easier bowlers replace them.

THE SESSION

A day consists of three two-hour sessions. The Australian cricket team, under former coach Bob Simpson and present captain Mark Taylor, has developed a method of playing to 'win sessions'. This is a way of managing the mental demands of a five-day game so that the players don't become overwhelmed by the prospect of 30 hours of cricket. A session is not a natural stanza, like an innings, but in modern times, 'winning the session' has become an explicit short-term goal.

THE INNINGS

Test cricket is broken up into four innings—two for each side. Obviously, the aim is to score more runs than the opponent, but every innings has varying traits.

The first innings of a match sets the scene, and is regarded as the most vital. Early in the first innings, the pitch is moist and fresh and offers 'life' to the bowlers, but should calm down during the first day. Most captains bat first if they win the toss, because by batting first, if you can survive that early freshness, you can put your team in a position where it cannot lose the match. On a normal wicket, a score of 350 to 400 is solid, and anything beyond 400 makes your team hard to beat. But on some pitches, which bounce unevenly, or hold a lot of moisture, or have an unusually heavy grass cover, or where the weather is cool or humid—any moisture, in short, favours the bowlers—a score of 250 or even 200 might be a good one. You don't know how good the first innings is until the other team goes out and bats.

The team batting second usually gets the best of the conditions, when the pitch is dry and even on the second and third days. This team will hope to establish a 'first innings lead' over its opponent. If it doesn't, it's in trouble, because as a match progresses, the pitch dries out, cracks and 'takes spin'.

Fast bowlers leave rough foot marks in the turf, at which spin bowlers can aim. This is why a spin bowler such as Warne comes into greater prominence in the second, third and fourth innings of a match: because the deteriorating condition of the pitch favours him increasingly.

Australia's proven method of winning matches in the 1990s has been straightforward. The aim is to build a big first-innings score, and set up the game so that Warne and McGrath can attack the opposition on the last day, when the wicket is crumbling. The reason Australia has done so well in recent years is because it has bowlers who can finish off the opposition in the final innings. While Warne has been injured, his place has been filled by a similar type of bowler, Stuart MacGill.

Less successful teams lack this penetration at the end of a match, and their opponents get away with a draw. South Africa, for instance, have a world-class fast bowling attack of Allan Donald and Shaun Pollock, but have regularly failed to bowl teams out in the fourth innings of Test matches.

Which leads to that most puzzling cricket result. What is the point of playing for five days, 30 hours, only to end up without a winner? And what can measure the perversity of fans who can call such a draw 'exciting'?

The answer is that cricket is more akin to high literature than to the dime-store novel. Cricket doesn't need a big, cheap climax. Nobody needs to die.

Lovers don't need to walk hand-in-hand into the sunset. The real pleasures of cricket, as in a good book, lie in the cracks and wrinkles of each step along the way. What counts are the stories within the story, which anyone can understand—you don't need to know the difference between a googly and a Chinaman to find the level of cricket's narrative that satisfies you.

4 January 1999

SECOND BEST TOO GOOD FOR PONTING

Malcolm Knox

WARNING: *the following contains material that may offend those who don't eat cricket statistics for breakfast, or those who think Test cricket only started in the 1990s.*

Among the many well-deserved plaudits Ricky Ponting has received at the end of his Test career is one that has been smuggled in uninvited. 'Unquestionably Australia's second-best batsman', I read the other day. Oh yeah? Having been up all night with my abacus and shelf of blood-stained Wisdens, I have two questions. One is about my own mental health. The other is about the cult of recency that would have Daniel Craig the best James Bond, *Fifty Shades of Grey* the best-ever book and Ponting the second-best Australian batsman.

One thing is unquestionable. Ponting belongs in the echelon of batting champions whose success has been the foundation of the Australian Test teams.

Since 1877, each era has featured these out-and-out champions, starting with Billy Murdoch, the first man to make a Test double-century and the first Australian to score a Test century in England at a time when the English believed, with some justification, that Australians were top bowlers and fielders but couldn't bat.

The Golden Age had the twosome of Clem Hill and Victor Trumper; bracketing the war was the career of the 'Governor-General', Charlie Macartney; then there was Don Bradman spanning two decades; in the post-war era was Neil Harvey, before the mantle was passed to Greg Chappell, then Allan Border, Steve Waugh and Ponting. Only the 1960s, which prospered under a committee of Bob Simpson, Bill Lawry, Ian Chappell and Doug Walters, lacked this singular batting master.

Ponting certainly belongs in this group, and beyond that all arguments are academic. Cricketers of one generation cannot be fairly compared with those of another.

Conditions and bowling attacks are too dissimilar. But cricketers can be compared with their own time, and on this basis Ponting is not all that close to being second on the list. He has averaged 52.21 in a time dominated by batsmen.

This table uses a blunt statistical instrument, but makes a case that Greg Chappell, Border, Murdoch and Harvey, in that order, have the greater claim to be considered second-best. The batsman's Test average is compared with Australia's overall batting average in that era.

This gives a fairer idea of how difficult it was to score runs. Harvey, for instance, averaged 48.41 in a tough time for batsmen, with England and the West Indies both boasting potent pace and spin attacks on generally helpful wickets. Australia's prevailing batting average was only 33.71 in Harvey's time, against which his average was 43.6 per cent higher. Ponting's is 31.9 per cent higher than his contemporaries.

Murdoch was such an important batsman that when he walked out of Test cricket for six years in 1884, his absence sent Australia into its worst-ever slump. His average of 32 may not sound prepossessing, but batting was diabolical on poorly-prepared wickets left uncovered day and night, at a time in cricket's evolution when bowling techniques were far ahead of batting. How good was Murdoch? W.G. Grace, the greatest cricketer ever born, averaged 32.29 in Test cricket in the same era.

The only two Australian batsmen outside Bradman who have exceeded their contemporaries more than Murdoch are Border and Greg Chappell. Both played against the mighty West Indian pace attack of the 1970s to 1990s. Border played much of his career in teams that struggled. Does that detract from his record, because he is being compared with some sub-average contemporaries? I doubt it. Few batsmen would say batting gets easier when you're the only one in the team who can make runs. Border's record, 50.7 per cent better than the prevailing average, is magnificent but will always be underrated because of his team's lack of success, when the opposite should be the case.

Chappell also batted against the great West Indian bowlers, as well as some great English and Pakistani ones, initially without a helmet. His Test average, of 53.86, is quite amazing when you see that contemporaries of the quality of Ian Chappell, Walters, Ian Redpath, David Hookes and Kim Hughes averaged a long distance beneath him. Greg Chappell's record positively glows when World Series Cricket figures are added. Against the best and fastest bowlers on sporting wickets—Australia only passed 400 twice in 30 innings in Super-tests—Greg Chappell's average of 54.42 was twice that of his team. Only one Australian batsman has ever got near that kind of performance, and it ain't Ponting.

Don Bradman averaged 154.7 per cent more than his contemporaries. For what it's worth, Sachin Tendulkar's average is 49.1 per cent better than India's in his era, and Brian Lara's was a mighty 77.7 per cent in excess of the West Indians of his.

These arguments don't prove anything, but they do raise questions about the unquestionable.

1 December 2012

SOMETIMES THERE ARE MORE IMPORTANT THINGS THAN CRICKET

Peter Roebuck

Marcus Trescothick is a good-natured young man. He comes from an affable, contributing family that continued to serve teas at his local club near Bristol long after the burly opener had joined Somerset. He was raised to be respectful, committed and loyal and throughout a distinguished career he has shown these qualities.

Yet there has always been an unease about him. Part of him is the superb cricketer, collecting runs, supporting colleagues, neatly taking catches at slip, occasionally taking wickets, even donning the gloves when required and never, ever drawing attention to himself save in the service of his side. Part of him, though, is uncomfortable with the exposure, the travel, the fame, the headlines.

He wanted to play cricket for his club, county and country and yet did not relish either the publicity or the pressures that arose off the field. He preferred to be at home, or among friends in the dressing rooms. He is a man of simple pleasures and simple desires thrust into a headstrong world.

When he arrived at Somerset in the early 1990s, he brought along with him a cricket coffin that contained not bats and gloves but several hundred chocolate bars. The elders at the club discussed how to react and tried to determine the significance of this accoutrement.

It emerged his parents had allowed him to avoid all contact with vegetables and fruit throughout his boyhood. Nevertheless, those candy bars bore a significance that has, perhaps, re-emerged only in the past few months. Here is a man who wants to surround himself with the familiar. A man who yearns for reassurance and finds it both in the scoring of runs and in the company of things he cherishes. Chocolate was a reminder of his youth when cricket was merely a matter of hitting the ball around a park.

Much to the mystification of his seniors, Trescothick took a considerable time to rise through the ranks at Somerset. His footwork was poor and he seemed inclined to edge catches to the slips cordon. He survived because he could bowl, catch and contribute. When the breakthrough came, it was sudden and certain. Somerset seconds chased 620 against Warwickshire at Taunton and the beefy left-hander ended the innings 323 not out. Within 12 months, he was representing his country. In his first match for England, at The Oval, he took to international cricket as a child takes to ice-cream. He looked at home. A country boy, happy even among city slickers.

Mark Lathwell, his contemporary, was different. He hated the crowds. Wanted to be left alone. Trescothick soon played Test cricket against the West Indies and beforehand practised hard at leaving the ball alone. Walsh and Ambrose held no fears for him.

Thereafter his career flourished. But something was lost along the way. A leadership quality that never quite matured, a selflessness that became compromised. Michael Vaughan played alongside Trescothick for England under-19s and he took the extra step into maturity. Eventually Trescothick began to fray at the edges. Every sportsman will recognise the signs. Every sportsman is more vulnerable than he pretends. That is why the Australians had not the slightest intention of teasing the west countryman.

Last winter Trescothick began to feel the seeds of unhappiness. Even beyond sport it is possible to go to sleep and wake up more tired. Strength seeps away, the will is slowly defeated. Once this mental cancer takes hold it is the devil's own work to stop it. Trescothick went home from India, started the next campaign afresh then slowly faded. He missed the Champions Trophy, hoped to arrive fully restored to play his part in this epic series. Within a few days of reaching Australia, he sensed it had been a mistake. Thankfully the error has been corrected before more harm has been done.

Every cricketer, and every Australian, will wish Trescothick well in the next few months. His friends will advise him to put cricket aside, and remind him that life has many more things to offer a capable young man than the scoring of runs and the winning of matches.

15 November 2006

THE AUCKLAND WARRIORS STORY

Steve Kilgallon

It was cool to like rugby league in New Zealand in 1995. They packed Mt Smart Stadium when the Warriors first arrived, and playing numbers skyrocketed so high they couldn't find enough fields to play on.

The allure, of course, faded, and league again became the outsiders' sport in a nation where everyone is an All Blacks fan.

Of late, there have been signs that league is again breaking out of the ghetto. Warriors chief executive Wayne Scurrah knew there was something of a shift going on last year when he walked past his local pub in uptown Herne Bay and his side's next game was chalked above the rugby union fixtures on the blackboard outside, then saw a bloke in a Warriors jersey jump out of a brand-new BMW. There have been flirtations with the rebuilt Eden Park, the bastion of rugby union and cricket that has guarded its gates from league ever since the 1988 World Cup final.

Periodic dissatisfaction with rugby union, sunny skies and a winning team at Mt Smart fleetingly draw the fairweather fans and the bandwagon-jumpers, and the Warriors have become adept at tailoring their appeal. But this franchise was founded on and still relies, for its identity, support and players, on understanding Kiwi rugby league's unique core constituency.

They are the 32 clubs of Auckland, playing on the muddiest fields with the most rudimentary changing sheds and the worn-out jerseys. Once league drew upon white, working-class rebels, who had shunned the school first XV and got the cane for their convictions, who waited for air-freighted copies of Winfield Cup games, screened on the clubhouse TV, to see what football was like when you were the big game in town. You didn't accidentally become a league player, you made a conscious decision, so it was no coincidence the game ran in families, who inter-married so you could trace the familial links between Kiwis of several vintages and surnames.

When Pakeha families drifted from the inner city, Maori became more urban and waves of migrants arrived from the Pacific Islands, league's core shifted ethnicity, but its essential characteristics did not. League people still live in working-class suburbs, in big families with small prospects, and the game remains an unusual choice when rugby comes and seduces players such as Jonah Lomu and Tana Umaga and claims them as their own.

The rugby league landscapes of Auckland and Sydney are wholly different. While league historians theorise that only the Second World War stopped their game becoming the biggest in New Zealand, this is not the majority sporting culture. This is the niche. Everyone knows everyone. New Zealand's best-known league fan, Peter Leitch, is a millionaire former butcher, covered in tattoos and rings, who one day last week was venerated at a local league function to the strains of *Working Class Man*, and the next accepted a knight-hood. Beating big-money Australian teams sits well in this psyche—every win a victory over big brother, and the commentators who say it won't happen (Phil Gould's pre-season 'Last, last, last' call is enjoying great play here).

When you can't get near an All Black, guarded by a phalanx of minders and media prevention officers, you know a Warrior will come to your primary school and read books. When a fan dropped dead at a recent game, the players stayed for hours after the match to comfort his young son.

Before he retired, the Warriors used Steve Price as their frontman. He was clean-cut, world-class, professional, well-spoken and liked by the ladies. But he was also white and Australian. Their coach, Ivan Cleary, might emote like a Grecian statue, but he has also understood how to mesh the cultures of his transplanted Australians and his indigenous talent.

The locals are now in the majority. And the new figurehead for the club is Manu Vatuvei. When the Warriors winger scores tonight, as he almost surely will, observe the routine. His eyes turn skyward, his mouth widens to expose a flash of gold teeth, a single finger salutes the heavens.

This is the man who sums up the Warriors. If New Zealanders were as crass as Americans, he'd be called their marquee player. In Auckland, he's simply a bloody good footballer.

The routine is a demonstration that Vatuvei is a product of his milieu.

The salute and the smile are a genuine nod to the man upstairs that, in the grand scheme of things, this really doesn't mean that much (it also explains the sheepish grin that accompanies those increasingly rare handling errors). It's a show of humility. Some might see something to the contrary in the gold teeth, but they are a mark of respect to his family: in Tongan culture, they are awarded by elders to those who have achieved.

Like many other Polynesian players, Vatuvei has bought a house for his parents. Until now, he has himself lived with his wife and daughter in a modest rented two-bed unit. Having last month shunned the money offshore to re-sign with the Warriors (despite being a near-national hero, it was another sign of the Kiwi sporting monoculture that he struggled to attract third-party sponsors), only now is he able to buy property for himself.

The club too, is wise with its dollars. While privately owned by millionaire businessmen, the Warriors are under instructions to aim for break-even. There is little wastage.

Vatuvei was raised with Tongan as his first language, and it was a mixture of paralysing shyness and still unpolished English that once made him a painful interviewee. Over time, a sly sense of humour and growing confidence have emerged—but never once could you accuse him of having tickets on himself. Neither does the club. To appeal in this market, you can't be precious.

Outsiders still hark back to the day at Parramatta in 2007 when Vatuvei dropped more balls than a wicketkeeper with a spot-fixing bung. He has long since moved on, and in New Zealand, there is little doubt they are witnessing the exploits of the world's best wingman.

Just as Vatuvei has matured, so, too, has his club; subtly nudging out the wayward without seeing the need to chest-beatingly declare a formal 'no dick-heads' policy, it has sailed through the past five years without a single player indulging in street urination or nightclub mayhem.

And what a cast of supporting characters Vatuvei has around him tonight. Another Tongan, Ukuma Ta'ai, took to league only because the foreman at his south Auckland meatworks told him he must. Jesse Royal, a former chef and coalminer, plays for half his mining salary, and will return underground next season. Another former chef, Aaron Heremaia, had virtually retired to the kitchen of his wife's Italian restaurant two years ago but made his Test debut this year. Fleet-footed winger Kevin Locke needed hand-me-down boots when he first played at his local junior club. Deeply religious centre Jerome Ropati analyses his personal performance with the members of his church group. And surely the NRL's first Niuean-Tokelauan, Alehana Mara, was raised by his grandmother but was too nervous to tell her of his forthcoming debut.

Above all, watch Vatuvei tonight. Ignore the precise, balletic leaps over cowering opposition wingers to field kick after kick; ignore too his unerring accuracy for aiming his 110 kilograms through multiple defenders and across the try line a millimetre from the flag, ignore even that he has played majestically all season despite a leg injury. Instead, watch him strain into his kick-returns, enticing five men into the tackle, before succumbing swiftly and playing the ball as they lie around him like toppled bowling pins to leave gaping chasms in midfield, and tell me this is not a supreme footballer.

10 September 2010

HEROES AND VILLAINS

Former Australian Test captain Ian Chappell recently wrote about how, when he went to Adelaide Oval as a young schoolboy, his father would urge him: 'Watch Miller. Watch what Miller does.'

Chappell watched Miller, and from then on idolised him.

Keith Miller was a hero to so many. Why he is such a special Australian character is revealed in this chapter with Peter FitzSimons and Spiro Zavos probing away at Australian cricket's matinee idol.

Sir Donald Bradman may be Australia's most famous cricketer, but he didn't touch the hearts as much as Keith Ross Miller, not surprisingly considering that Miller had the common touch. He was renowned for never forgetting a face, never forgetting a name. I first met him on a Sydney harbour cruise with his old Aussie Rules adversary Jack 'Captain Blood' Dyer, with the pair involved in a promotion revolving around the arrival of the Swans in Sydney. It was a merry afternoon of booze, food and tall stories. An article, accompanied by a photograph of the two arm-in-arm wearing their old VFL football guernseys (St Kilda and Richmond), appeared on the front page of the *Sydney Morning Herald*. Miller telephoned at dawn to thank me. I was gobsmacked. Keith Miller thanking me?

I didn't see the great man for about three years. One afternoon I was walking along George Street in Sydney, with my father, another to idolise Keith Ross Miller. Miller was on the other side of the street heading towards Circular Quay, saw me, and yelled: 'Greg, get over here. We're going to the Cricketer's Club for refreshments.'

Father was suitably impressed. An afternoon with Miller was one well spent. Father couldn't wait to get home that night so that he could telephone his brother-in-law Rex, a sporting obsessive, just to say: 'Have a guess who I had a drink with today?'

Rex laughed along, uttered 'yeah sure, sure, sure', but never truly believed him.

There is heart and soul in numerous other Australian sports identities, in particular Tour de France victor Cadel Evans, with cycling writer Rupert Guinness who has followed his every step for many years providing the details in two articles in this chapter.

On the other side, there are also the more mysterious characters such as Khoder Nasser, who has hovered around rugby league players and boxers for some time. Greg Bearup brilliantly delves into the unpredictable Nasser world.

GG

THE GREAT MAN

Peter FitzSimons

You have to imagine the scene. It was in September of 1945, in London. Japan had fallen the previous month. Little by little, normal life was just starting to right itself, and that included playing cricket at Lord's.

On this fine autumn day, the first of the Victory Tests was to be played— five encounters between the top cricketing men of the armed services of both Australia and England.

Sitting in the players' pavilion, the dashing Australian pilot Flying Officer Keith Miller was enjoying the sunshine and watching as one of his own, with bat in hand, slowly made his way out of the pavilion and on to the ground proper to take his spot at the crease. His name was Graham Williams, a former South Australian Sheffield Shield player who'd been shot down in the Middle East five years earlier, and spent the rest of the war in a German POW camp.

He'd been liberated only two weeks earlier, had lost an enormous amount of weight and an article had appeared in *The Times* that very morning, detailing his story and that he would be playing.

Miller, sitting at the kitchen table of his Newport home, takes up the story, choosing his words carefully so as to get the feel right. 'So he started to walk out. I can see him now, his back straight, looking all around at Lord's—it was made to hold 28,000 but there were 30,000 there that day. Lots were sitting on the grass. Naturally, as he walked out, people began to whisper to each other, "POW", "shot down", "released two weeks ago" and that sort of thing. And as he walked out everyone quietly stood and started this clap . . . clap . . . clap . . .

'Now I have heard people clapping at Lord's many times. I've heard applause for wonderful batting and bowling from great players. But this was an applause with a difference. It was muffled and ongoing. Everybody stayed standing as he walked and continued this beautiful, hushed applause.

'And I can see him walking out there, his head going from side to side, looking around him, saying: "Where am I? Can this be true?" Poor fella, had lost quite a bit of weight.'

Quickly now, before he loses a little control, Miller finishes the story. 'I often think what a marvellous piece of music that kind of applause would make . . . Beethoven could have put it to something stunning.'

And then Miller reaches for his handkerchief, wipes his eyes and falls silent for a full two minutes at the memory. It was the moment he remembers perhaps best from that whole time—on the cusp, as it was, between his war days and his even more legendary days wearing the baggy green cap of Australia. Not that the former didn't have an enormous effect on the latter.

'It changed me,' he says simply. 'All the death and the injuries and all the terrible things that go with a war. It means that when you come back, well . . . you don't want to muck around, you want to live it to the fullest.'

In terms of the effect the war might have had on his approach to cricket, a reply he once gave when asked why he never seemed to get too excited upon the taking of a crucial wicket, sets the tone: 'I guess you don't do those sort of things when you've known what it's like to have a Messerschmitt up your arse.'

(And fair enough, too. His was a charming insouciance that damn nigh inspired a generation. And not just in Australia. People like Michael Parkinson and the British Prime Minister, John Major, had him as their childhood heroes, and, as a matter of fact, both men remain in regular correspondence with him, the latter through regular Christmas cards from 10 Downing Street.)

If Miller was famous for his devil-may-care attitude in his approach to both the game and to life, though, it wasn't as if he had been a particularly buttoned-down sort of bloke during the war, either. He'd only gone into the air force in the first place because a mate of his with whom he was joining up hadn't been accepted to the navy, and so Miller had taken it upon himself to take both their papers next door to the air force recruiting office instead. And that would learn 'em.

Even in the thick of action, he was still a law pretty much unto himself . . . Once, on a mission in Germany, he'd broken off from the main protective pack of planes and gone for a burn up the Rhine on his own until he got to Bonn, then circled it a couple of times.

Why exactly? 'Because that was where Beethoven was born, and being a bit of a ratbag, I guess, I was just curious to have a look at it.' So he did.

Then he flew back to join the rest of 169 Squadron, back on the ground at Norfolk. How many missions did he fly during the war? 'We don't ask those questions,' he replies with a gently dismissive hand. Oh yes we do—how many? 'We don't ask.' I guess we don't after all. And that is Miller now.

He is old and no mistake, with the 70-something seasons that have washed over him having admittedly wreaked the odd ravage as they've gone. But his presence, and vitality, are totally intact. He has the air of one who has seen some things in his life, done some things out of the ordinary, and in all humility is extremely happy with the view that a backward look at his life presents. Without being too mealy-mouthed, one feels privileged to be in his company.

And where were we? After the war was over . . .

In the company of his new American bride, Peg—which gracious woman is now serving her husband of 50 years coffee as we speak—he returned to Australia and walked into the Test cricket side. One DG Bradman was the captain when Miller made his debut in Brisbane. As far as Bradman goes, Miller is an enormous admirer still—of both the man and the cricketer—though he does acknowledge they had one or two differences in their approach on the field. That was apparent from the very first Test he played.

The Australians had batted first, amassing a score of some 600 runs over the first two days—including the usual 180-odd from The Don. Overnight, though, a Queensland tropical storm had hit, making the 'sticky wicket' all but unplayable for the English when they took to the crease.

'All the England players were war boys,' Miller recalls, 'and they were my best mates. [At one point] I'm bowling and there was little Billy Edrich [facing]. He was the toughest little guy you could ever meet, a lovely man, Bill, and he got a Distinguished Flying Cross flying over Germany in the early part of the war, when it was like winning a Victoria Cross.

'And I'm bowling . . . and I keep hitting him . . . bang . . . bang . . . and I thought 'Oooooh, that's [my mate] Billy', and so I started to ease up, started to slow down, fill in time, thought "we'll win this anyway and that's it" . . . so I slowed down.

'So Don came up to me, and he said, "Nugget, bowl it faster, it's harder to play this stuff on these pitches." Well that one remark . . . I thought, "Here's my mate [Billy]" . . . And then I thought, were we playing cricket in England, where it's a sport, a real sport, it [would have been different]. Here we've got, the war's just over, and we've got Don who was only in the war five minutes here—and here's all these fellows, all been to war in the real tough parts of the war . . . just come out here for a lovely trip . . . and suddenly they run into this.

'And when Don says, "Oh Nugget, bowl faster, it's hard to play that type of stuff on this pitch" . . . I just thought, "We just finished one war and it's like walking into another war." And that really turned me completely against Test cricket as it was played then. That took the sting out of me, as far as playing cricket and enjoying it. Test cricket suddenly went from a sport to a war. I [got through] it but for quite a while it stuck in my mind, that.'

He certainly did get through it. Whatever Miller's qualms at the time about taking Test cricket as ultra-seriously as his captain, he would soon cement his spot regardless and go on to be the most revered cricketer of his generation. Not that he has any idea for all that, of just what his batting aggregate, bowling figures or averages in either discipline were.

'Statistics? No, I thought it was a bloody lot of crap. If I got a hundred, I got a hundred. If not, then not, and that was it . . . Batting average? Wouldn't have a clue . . .'

For the record, over 55 Test matches he scored 2958 runs for an average close to 37, and took 170 wickets at 22.97. These figures may measure modestly against a very few other Australian cricketers, but by all accounts Miller's greatness was as much one of style and timely contribution as brute aggregates.

As one of his biographers, Mihir Bose, wrote: 'Miller's career straddled the closing years of the Age of Bradman and the opening years of the Age of Professionalism. He was easily the most distinctive cricketer of either age: to neither did he really belong. The Age of Bradman distrusted him because he refused to harness his undoubted gifts for the cause: ruthless, mammoth run-getting in pursuit of total victory. The Age of Professionalism feared him because it could not always curb those gifts.'

Bose also noted that Miller's figures 'do not tell of the runs he inspired or the wickets he helped his partners take or the influence he exercised over his contemporaries'.

One way or another, the Miller legend grew. One of the stories about him that resonated particularly well with his fellow Australians was that one day, walking on to the SCG as captain of NSW in a Sheffield Shield game, he was advised that he had not yet designated a 12th man, and so solved it instantly by turning to his troops and addressing them thus: 'One of you blokes bugger off, the rest of you scatter.' Problem solved, and field placements done. True or not, Mr Miller? 'TRUE. I used to see fellows coming on the field and being like conductors of an orchestra, endlessly giving directions about where everyone had to be and what they had to do. I took the approach that everyone knew roughly their position and I could do a bit of fine-tuning from there.'

Some years after Miller, Doug Walters would achieve rightful fame by belting the last ball of the Test match day for six to bring up his century. Miller achieved similar acclaim for hitting the first ball of the day for six in a Test match against England, in Adelaide, though to be fair, as he notes: 'I hit Doug Wright over the square leg boundary, which at Adelaide Oval is not very big. Actually, I could have hit it over with a toothpick . . .' Like I said, more buckles on this man's swashes and he'd keel over from the weight.

What about the story, though, that in the Ashes tour of 1948, Bradman's Australian side had massacred Essex all day long to plunder a tally of over 700 runs, and that Miller—tired of the slaughter—had taken his turn at bat, got out first ball and immediately turned to the wicketkeeper and said, 'Thank God that's over'? Then walked back to the far pavilions. Is that true, Mr Miller? 'We don't ask those questions.' Damn right we don't, and I for one don't want to hear another word about it.

Despite Keith Miller's domination of the game for well over a decade, and the undoubted regard in which he was held by both the public and his team-mates, he never captained Australia. 'That is a matter of absolutely no regret to me. I was quite happy being No. 2. Bradman was a good captain, so was Ian Johnson and so was Lindsay Hassett. Not being captain meant that I didn't have to make any speeches and was free to just play cricket.'

There were, nevertheless, other forms of recognition of his contribution. Perhaps the greatest was the one accorded him two years ago, when his portrait was hung in the Long Room at Lord's. He flew to London for the occasion—just as he had so many times before in his cricketing and ensuing journalistic career—and the memory delights him still.

'The highest accolade you can be paid in cricket,' he says with no little pride, 'is to be selected to have your portrait hung in the Long Room at Lord's. And the only other one there, of all the thousands of Australians that have played . . . [well], I'm the only one there with Don Bradman.'

Bradman is, of course, still going strong in Adelaide, at the age of 87. As is Miller still going strong, though he has had his health worries. 'I went down to the Melbourne Cup about four years ago,' he recounts. 'On Saturday I went to the Derby, and on Sunday morning I was talking to some people, and the whole room started to wobble, and I had a stroke. I was 16 days in the Repat hospital, and then I came home and fell over and broke a hip. I had three operations on this one hip.' There was also a brief battle with cancer. Miller won, but in the fight lost part of his left ear. 'I spent a lot of time in the sun playing sport, never wore a cap, and they had to take a chunk out of me.' Not to worry, though . . . 'Now, health-wise I'm great,' he says. 'The only thing that gets me is my hip.'

With his lack of mobility a remaining problem, though—he is obliged to get around with a walking frame—these days it is not possible to get out and about like he once did, seeing the many friends he has over the world. But that does not stop him talking on the phone.

Even in the hour we have been speaking, the phone has rung perhaps five times. Miller grumbles a little, but as he acknowledges, his whingeing is just for show. 'People are calling out all the time. I say "bugger it", but what would I do without it? I talk to Alan McGilvray every day. My great mates to talk to on the phone were Alan McGilvray, Harold Larwood and Bill O'Reilly. Alan McGilvray is one of the finest men I've ever met. Very direct.'

Sadly the other two are no longer alive. Miller misses them, and no mistake. 'Tiger O'Reilly was a marvellous man,' he says, 'forthright and down to earth, and did he talk sense . . . and pull no punches.'

Harold Larwood? 'Lol loved a beer and a cigarette,' Miller recounts, 'and when I'd call him up I'd sometimes start, "now Lol, before I talk to you, put down that beer and that cigarette". And he'd always say "how do you know I'm smoking and drinking . . .?"'

One day, as he contemplates occasionally, he'll go, too. Between now and then, though, he hopes he has a lot of talking and playing with his grandchildren (who are always around the house), talking to his wife and his children, chatting to his mates, reading the papers and following a variety of sports, but . . . 'But put it this way,' says Miller, 'if I dropped dead tomorrow I couldn't ask to have lived a better life.' Amen to that. And so say all of us.

16 October 2004

FROM THE OUTBACK TO THE TOP OF THE WORLD

Rupert Guinness

Cadel Evans is in the back seat of his team van. Beads of sweat pour from his furrowed brow and chest after another day in the saddle of the Tour de France in which he has again fended off the attacks against him. Outside the tinted windows, cameras and microphones and fans circle, trying to glimpse the star within. It is comparatively dark, cramped and stuffy inside compared with the 15-metre airconditioned bus to which he usually retires after a stage. One by one, his teammates enter to seek relief from the mayhem, and it becomes stiflingly hot.

Evans, 34, who has just finished 20th at four minutes, 26 seconds to the winner of Stage 17 from Gap to Pinerolo in Italy on Wednesday—on a day when he had to chase down and catch Spain's defending champion Alberto Contador (Saxo Bank-SunGard) and compatriot Sammie Sanchez (Euskaltel-Euskadi)—apologises for the cramped conditions. Being in the BMC van is a world apart from 2008 when Evans was riding for the Belgian Silence-Lotto team (now Omega Pharma-Lotto), and finished second overall for the second straight year, after his campaign was devastated by a crash in the Pyrenees on Stage 9. When the team van door opened that day, it was to throw me his cracked helmet and say: 'There's your interview.'

That year, Evans was highly fancied to secure his first Tour win after placing second to Spaniard Alberto Contador in the previous edition at the second lowest margin of 23 seconds. Even the great Eddy Merckx felt that a win by Evans was a 'fait accompli', as did the head sports directors from 15 of the 22 teams in a poll taken and published by the French sports newspaper *L'Equipe*.

It was not to be. In the 53 kilometre time trial from Cerilly to Saint Amand Montrond, Evans placed seventh but was only 29 s faster than Carlos Sastre when he needed 1.34. Asked if he learnt a lesson from that near-miss in time for today's 42.5 km time trial in Grenoble, Evans smiles: 'A friend who is quite high up in the business world in Australia and the world said to me recently, 'I want to give you some advice . . . one thing: trust your instincts.' Did he not trust his instincts before? Evans again smiles, and says: 'You also want to be able to control the environment around you. To an extent that can control you sometimes. So, yeah, I learned about that. That's part of having a team—and not just a team that will ride for you on the road and support you when you are good, but supports you when you are bad or not going well.'

Evans is still very much the loner who misses the tranquillity of his early days in Katherine in the Northern Territory where he never saw anyone for weeks, and was later raised in the Aboriginal community of Barunga where his parents—Helen and Paul—moved for 'adventure' before relocating to Upper Corindi in northern NSW to live when he was four and then divorcing two years later.

Today, Evans lives with his Italian wife Chiara Passerini in the small Italian village of Stabio with their beloved dog Molly. An Italian gospel choir singer and pianist, Chiara was there in Mendrisio, Switzerland, when Evans won the world men's elite road championship. She has experienced the highs and lows of her husband's career, but doesn't know how she will feel should Evans add a Tour crown to his name. 'When he won the worlds it was huge. Even when I think about it I cry,' she says. 'I won't think about it because there are still a few days to go.'

Having made two surprise visits to see Evans in this Tour, Chiara will be in Paris on Sunday to see the fate of her husband's long quest for glory—with Molly in tow. She says Molly has a calming influence on Evans: 'She's a good distraction. He likes to cuddle Molly . . .'

As Evans looked to Saturday's 42.5 km individual time trial in Grenoble, which could reward him with his—and Australia's—first Tour victory in Paris on Sunday, he revealed that he has only now learnt to enjoy racing in the Tour, and feels he has only begun to earn respect within the peloton. 'It's a very closely raced Tour, and the contenders are very closely matched . . . I have really enjoyed it,' Evans says.

Told that it appears he is embracing the role as a major Tour favourite, where in previous years he would baulk at the suggestion, Evans says: 'Everyone is really looking after one another, and in difficult moments that makes it that little bit easier. It's something you earn, and I feel I am earning it.'

That he feels he is still 'earning' respect within the peloton in a career that includes one world road title, two second places in the Tour (2007 and 2008), and a third in the Vuelta a Espana, says something about the journey to the summit of world cycling.

Evans was still very much in the frame to win the Tour when the race resumed on Stage 19 from Modane to l'Alpe Huez on Friday. It has also helped Evans that he came into the Tour on a reduced program and with wins in the Tirreno Adriatico race and Tour of Romandy. It has also paid dividends that he has been able to tailor his program at BMC, which he joined in late 2009 to find the environment he has needed.

Evans first heard of the Tour—the race that is now his rasion d'etre and the driving force behind every pedal stroke he makes, in 1991. At the time, only one Australian had ever worn the yellow race leader's jersey that he hopes to win for keeps this weekend—that being Phil Anderson in 1981, who finished fifth twice.

The Tour has gone from being a dream into a reality since 2005 when he came eight overall on debut, then backed that up in 2006 with a fourth place before his second places in 2007 and 2008. Then came two years of heartbreak that led many to suspect his Tour days were at an end.

This season has turned those suspicions on their head, as Evans has enjoyed his best ever build-up to the Tour with up to 10 days less racing and more time training at high altitude—the benefits of which he really hopes will become clear this weekend as the Tour nears Sunday's finale in Paris.

As long as the goal of winning the Tour has been his, Evans has still never found himself imagining it in his head, as some riders have—or still do. 'Not really. As a rider, for so long I would just think of the process and what is needed [for a team] to get the ultimate performance. My ultimate goal is to get the best I can and get the maximum capabilities on the board. If that is good enough to come second, then no more—so be it. But it may still be possible to be a little better than second place so of course I hope to do that.'

As topsy-turvy as the battle has been for the race leadership this year, Evans is still ready to leave his biggest imprint on the Tour with a winning, or yellow jersey-securing, ride in Saturday's time trial on the same difficult, hilly course that was used in the recent Criterium du Dauphine.

Evans plays down the billing of a time trial as 'the race of truth', saying: 'It's as if you have to do it and stay calm and go as hard as possible.'

But his penchant for detail gets the better of him when pressed: 'You are only riding a bike from point A to point B, but in terms of technique there is so much in terms of pedalling, breathing, and there are the corners. Just to concentrate and ride out beyond your limit is very taxing actually. It's more technical, but you are also trying to get it out physically. Extracting the two—both at once—is emotionally and mentally quite demanding.'

23 July 2011

CADEL ACHIEVES ANOTHER HEARTFELT DREAM BECOMING A FATHER

Cadel Evans is recognised wherever he goes as the reigning Tour de France champion. But the halo of fame was nowhere to be seen on a sunny autumn day in the hills north of Milan last October.

As Evans and his wife, Chiara Passerini, a pianist and gospel choir singer, mingled with about 50 couples who had adopted Ethiopian children, absent was any thought of this year's Tour defence and how their lives had changed since his historic feat to become the first Australian winner last July.

They were attending a gathering of members from a local association that supports families who have adopted Ethiopian children—or couples such as Evans and Passerini, who were in the throes of the two-year process.

As the smell of roasted chestnuts baking on a barbecue wafted into the forest, a smiling Evans and Passerini wandered among the laughing parents eating from wrapped newspaper as Ethiopian and Italian children played around them.

Evans and Passerini were welcomed not as celebrities, but as people who shared the dream of becoming parents, wanting to provide a child from a disadvantaged country the opportunity of a new, happy and loving life.

Their plans, at the time, were private to all but a handful of confidants. Such is the exhaustive process that requires documentation duplicated in

Italian and English and on exactly the same forms, they knew their adoption was never over the line until a final decision was made by an Ethiopian judge. They didn't know, either, when they could be asked to visit Ethiopia to meet and share quality time with their prospective child. Whatever the timing, they would have to take it or risk their application being unsuccessful.

Fate favoured them. On December 28, Passerini made public their intention of adopting a baby Ethiopian boy to the *Herald* while she and Evans were in Ethiopia. She said the adoption was the real reason for their early departure from Australia on December 16. It had been believed that Evans had sought the peace and quiet of a return to his Swiss base to train after a hectic visit to Australia.

'We came here to bring home our little '12-month' boy after months of paperwork,' Passerini told the *Herald*. 'We always felt the strong wish to adopt, so we decided to start our family through adoption. It certainly wasn't an easy process.'

That little boy, 15-month-old Robel—who was abandoned in the streets of Shashamane at the age of six months—now lives with Evans, Passerini and their dog Molly at their Swiss home in the village of Stabio, near the Italian border.

A new life has begun for them all. And on Thursday, at his BMC team's official launch at their training camp in Denia in Spain, Evans spoke about the emotion he felt when a judge officially handed over custody of Robel.

'You come back from the courtroom in a taxi, and this time you can walk out the door [of the childcare centre] with him. It is quite bizarre,' Evans, 34, told AAP. 'It happens like [clicks his finger]. It is a flood of emotions and it has been an amazing process. We are still learning about him. After being abandoned at six months old . . . it is a big change.'

28 January 2012

POWER AND POISE GAVE GERRANS
THE TELLING EDGE

Rupert Guinness

To look at Simon Gerrans, who won the recent Milan–San Remo classic in Italy, there is not a lot of him. But looks can be deceiving.

The magnitude of the engine within the 66-kilogram, 170-centimetre Victorian, and what it takes to win a one-day race of this stature, was revealed this week when his team, GreenEDGE, released his SRM PowerMeter data, allowing fans to take an inside look at the race.

Gerrans's win on March 17 was one of the great feats of Australian cycling. The race is one of five one-day 'monuments' in the sport, alongside the Tour of Flanders in Belgium that is on tomorrow night (Sydney time), the cobblestoned Paris-Roubaix (April 8), and the hilly Liege–Bastogne–Liege (April 22) in the Belgian Ardennes and Giro di Lombardia in Italy (September 29).

The image of Gerrans winning ahead of second-placed Swiss Fabian Cancellara (RadioShack–Nissan) and Italian Vincenzo Nibali (Liquigas) in the Australian champion's jersey he won in January only added gloss to the occasion. But a study of his data heightens the significance of the victory considering the physical demands of the 298-kilometre race—the longest one-day race on the professional circuit.

Australian Institute of Sport sports physiologist David Martin provides sports science support for Australia's Olympic cyclists and says Gerrans's average power output of 220 watts over seven hours, including 15 surges of 900 W to 1100 W in the last hour, is enough to run four laptops for a working day, or a 200 W lightbulb for seven hours. His peak power-to-mass ratio is

2 per cent of the power of a formula one racing car, 50 per cent of a 1953 FJ Holden, or the same as an M1 Abrams main battle tank.

Martin says the data reflects how Gerrans, 31, executed the near-perfect race by not wasting energy early so he had enough power for the back end to go with the decisive moves, chase down Cancellara's attacks on the descent of the Poggio and finally win the three-way sprint.

Furthermore, Martin believes power data shows Gerrans's ride was a greater display of strength than has been recognised by those who said Cancellara was strongest and Gerrans was street smart.

The key was in the first 100 km, when Gerrans's power output kept low and his heart rate averaged 120 beats a minute—it did not pass his 175 threshold until the Turchino Pass at 145 km.

'In the classics, the goal of the team is to protect the fittest cyclists so they have the best chance of a win,' Martin said. 'That's the job of the team and Simon said they did their job perfectly.

'To have a heart rate that is essentially around 120 for almost two-and-a-half hours is outstanding and reflects that the team looked after him very well. The reason for the low heart rates and low power output early is because they are drafting. When they are riding at 60 km/h, if the lead rider is at 100 per cent power output the person on his wheel is only at about 60 per cent to 70 per cent.

'So if you have someone riding at 400 W the person sitting on their wheel can afford to be at 300 W or even less. The more cyclists in front of you the better the drafting effect is.'

Even on the second climb, La Manie, five hours into the race, Gerrans's heart rate was only near threshold when his power output rose to 400 W for 11 minutes when the race tempo wound up to try to discard fancied sprinters such as Britain's Mark Cavendish (Sky).

'Simon is not a big guy, so 400 W is a substantial effort over 10 minutes,' Martin explains.

It was after La Manie, as the race hit the coast and the hilly run to San Remo, that the intensity really picked up—especially on the two most decisive climbs of the race, the Cipressa and the Poggio.

On the Cipressa, at 276 km, Gerrans's output over 10 minutes was 390 W, but as the pace quickened there was the first of 15 1000-plus watt surges. On the Poggio, Gerrans averaged 400 W for seven minutes, but when Nibali attacked near the top, with 7.2 km to go, Gerrans generated a peak power output of 1200 W (100 W less than his winning sprint). The attack was decisive and sustained—about 1000 watts for 10 seconds followed by 800 watts for 10 seconds as Cancellara caught up and led them over the top.

On the descent, Gerrans recorded seven 1000 W–plus surges on the turns where Cancellara gained a lead and then two more, one in the final two kilometres as Gerrans took a 300 m turn in front as their lead dropped to seven seconds, and then again in his winning sprint.

Martin believes observers underestimated the effort needed by Gerrans to beat Cancellara.

'To get away in the break was phenomenal,' he says. 'It's not like Simon was the only guy that read it. Others were thinking: "This is my moment. This is happening. I've got to get up there." But they couldn't. You have to put yourself in it to win it. That is exactly what Simon did.'

That Gerrans was still able to produce almost 1300 W of power in his final 10-second sprint to take first place shows that 'at the end of a very long day he was able to generate near peak power'.

'It's a great indication of pacing his capacity—that's probably the big trick to winning in the classics. A lot of fit guys are out there who, given the right opportunity, could do something amazing, but little things use up their high intensity capacity,' Martin says. 'By the end of the race most . . . don't have anything left.'

Gerrans did have something left—and that proved to be enough to win.

31 March 2012

EVERYTHING YOU WANTED TO KNOW
BUT WERE AFRAID TO ASK

Richard Hinds

Your mother had seven brothers, most of them decent footballers. They brought their kids to family gatherings. So, the way Paul Gallen tells it, you just expected to be driven head-first into a concrete driveway.

This time, however, the cousins' spear tackle was a bit too reckless. The four-year-old victim was stunned. Momentarily, the game was abandoned. But—sighs of relief—no harm done. The concrete was OK.

And Gallen? 'One of my aunties was a nurse, and she called an ambulance, just as a precaution,' he says. 'I had a bit of a sore neck. All good.'

You have been talking with Gallen for only a few minutes. But, immediately, you start aligning the stories with the reputation. As Gallen speaks with surprising candour about his early life in the western suburb of Wentworthville, the anecdotes seem to dovetail with the image of the famously hard-headed Cronulla forward.

Toughened up in the playground. Driven by anger as much as ambition. Here—you are thinking—is the genesis of the Sharks' warrior. The brutal protagonist whose face is sometimes so contorted by his aggression that friends and family can barely recognise the affable man they know.

As Gallen takes you through his childhood, the amateur psychologist rushes to judgment.

Angry after his parents' divorce, there is the 14-year-old who gave up the game for a year and fuelled his teenage aggression through the throttle of a motorbike instead of the fury of a hit-up. The kid so uncontrollable that his mother kicked him out of home. 'I just couldn't handle that Mum and Dad broke up,' he says. 'It was just a bad situation. I was a little bit angry, I suppose. She had to cope with the other kids [two brothers and two sisters] who were all younger than me.'

Here is the 16-year-old who was rejected by the Wentworthville Magpies. Who worked his way into the first team at Marist Brothers, Parramatta. Who found he could cut it with Nathan Cayless and the school's other stars. Who was picked for Parramatta's SG Ball team, then impetuously threw that chance away.

'Why not play with my mates at "Wentie"?' the teenage Gallen was thinking. So what if the Eels did not allow it? No one would know. Except Gallen scored a try, copped a late hit, joined an all-in brawl and was hauled before the judiciary. Parramatta found out, and he never played for the Eels again.

And so, even before Gallen gets to the bit where the Sharks recruit him out of school, it is tempting to think you have Gallen's measure. To cast him as the angry kid from the broken home who takes out his aggression on the field. The wild bloke with no respect for boundaries or consequences. Just join the throng and click the button beside his name on the website poll of the 'NRL's most hated man'.

Except, after a while, you have stopped merely listening to what Gallen says and you also hear the thoughtful, even gentle way he says it. There is no anger in the way he talks about that angry 14-year-old. No bitterness even in how he describes the furore that engulfed him after he was accused of racial vilification. The things that have happened to Gallen clearly do not define him, or even necessarily drive him. 'That's my job now, that's how I see it,' says Gallen of the ferocious nature of his play. 'If I don't go out and do what I do, someone is going to take my spot.'

That pragmatic rationale might not appease the opposition fans who jeer when Gallen barges into the fray, or even excuse some indiscretions. But, as he has come to accept: 'Perception is fake. I try never to judge people on what others have said about them.'

Accordingly, he does not judge himself by newspaper labels: 'Hitman', 'Enforcer'. Nor, conversely, by the applause when he walks into the leagues club after a big win, and his amused friends turn and ask: 'Do they really know who you are?'

So, if not the raging pantomime villain, who is Gallen? 'Pretty normal bloke, I think,' he says, smiling. 'If you asked my friends of 20 years, I don't think I've changed.'

Perhaps only in one regard. Gallen has, with his fiancee Anne, a two-year-old daughter, Charly, and another child due in four weeks. Fatherhood has been 'a life-changer'.

'I was praying for a boy,' he says. 'When she come out, she had the forceps on her head, and I thought "Geez, that's a rough head. That's a boy for sure." But she's awesome.'

A bloke who clearly relishes his very physical work, Gallen is thriving this season in a new role where his average tackle count is down to about 20. 'Give me only 50 minutes per game, like the props,' he says, 'and I might play until I'm 40.'

Gallen still likes a bourbon and Coke. But he can't remember the last time he closed the bar. There is plenty to go home to. Not that his career has been littered with off-field problems.

'People around [Cronulla] are nice,' he says. 'If you are nice to people, you shouldn't have too much to worry about.'

If neither fame nor infamy has changed Gallen, it has had one profound effect on his life. Five years ago, a woman rang the club claiming to be his half-sister. Gallen rang his father, who confirmed he had a daughter by another relationship.

The woman, Alison, had worked out the association because of Gallen's public appearances, and came to a game. 'I walked into the leagues club, and I looked straight at her and I knew it was her,' Gallen says. 'She looks a bit like my sister Julie. I could just tell.'

Alison is now close to the rest of the family.

Gallen does not like to trawl through the list of incidents that have, in some eyes, shaped his reputation. Not because he does not take responsibility, but because he believes he has often been misrepresented or held to a higher account than others.

'If you compare me and Petero Civoniceva, people would say I'm a mongrel and he's the nicest guy in the world—which I'm sure he is. I love him. Petero was sent off last year, he's probably been put on report this year already. If you have a look at me, I don't think I've been suspended since 2008. If you break it down and look what I've done, particularly lately, it's not that much.'

Gallen was condemned three years ago after he allegedly tried to rip the stitches from a wound on Anthony Laffranchi's face. He says he got an idea the previous week watching Melbourne players move a bandage on the head of

Sharks teammate Luke Douglas. 'I just saw the [Laffranchi] cut and thought, "I'm gunna make him bleed." I didn't try to rip the stitches out. I just wanted to move the bandage so he had to go off. They got a penalty in front of the post and kicked two points. I probably could have been a bit smarter about it.'

Even more injurious to his reputation was the accusation he had racially abused St George Illawarra's Mickey Paea. Gallen does not deny the specifics, but notes the charge was 'bringing the game into disrepute, not racial vilification', and remains disappointed he was fined $10,000 while others involved in similar incidents were not.

There is a trace of naivety in Gallen's belief people should remember he was awarded a penalty after Paea stepped on his hand. What he resents most is that the inevitable media coverage created a vast gap between what the public came to think of him, and what those close to him know.

'I'm not a racist person,' he says. 'It's just something that annoys me that you get labelled as that. That was probably the lowest point of my career.'

He was asked late last year to be an ambassador for a largely indigenous club in Gladstone in Queensland, an honour in maroon territory. He is trying to fit a visit into his schedule. 'Hopefully I can get up there and give one or two of them something to strive for in life,' he says.

He was bitter with the media for some time after the Paea incident and made public appearances for the NRL only grudgingly. Last year, he started to open up again. While his tackles remain brutal, his image is softening.

The perennial villain was startled when he drew the most votes on the poll to choose this year's All Star team. 'That came out of the blue,' he says. 'Maybe I'm impressing a few people.' Or perhaps, as people get to know him, the gap between perception and reality is closing.

HITS AND MISSES

2001: NRL debut for Cronulla

2003: Sent off for high tackle

2004: Suspended for two weeks for contrary conduct after a fight

2005: Wins Sharks' Chairman's Award

2006: Suffers bulging disc. Wins first City rep jumper, his first NSW Origin jumper, and his first Australian jumper for the PM's XIII

2007: Signs a four-year contract. Accused of diving. Reported twice for high tackles, serves one suspension. Chosen for third Origin match.

HITS AND MISSES CONTINUED

2007: Charged with contrary conduct after headbutting, suspended for one match. Accused of off-field scuffle with Reece Williams, and concedes he consumed 'too much alcohol'

2008: Accused of Laffranchi incident. Selected for all three Origin games but gives away three penalties in final match. Reported for high tackle

2008: Makes World Cup squad

2009: Plays Anzac Test. Accused of racially abusing Mickey Paea. Steps down as Sharks captain. Issued with a criminal infringement notice for urinating in public

2010: Omitted for first Origin but selected for final two games. Reported for a high shot on Nate Myles

16 April 2011

PUP GROWS UP

Malcolm Knox

Michael Clarke loves a shower. Loves it. Coming in for a break from a Test innings, he rushes out of his gear and into the bathroom. Even waiting to bat, he will grab any opportunity to get wet. He laughs in a way that suggests he has had to justify his habit to teammates for years. 'I shower to try to relax and cool down. If I've been waiting an hour and a half and am next in, I'll definitely have a shower. I love a shower.' He showers because he sweats, and he sweats because he can't wait. Michael Clarke is quick and bright. In person, he is good evidence for the idea that sporting performance reveals personality. Busy, effervescent and likeable on the field, so he is in conversation.

First in line to the most prestigious job in Australian sport, Clarke's nervous energy is anything but uneasy. A consolidated 47-Test regular in the Australian cricket team, a one-day and Twenty20 veteran and sometime captain, he says he loves his cricket more than when he was an obsessed 15-year-old and is very happy with an off-field life of handsome financial rewards and a glamorous fiancée. 'Without doubt I'm as happy as I've been in my life,' he says, and if he's not being genuine then he's a terrible loss to the theatre. He exudes the kind of lust for life that propels young children out of bed at sunrise every day. He isn't nicknamed 'Pup' for nothing.

But Clarke's energy needs somewhere to go, and he can't wait to get down to business: score runs, win Test matches, redress the blemish of losing the Ashes the last time Australia toured England, in 2005. It's the anticipation he can't bear.

'I get really nervous waiting to bat. I listen to music, talk or read the paper, or get up and burn off some energy, try to calm down. But I just want to get out there. Maybe I should have been an opener.

170

'The hardest part of batting is getting from your seat in the changing room out to the crease,' he says. 'That walk is a lonely time, especially if you've got doubts.' But doubts have only rarely impinged on a career with a single, upward trajectory. Born in Liverpool, Clarke is a loyal Sydney western suburbs boy. His father played cricket for Western Suburbs and local rugby league, before owning an indoor sports centre in which Michael was hot-housed.

'My whole life was rugby league in winter, cricket in summer. They were my Dad's two sports and I just wanted to follow him. But soon the cricket took over, and it was cricket all day every day, in winter indoor nets and sessions with the bowling machine, then when it got warm, outdoor cricket.'

He was awarded a contract with New South Wales at age 18. 'I was doing everything I wanted to do and getting paid for it.'

By 21 he was chosen for Australia, first in the shortened game and then, in India in 2004, in Test cricket. As a 23-year-old he went to the final frontier where Australia had not won a series since 1969, and scored 151 in his first innings at Bangalore against all the pressure and mayhem of Indian spin and pace bowling in Indian conditions.

Under Adam Gilchrist's captaincy, Australia wrapped up the series by the third Test. Then Clarke (after taking six wickets for nine runs with his finger-spinners in the lost fourth Test) came home and scored another century, against New Zealand, in his first Test innings on home soil. He was confident, but not cocky: a Ricky Ponting with smoother edges. Shane Warne more or less adopted him, anointing him with his No. 23 one-day shirt. Clarke wore an earring and dyed his hair. Red lights were flashing, but for a while he avoided the crash and burn. His seniors noticed that even though he admired Warne, he didn't make an idol of him; still only a boy, Clarke was his own man.

'You're pretty much on your own when you first come into a team, and it's hard,' he says. 'What was great about the leaders in that team—Ponting, Warne, Gilchrist, Glenn McGrath—was that as a young guy I was never told, "Shut up and sit in the corner." Those guys allowed me to be the person I was, even voice an opinion . . . not that I said a whole lot.

'I was more interested in learning from those guys. But the great thing about their leadership was that there was no pressure or intimidation. For example, I never drank beer. I was never told I had to, never pressured.'

It was nothing but blue skies for Clarke until the team toured England. Early on the 2005 Ashes tour, unity cracked. Andrew Symonds was out drinking all night in Cardiff, and was dropped when he turned up still drunk the next morning for a one-day game against Bangladesh. Australia lost.

The squad regrouped and won the first Test, at Lord's. In his second innings at the home of cricket, Clarke scored a dashing 91 off 106 balls.

A century seemed inevitable. He drove loosely at a wide ball from Matthew Hoggard, edged it against his boot and it rolled into the stumps.

The series, for the team and Clarke, turned in the next match at Edgbaston. Late on the third day, Clarke and Warne were building a potentially match-winning partnership after an early collapse. It augured as a dream coming true for the friends until on the third-last ball of the day Steve Harmison bowled Clarke, on 30, a searing short ball that crunched his hand. He followed up with what looked like a beamer, heading for Clarke's chest. Wrong-footed, Clarke was glued to his heels as the ball looped softly, beat his defence, and bowled him. His England series wasn't bad—he made a start in every innings but one—but he didn't make the big score.

'The batting never got easier, no matter how long I'd been in. I'd found that the longer I was batting, the easier it got. But in England when you got through the new ball, it'd start reverse swinging, and if I got through that they'd put fielders out deep to stop me hitting boundaries. I was a young kid, I wanted to put on a show for the crowd, and I couldn't accept that my freedom to score was being limited.'

Clarke retained his place after the lost Ashes series, but failed at home to the West Indies and spent several months on the outer. It was a deep pothole in his hitherto smooth ride.

'There's no doubt it hurt. It hurt a lot at the time, mostly because we'd lost the Ashes, and then because I was dropped.'

It must have felt a heavy fall from grace. He made a double-century for NSW and was reinstated, as a temporary replacement for injured players, for two Tests in Bangladesh in 2006. He was not a part of Australia's selected team to contest the Ashes at home in 2006–07 until Shane Watson withdrew with injury. In Brisbane, Clarke made a half-century. In the second Test, Australia's famous last-day victory in Adelaide, he scored his first Test century in two years. The comeback enables him, now, to place his omission in a narrative arc.

'Getting dropped was the best thing for my career, because it allowed me to get away from the game . . . and understand the things I'd need to be successful.'

Nearly every great Australian player has been dropped early in his career—including Bradman. But being dropped, and coming back, doesn't guarantee long-term success. Clarke has now played 47 Tests. Clarke averages 47 runs an innings. He is at a crossroad where his performances during the next four or five seasons will determine whether he steps up a level and averages in the fifties, like the elite—or slips back like so many others.

'One thing I've learnt is not to look too far ahead,' he says. 'Don't look too far backwards at the horrible times, and don't look too far ahead. Since I was dropped, I've chilled a lot as a person and as a player. It's impossible to think of outcomes. Who knows, I might have a few ducks and my average will be back to 40. But my mindset is that, although I'm not starting my career, I'm still learning so much about the way I play. I feel I'm twice the player I was when I made my debut.'

Returning from exile, he tightened his technique, decided that a good forward defence or a good 'leave' can be just as powerful in asserting dominance over a bowler as hitting a four. He learnt to make hard runs. 'If I make a hundred off 300 balls, it doesn't faze me anymore.'

Clarke is either a very happy dynamo or a superb liar.

'I'm stoked where I'm at the moment, 28-years-old and vice captain of the greatest sporting team in the world in my opinion. My love of cricket is stronger now than when I was 15.'

Having just been appointed a 'Gillette champion' for Australia, joining fellow sports luminaries including Roger Federer, Thierry Henry and Tiger Woods, Clarke is, like any true sports fan, beside himself with excitement.

'Look at those three guys. I'm stoked. I've met Roger, and hope I meet all three of them.' Will he ask for autographs? 'Probably. Definitely photos.'

Clarke's admiration for those three extends to their off-field behaviour. Australia's first wave of full-time professional cricketers—the likes of Border, the Waughs and Warne—were not always at ease with the exposure of their private lives. As one of the second wave, Clarke says he always expected such scrutiny. This extends to public curiosity over his engagement to model Lara Bingle.

'I guess I accepted at an early age that there's more to this than what you do on the field. Your performance in your sport is the main priority, but the public looks at what you do off the field just as closely.'

But the off-field and on-field soon become entangled. Clarke and Symonds had a falling-out when the Queenslander took an infamous fishing trip rather than going to a team meeting when Clarke was Australian one-day captain last year. They say the friendship has been rebuilt, but, as 2005 showed, a long Ashes tour strains cricketers' private lives. That tour was characterised by the divided loyalties caused when players brought their partners and children. When the team started losing, some former greats reasserted their belief that families and tours should not mix.

Clarke, who was single during the 2005 tour and says the politics 'passed me by', is an adherent of partners being allowed to join long tours.

'Having a relationship is never easy, especially when you're away so much. I'm all for having partners on tour. I love it when Lara comes on tour . . . I can't imagine being away from her for five months.'

There is no understating the importance of this Ashes tour. For those who were there in 2005, such as Clarke, Ponting and Simon Katich, there is the spur of unfinished business. Can Clarke perform as well in England as he has elsewhere? Can Australia? For Australia to win the series, it's hard to imagine them doing so without Clarke batting as well as he did in 2006–07.

'Sure, I want to do well, but it's not all about 2005,' he says. 'We've got a whole new group of guys, some of whom haven't played in England at all, let alone in 2005. The key is that the senior guys need to lead the team with bat and ball and in the field, take on the grunt work, and let the younger guys enjoy what is one of the greatest tours you can ever go on.'

Clarke goes there now as a senior guy: the VC, trying to impart the lessons he learnt from his elders to newcomers like Phillip Hughes. He relishes leadership. Most Australian captains have craved it. It is only when he is asked if he 'wants it' that Clarke pauses, knocked momentarily off his stride. It's not always the done thing to be openly ambitious. Carefully he replies: 'You don't need a (c) or a (vc) beside your name to be a leader in the group. Look at Warney—not the captain, but definitely a leader.

'It's for others to say whether I'm a good leader or a bad leader, I just want to earn respect. But I have to say that I think it brings out the best in me . . . statistics don't lie. I've batted a lot better when Ricky's been asking me to step up.'

His greatest fear is missing the opportunities when they come.

'I usually know within the first few balls if I'm "on",' he says. 'You look at Ricky Ponting, and out of [221] Test innings he's had 37 great days, when he's scored a century. Even for the best, it doesn't happen very often. You really need to grasp it. The days you get angry are when you're "on" and you miss out.'

One thing he can't promise is to exude stillness and calm, to stop sweating and showering. That, after all, would not be Michael Clarke. Talk about going back to Lord's and this time grasping the opportunity he missed, and he is the excited kid again.

'Lord's, what a ground, it's amazing. I can't wait to get back . . . and I guarantee if I get to 91 this time, I won't be playing the shot I did in 2005.'

4 June 2009

THE METHOD IN RICKY'S MADNESS

Adrian Proszenko

Ricky Stuart sensed the natives were restless. It was during his stint as Roosters coach when word filtered back that the players felt flat and tired. That he'd been too hard on them at training.

Never one to shirk from an issue, he gathered the whole team together to address the elephant in the room.

'Everyone feeling flat or tired,' Stuart dared. 'Raise your hand.'

Legend has it about half put their hands in the air. The smart ones kept their mitts firmly tucked into their pockets. 'Everyone with their hands down can go home,' he said before eyeballing the weary.

'The rest of you . . . you're doing 400 m sprints. Then we'll see how flat and tired you are.'

Welcome to the method and madness of Ricky Stuart. A man who bleeds blue, doesn't mind picking the odd one and, according to none other than Jack Gibson's right-hand man, Ron Massey, could well be on the path to super-coach status himself if his Blues get up on Wednesday night.

What the above anecdote doesn't demonstrate is how much he cares for his players. Hopefully the next one will.

In the aftermath of the Roosters' gut-wrenching 2004 grand final loss to the Bulldogs, Stuart and his charges trudged back to the club to commiserate with the fans. Several were ripping into one of his players, who made the sort of gaffe which costs you a lap of honour. Stuart was so protective of his charge that he had to be physically restrained, ending the heckles once and for all.

It's that sort of devotion to his men that has him primed to make history at Suncorp Stadium. On only two occasions have the Blues come from behind to win a series. The first time was in 1994, when Stuart was the halfback. The only other time was in 2005, when he was the coach. Coincidence? Unlikely.

Fittingly, the man in the opposing coach's box is his good mate, Mal Meninga. On the surface, you couldn't find two more different personalities. Mellow Mal and Rampaging Ricky. But appearances can be deceiving. Just ask the man who coached them both at the Green Machine, Tim Sheens.

'They're not as far away from each other as you think,' Sheens revealed. 'They're two of the most competitive blokes I've ever been involved with. If you wanted to play Mal in marbles, he'd want to beat you. Ricky would probably want to beat you. And then steal the marbles.'

That competitive fire has sometimes got him into trouble. It's also put him offside with some of his closest allies. Like his fallout with Meninga after last year's decider. Or the time that Phil Gould, in one of the most cutting and eloquent sprays of all time, described him as the most 'pig-headed and ungrateful person I've ever met in football'.

Or when 'Sticky' savaged Sheens for his unsolicited advice regarding the selection of Robbie Farah.

But it seems no one can fall out of love with Stuart for long. Having made up with Gould over a long, long lunch some time ago, he accepted an invitation from Gus to prepare for game one at Penrith. Meninga remains on his speed dial. And the supposed Sheens feud was just a couple of mates having some fun at the expense of an obliging press.

Ricky Stuart circa 2012 is a different bloke to the one who terrorised opposition forwards—and his own—as a halfback for Canberra, Canterbury, NSW and Australia.

Back then, the stories of his competitiveness were legendary.

There's the yarn about how he used to drink his bourbon and cokes after a game and throw the ice at one of the biggest monsters in his pack.

Sheens told his prop to put Stuart in his place.

The response: 'No way. If I clip him, he'll clip me back. And then he'll clip me again when I'm not looking.'

As a Raiders player, he loved watching the opposition troops climbing out of the bus, rugged up in their overcoats and moaning about how cold it was in the nation's capital.

So when he was in charge at the Sharks, he ordered the squad to dress in shorts and T-shirts for the trip.

Anyone who so much as mentioned the weather was fined.

Apparently, he has mellowed, according to Brian Canavan, his chief executive at the Roosters and the man Stuart worked closely with in producing the blueprint for a shot at dethroning Queensland.

'Comparing him now to what he was like at the Roosters, he's now far more rounded,' Canavan said. 'Far more circumspect. He's extremely passionate and it's good to have people who are calm around him, guys like Ron Palmer.'

Now his players are buying in. The passion. The loyalty. The unstinting belief they are better than a team which has beaten them six years in a row.

Even Mr Queensland himself, Wayne Bennett, heaped praise on Stuart for reigniting Origin interest in its most lopsided period ever.

'Ricky is the driving force in all of that,' Bennett said. 'And he's the driving force in the way the team is playing.'

Stuart speaks to Massey at least once or twice a week. As sounding boards go, 'Mass' is the best in the business. Having worked with Gibson and Bennett, he is also well placed to compare the trio.

'He's more emotional than they were,' Massey said. 'Jack was never a big one on speeches and things like that, but the players listened to him. Similar things with Wayne Bennett. It's the attitude he's got. He and Jack both had the title of being a super-coach and Ricky is just behind them.

'If he has more success, he'll be fair dinkum up there as a contender as a super-coach.'

1 July 2012

THE MAKING OF A MAN

Brad Walter

There is a flat patch of ground in a gully near the outdoor boxing ring Anthony Mundine set up at the remote Aboriginal settlement of Baryulgil to prepare for Wednesday night's bout against Danny Green. The locals refer to it as the Bull Ring.

'Anyone who got into a fight—the drunks and that—would have to sort out their differences first thing the next morning in the Bull Ring,' Mundine's father and trainer, Tony, recalls.

'They'd fight with bare fists until one person dropped. There would be broken teeth and broken noses. As kids, we'd all gather round and watch. If someone didn't want to fight, they'd be dragged out of bed.'

Perhaps it's where the Mundines developed their boxing genes. Although Tony—like Anthony—doesn't drink or smoke. Their upbringings, however, were vastly different, and unlike his father, Mundine's background is no *Rocky* script.

Born in Newtown and raised in Earlwood, Mundine was always destined to be an elite sportsman and by 15 had toured the US with a combined NSW–Queensland basketball team and was on a rugby league scholarship with St George. Choosing the latter, he became a star with the Dragons and played for NSW, ensuring he always enjoyed the best conditions and facilities.

In contrast, Tony Mundine worked from the age of 13 in the asbestos mine near Baryulgil that is blamed for so many of his friends and relatives being buried in the village's graveyard. Like so many boxers, he used the sport to build a better life for himself and his family and believes his tough start helped him get to within one knock-out punch of the world middleweight title.

It's why Anthony Mundine decided to go back to basics for the Green fight with his primitive training camp in Baryulgil, a 12-hectare tract of land bequeathed to three Aboriginal families—the Mundines, Daleys and Gordons—by the cattle-ranch owner they worked for to help them escape the welfare laws of the 1920s that led to the stolen generation.

'Anthony is a city boy, but the country life is a good life,' Tony Mundine says. 'When Anthony first started training, he was doing all new stuff like running machines and weights and all of that shit—the same as what Danny Green is doing now. Weights will do no good for you.

'To be a boxer, you have got to have muscles like a baby, you've got to be quick and able to fire like a bullet. If you are pumping weights, naturally your muscles are going to get hard and you're going to stiffen and get tight. You might think you look good but from maybe the sixth round or seventh round onwards you're going to feel the [negative] effect.

'The old school way is still the best: get a lot of exercise the natural way like sit-ups and doing a lot of mileage. In the old days, it was . . . harder and . . . tougher. You've got to remember the guys who have beaten my son—like [Mikkel] Kessler and [Manny] Siaca—haven't had two amateur fights [as Mundine had before quitting league to take up boxing in 2000]. They have done this sort of training before.'

Mundine trained up to four times a day, running the dusty roads around the settlement, working out in the makeshift gym that comprised a concrete block wall and three timber posts supporting rafters from which hung punching bags and a speed ball, and sparring in the ring that had previously been used in the Russell Crowe movie Cinderella Man.

It was a regime that began at about 6 am each day and could finish at 10 pm, sometimes after workouts with three sparring partners under the glare of headlights. The training—overseen by Tony Mundine and famed American trainer Roy Jones snr—was physically demanding, but the main benefit for the Man of returning to his father's birthplace was mental.

'In Sydney, there are a lot of distractions and especially with this being the biggest fight in Australian history, it was good to get away,' Anthony says. 'I had to adjust, I had to adapt to a different environment and it challenged my mind as well as my body.

'Any fight that I've lost, mentally I was there but to get into a real war mode before the battle you need solitary so you know why you're there. I know why

I am here and it is because of Green. No matter what he's got or what he's done, how much skill he has got or how much power, it's not going to affect me.

'This fight means a great deal to me—this is the fight that is going to catapult me to where I want to be in the boxing ranks. From now on, I can't see myself getting beat unless I beat myself. I've blossomed and progressed as a fighter, mentally, physically, skilfully and in every way.'

According to Jones, Mundine is still a baby in boxing terms, having had just 28 fights since quitting league in 2000 to pursue his dream of winning the world title that his father was denied during a 15-year professional career in which he stepped into the ring 96 times.

Of those, five have been world title bouts, and Mundine, who will turn 31 next Sunday, has won two.

'He was renowned in rugby [league] and everyone just thought of him as an athlete and a star when he first came into the sport,' Jones says. 'But everyone has to take their punches straight, if you know what I mean, and he'd never done that. Everything he has ever done before has been high tech.

'Going to Baryulgil was like giving him a taste of the inconvenient things in life. I think the main thing it did was made him more aware and made him realise that this is a different sport. It kind of toughened him up a little bit.

'He'd never had a taste of it before and he didn't like it, but no kids these days like it. It was just to get him out of the element that he's in now, just to give him a slight taste—not that he had to stay there—of what not having things was like and see what sort of effect it had on him.'

While he is focused on beating Green and eventually regaining his WBA super-middleweight belt, the time at his bush camp has sharpened Mundine's consciousness of being a role model for young Australians, and unlike many other athletes, he is comfortable with that responsibility.

'I touch a lot of youth, give them self-esteem, give them pride, and as long as I'm doing that, and saving a few lives along the way—not touching drugs, not touching alcohol—I feel like I'm doing my job,' Mundine says.

13 May 2006

LEISEL LIKES A LAUGH—AND MUCH MORE

Stephen Wood

Even when she's trying to be funny, Leisel Jones can't win. This was the ruse: she had finally lost it. She'd smashed a glass in the reception of an overseas hotel, been thrown off the team, and was heading to court. It wouldn't be long before the press found out.

'That's the last practical joke I'll ever pull,' she says. 'We had it all set up. Rohan [Taylor, her coach] likes to pull pranks on Grant Stoelwinder, and we were at a world cup event last year so Grant says we have to get Rohan back. I was, like, "Yep", so I sent this message to Rohan telling him I'd been kicked off the team for, you know, something ridiculous—that I'd been sent home on the first plane, that he couldn't contact me, and that I'd be in court on Monday. But it failed miserably. Rohan gets to the hotel, sees me, and doesn't have any idea. He didn't get his messages.'

The message is not lost on us: Leisel likes a laugh. She has been diligent in showing us since 2004, when she stuck out her glass chin, played the straight man to a blonde bombshell, and dented Australia's reputation as a country of good sports. That nadir, her personal and professional breakdown at the Athens Olympics, forced her to confront demons most leave to the death bed. She did so while strangers called her out, sometimes to her face. The result— the new wisdom she revels in—was that Jones emerged with an understanding of dry land and her place on it. In the strange cult of professional swimming, it is nothing short of enlightenment.

'After Athens it really opened my eyes,' the 24-year-old says. 'I was very shy as a kid and I didn't let my personality shine through the media. I was absolutely guilty of that. I was always very protective, and that can come across as arrogant and rude.

'Only recently have I relaxed and given myself and opened up, but I feel super comfortable. I have accepted who I am. Now, whatever answer I give, that's me. If you don't like it, too bad; if you do, that's good, too.

'You know, I was trying to figure out who I was when I was young. Am I the funny person or the quiet person or am I the . . . My favourite personality is the funny one. In training I'm a bit of a joker. I like to keep it lighthearted; I'll be open and talk about everything. Everyone knows I'll be the first one to crack a joke at 4 am.'

Of course Leisel likes a laugh. She also likes painting her nails, watching movies and baking desserts. She does a mean soufflé that might make the grade on *MasterChef*. But don't be fooled. At twelve years of age she watched her father abandon her and her mother; two years later she graced the Olympic Games. She has won eight Olympic medals, broken several world records, and rises at four o'clock in the morning six days a week. If she achieves her aim of competing at London 2012, she will become the first Australian swimmer in history to make four Olympics. She has not ruled out a fifth, when the iconic records of Dawn Fraser and Krisztina Egerszegi might be in sight. Even though he has suffered illness and asked for forgiveness, her father is unlikely to be given a second chance. And disregard her line about never trying a practical joke again: Jones is driven by a pathological desire to succeed and an immaculate sense of ambition. She is not like you. You don't construct a legend on totem poles of normality, and Jones knows it. She's known it for ten years.

When TV news helicopters landed on her school oval when she was fourteen, Jones realised her life would be unusual. 'You can't fathom what it feels like,' she says now. 'You feel so ostracised. It was, like, "I'm so different. Why me, why have I been chosen?"'

It was the middle of 2000, and Jones—born 'the only white baby' in a hospital ward in Katherine, Northern Territory—had just moved to a new school in what would become her de facto home town, Brisbane. 'It was not the best way to fit in,' she says. 'You know: "Welcome to school"; "Yeah, thanks, I have helicopters following me around."'

In January of that year she swam one minute, 10.74 seconds in the 100 metres breaststroke at the Queensland age championships. By August she was winning silver at the Sydney Games in 1:07.42. In seven months she took more than three seconds off her best time. It created a hysteria and highlighted

Jones's natural gifts. She had the three factors required to excel at breaststroke: a powerful arm pull; a powerful kick, enhanced by knock knees that allow her to jack-knife her ankles close to her hips; and timing to bring the mechanics together. 'She had a funny build for a girl,' says her first coach, Ken Wood. 'But she was also a hard trainer. I remember her ducking out the back after sessions to vomit.'

Yet for the fuss of the Sydney Games, the Jones enigma began a decade ago this month, at the Olympic trials. Nadine Neumann, an Australian Olympian at Atlanta in 1996, got a personal taste that did not endear her to the teenager. 'Leisel and I had just swum the 200 m [breaststroke at the Sydney trials], and we both failed to qualify,' says Neumann. 'For me, it meant the end of my career and I was devastated. At the warm-down pool, Leisel was upset she hadn't made the 200 team, and my father went over to her to say she needn't be disappointed, that she'd swum well and had a bright future.

'Leisel and her mother [Rosemary] just turned their noses up at him and walked away. She probably wouldn't remember it now, but I felt angry. It was like she did not care for those who went before her, and I thought, "Who are you, you little upstart?" She was inexperienced and very ambitious.'

It was an indication of Jones's struggle to reconcile her standards and short-comings. At the 2001 world championships in Fukuoka, Japan, she was second in the 100 m. Two years later, in Barcelona, world championships gold eluded her again. 'In 2001 she got silver and was crying,' says Wood. 'I said, "For Chrissakes, this is the world championships!" She should have been crying with joy, but it became a problem.'

If Jones forgot the Neumann incident, her reaction to defeat at the Athens Games left her exposed. Third in the 100 m, behind compatriot Brooke Hanson and Chinese victor Luo Xuejuan, Jones cut a petulant, tortured figure at the medal ceremony. She did not congratulate Hanson or talk to her rival for five days. Many weighed in with opinions on her behaviour and mental state. Some called her a 'choker'; Fraser, infamously, called her a 'spoilt brat'.

Ian Hanson, the media manager for Australia's swimming team between 1991 and 2009, says: 'Athens was not an easy time. I did think it could get out of control. You can say what a sourpuss and a sore loser [Jones was] but I did not think it. In fact, from my observations her real demeanour was not coming through in the public eye. She appeared to handle herself better than the presentation suggested she did.'

Grant Hackett, who won a gold and two silver in Athens, says: 'She was probably naive and an immature athlete, and she didn't understand how things would be portrayed. Unfortunately, mud sticks sometimes, but even though her reaction was not in the best light, she didn't hurt anyone. The perceptions of the last few years have been unfair.'

Brooke Hanson told *Sport&Style* that after Australia had won gold in the 4 × 100 m medley relay in Athens, Jones apologised to her for her behaviour, for having acted like a 'spoilt brat'. 'I hope you can forgive me,' Jones said. They hugged and became friends. Today, Jones admits Athens was 'the worst', but says she had no idea her reaction at the medal ceremony would cause a problem and insists she had not become 'professionally spoilt' by her dominance of the stroke in the build-up to Athens.

'It's so funny that a picture can capture one moment,' she says. 'I see it all the time in paparazzi photos. You've captured one instant when your eyes dart to the left, or your mouth is open, and it translates into something different.

'I understood what it took to get there. People said if you win gold in your first event, it's the worst thing because you don't know what it's like to work hard and be beaten. Well, I had the best start because I [got silver in 2000 and silver in 2001].

'You [Fraser] don't understand the situation or my upbringing. If anyone had to work for anything, it's me, because we [she and her mother] had houses repossessed and got out of bankruptcy. My definition of a spoilt brat would be very different to that.

'I don't have bad memories of Athens. I still have the wreath [from the medal ceremony], and I don't have any negative feelings. In fact, I'd like to go to Athens for a holiday, really.'

Wood made a startling admission to *Sport&Style*, that he should take some blame for what Jones went through. 'I put too much pressure on her, telling her she was the best in the world all the time,' he says. 'I gave her a [mock] gold medal [before Athens], just to give her confidence, but maybe it was too much.'

It was all too much. Jones returned home to a villain's welcome. She left Wood to join a new coach, Stephan Widmer, who helped her confront her self-esteem issues—the fact that, in his words, she 'was just a swimmer, and if that went wrong her whole world fell apart'. He used $2500 of funding to enrol Jones in a personal development course run by a life coach. Within twelve months Jones had won her first major gold, in the 100 m at the world championships in Montreal. 'Oh my god, thank you,' she mouthed to the heavens when she touched home in first place.

Jones admits she is scared of retirement. The desire to extend her career helps to explain why she took a year away from major competition in 2009—such respite is bound to aid longevity. But it ignores the bigger picture: that she refuses to quit until she is recognised as one of this country's greatest swimmers. 'I think, "Why retire now?"' she says. 'I've got more to give.'

She would likely have a different attitude had she not enjoyed her finest moment at the Beijing Games in 2008: her first individual gold, in the 100 m. It was, she acknowledges, the 'cut-off' point in her seven-year battle with herself. 'After Beijing I dealt with a few things,' she says. 'Winning was just . . . relief. It wasn't even happiness. But maybe it helped me accept [the past] more, and proved to people I was capable of winning. It was almost like proving to people what I knew inside. I knew I was capable, I just couldn't get it out.

'In that time I questioned myself. I don't like the word "depression"; it's too loosely bandied around. But I felt horrible. You feel your self-worth is in a gold medal. Yes, I thought about quitting [before Beijing], but then I have thought about quitting when I've been on a high as well.'

Strangely, Jones's triumph in Beijing presents her with another challenge. She has finally won an individual gold, but it is only one. Fraser won three in the same event in as many Games, a feat matched since only by the Hungarian Egerszegi. Another Australian, Shane Gould, won three at one Olympics. 'I've achieved everything I ever wanted,' Jones says. 'I've done three Olympics, world championships, I've been around the world and made good friends. But I still have the inner drive to do more, to be not just good but . . . great. One of the greatest compliments you could receive is being one of the best in your sport, ever. It's a respect thing.

'That's my competitive nature. I want to make sure I get everything out of [my career]. I would hate to retire and go, "Oh, if only I had done the work I could have achieved more." London is not that far away, it's just around the corner. No one's ever done four Olympics [as an Australian swimmer], so that would be so nice—a nice thing on the CV, good for a job application.' She adds that she wants to be great 'for me, not for anyone else, for me'.

She would even contemplate a fifth Games, in Rio de Janeiro in 2016. 'Oh, anything's possible,' she says. 'Physically I could go on past London, easily. I thought [I would retire] after Beijing, but, no, I'm still physically fit and enjoying it.

'It depends if I've achieved everything I ever wanted. You know, if I'm not going training then someone else is; if I'm sleeping in then someone else is doing the hard yards and they're benefiting and you're not. I'll always be competitive, no matter what I do. Even if I did Little Athletics, which I was rubbish at, I still want to win.

'That's not a bad thing. It makes you strive to be better. Anyway, sleeping is boring—I'm scared of sleeping in. I really struggle to not do anything. I hate sitting on the couch; I like seeing how many things I can fit into a day. I don't know where that [desire] comes from. It comes from within, I think.'

So after her soul-searching, the time spent 'finding herself', and the unsolicited advice, who is Leisel Jones? 'Who knows!' she says with a guffaw. 'I've got a multi-personality, a split personality! I can accept all of them; they're all part of me, and on any day I can be any personality I choose.'

It is the first time she has equivocated, though it is hardly damning. To a person, those who have played a role in the drama—Neumann, Hanson, Hackett, Wood, Widmer, Taylor—stress how impressed they have been with the transformation of Jones's character and the balance she has achieved. Perhaps Taylor, her coach, puts it best when he says it has been a process of 'becoming a woman'.

Jones is wise enough to know that 'you make plans for life and it doesn't go anything like'—the end of her engagement to former AFL footballer Marty Pask is evidence of that. Wood also hints at Jones's enduring hardness when he says that, despite her dad's absence, she 'never needed a father figure' and that 'you can't get too close to Leisel'. But Jones isn't taking much notice any more. 'Yeah, it has been a crazy ten years,' she says.

'In ten years' time I think I'll step back and be proud, and realise the enormity of my achievements. But for now I am enjoying racing for what it is. I'm not trying to cure cancer. When I was on the blocks in the final in Beijing, I told myself that it's just sport, that it will all seem so insignificant in the future, and that no one will have their heads chopped off if I don't swim well. In Athens I took it differently—it was serious, "my whole life depends on this, I've gotta make a living".

'I've been through tough times but now it's smooth sailing. Some people have rocky roads ahead but I've done it. I love life. What is my bad day now? When I can't find my soy milk at the supermarket.'

Come on, Leisel, is that *really* your worst day?

'Exactly.'

It sounds too good to be true, and it probably is. But that's not the point. The point is she's challenging the proverb that when ambition ends, happiness begins.

6 May 2010

LORD OF THE RING

Greg Bearup

Vince Sorrenti was the guest comedian at the Men of League's gala dinner at Star City on Wednesday night. One of his jokes went along these lines: 'David Gallop is caught in a lift with three people—Osama Bin Laden, Khoder Nasser and Adolf Hitler. Gallop has a gun, but only two bullets. What does he do? Shoots Khoder twice!'—Bec & Buzz, The Sunday Telegraph, October 2008.

It's the day before the June 30 fight and cars, bulging at the hinges with blackfellas, are on the move from the big Aboriginal settlements of NSW and southern Queensland. Many have already arrived and their occupants are gathering at a riverside cafe. Freddo 'The Bush Tucker Man' Robinson, a gnarled little Aboriginal bloke from Grafton with a patch over one eye, tells me he's been employed by the Mundine camp for the past six years as a corner man and 'masseurist'. 'It's changed me fuggin' life,' he says. 'I live for this. I wouldn't even walk into a pub these days.'

At the centre of this group sits the imposing figure of Tony Mundine, father of Anthony. The 'man who made The Man' is sipping tea sweetened with honey. He's monitoring this modern-day walkabout, relayed to him by various messengers, while Khoder Nasser casts a bemused eye over the comings and goings.

'There's a big mob, I just discovered, comin' all the way from Bourke and another from Brewarrina,' Tony, 60, explains. 'They'll be needin' a coupla dozen tickets, at least. Maybe more.' He should be focusing on his son, Anthony, whom he trains and who is fighting tomorrow night. But he sees it as his personal duty to ensure that no Aborigine, having made the effort to get to Brisbane, should pay for a ticket.

'Money's only paper,' Tony tells me. 'It comes and it goes.' I ask him how many relatives he reckons will be at the fight. 'All of 'em,' he says, surprised by the question. 'All of 'em.'

Nasser, the man whose job it is to control the flow of tickets—and to organise the fighters, the venue, the pay-television deals, the glove men, the hotel rooms, the media interviews, the press conferences, the scales, the sparring partners—is reaching into his bag for another wad of freebies.

He's had to master more than just the fight game to do this job: he's now an expert on Aboriginal familial and clan relationships.

'Yesss,' says Nasser with a drawn-out laugh. 'There'll be all of Tony's relatives and then some he's never met. After the fight they'll be hitting him up again for the petrol money to get home.'

'What can I say?' asks Tony, muscular arms folded across his chest. 'I'm da black Santa.'

This is the 42nd time Khoder Nasser has managed an Anthony Mundine fight and every one has been a shambles in some way—but somehow they've all gone ahead. With Nasser at his side, Mundine, 35, a three-time World Boxing Association Champion, has become a very rich man—rich enough to buy his mum and his sister a house each in Sydney and to sling a couple of thousand here and there to broke and broken mates and relatives.

Nasser and I leave the cafe to pick up his other client, the rugby league defector turned rugby union superstar Sonny Bill Williams, for the drive out to the weigh-in at the Brisbane Entertainment Centre. SBW, as he is known, is one of the feature fighters in the 'KO to Drugs' bout, a charity event the Mundine camp stages each year to raise $50,000 for drug rehabilitation.

Williams has possibly the most perfect male body ever assembled. He's 193 centimetres tall with enormous shoulders and arms and a torso that tapers down to a chiselled stomach. There's not an ounce of imperfect flesh. He jumps into the black rented Range Rover, pulls his hood over his head and moves to the beat of a muthaf . . . a rap as Nasser barks instructions into his mobile.

'F— me!' the manager exclaims, exasperated, as we are halfway to the venue. 'F— me. We've done 41 f—ing fights, how could we forget the scales for the weigh-in?'

It's soon evident there's nothing conventional or ordinary about this circus, least of all the ringmaster, Khoder Nasser. He runs a hugely successful multimillion-dollar sporting business without a secretary or other full-time staff, a laptop or even a notepad. Everything is in his head or buried deep in his BlackBerry under a mountain of text messages. He doesn't own a computer. He's never signed a contract with Mundine or Williams, the two men who provide him with his livelihood. Their deal was sealed with a handshake. 'If they're not happy with me,' says Nasser, 'why should they stay with me?' The 39-year-old generally goes about looking like a homeless man scrubbed up after a night in a hostel. Today he's dressed in an old, frayed sportscoat with tracksuit pants, a French soccer shirt and sandals, with one of the straps undone because he has a blister. His bushy mop of thick black hair pokes out from beneath a blue cap.

Despite his bagman appearance, he manages a ragged handsomeness, a cross between Robert De Niro and Diego Maradona. He has a Mediterranean temperament, hurling abuse one moment and hugging someone the next.

He has managed Anthony Mundine for the past 12 years and oversaw his controversial switch from rugby league a decade ago, when Mundine walked out on a record $600,000-a-year contract with the Dragons to take up boxing, the sport of his father.

Mundine is now Australia's most financially successful boxer ever and, having won three world titles and reached the pinnacle in both rugby league and boxing, can justifiably lay claim to being one of our great sportsmen. And yet, because of his outspoken views on racism, his conversion to Islam, his often-stated belief in his own greatness and comments such as, 'It's not about terrorism, it's about fighting for God's laws and Americans brought it upon themselves for what they've done' (in the weeks after September 11), he's disliked intensely by a large percentage of the sporting public and sections of the media, particularly News Ltd, which owns the game he scorned.

Nasser has always been portrayed as the Svengali behind Mundine—the one who encouraged the brash talk and lured him to Islam—but after he became Williams's manager, the knives were sharpened. 'When Sonny first came to me and asked me to manage him, I tried to talk him out of it,' Nasser tells me. 'I said to him, "You don't want me, they'll try to f— you." And they did.'

'Already guiding the career of one of the most disliked athletes in Australia, in Anthony Mundine, Nasser has recently taken charge of one of the most popular, Sonny Bill Williams,' wrote *The Daily Telegraph*'s Paul Kent in 2008, 'and within a few short months appears to be already leading him down the same road as Mundine.'

Unhappy with the $400,000 a season the Canterbury Bulldogs were paying his client—and his treatment by the club—Nasser secretly negotiated a $1.5-million-a-season contract with the French rugby union club Toulon, even though Williams was only part-way through his five-year Bulldogs deal. And so, without telling his teammates, SBW jetted off to France to play union as lawyers tried to serve summonses on the pair. (The matter was later settled with a $750,000 payment to the club, Mundine stumping up the money.) 'What Khoder Nasser is doing with Williams amounts to nothing short of high treason,' continued Kent. 'A shameful bid to exploit Sonny Bill, a deliberate kick in the guts to rugby league.'

News Ltd columnist Rebecca Wilson said Sonny Bill had 'no basic values' and was 'a disgraceful example of how greed is turning many of our footballers into mercenaries who don't care about anyone except the bloke in the mirror'. (The *Australian Financial Review*'s Neil Chenoweth pointed out that this was all a bit much, coming from the organisation that had shafted the community-based Australian Rugby League a few years earlier to set up Super League, even after News Ltd's chief executive, Ken Cowley, had publicly declared, 'Whatever happens we will not start up a rebel league.') Sonny's departure may have been a kick in the guts to rugby league, but it was a jackpot for someone who earns a living as a professional sportsman.

After two years in Toulon, the 24-year-old Auckland-born Williams—or '$BW', as they refer to him at News—has just turned down a record $2 million a season from the French club to play provincial rugby in New Zealand, with the likelihood of being picked for the All Blacks in next year's Rugby Union World Cup. If he succeeds, he will become an international superstar and his earning capacity will have outstripped, many times over, anything rugby league could have offered.

Khoder Nasser has plenty of knockers, but the people he represents have no complaints. 'The thing that I love about Khoder is that he's ruthless,' Anthony Mundine explains to me. 'His number one priority is his client and getting the best deal for the person he represents. He doesn't care if he pisses people off. In fact, I think he loves it.'

The legendary boxing trainer Johnny Lewis, who was initially wary of Nasser, says he is the best boxing manager/promoter Australia has ever produced and credits him with reviving the sport here through his savvy management of Mundine.

'Anthony may be The Man, but Khoder is The King,' Lewis tells me. 'If I had a young boxer with big potential, I'd get down on my knees and beg Khoder to manage him. I think he's a genius.'

Nasser explains that whenever he makes a deal he canvasses all the possibilities but keeps one final option up his sleeve. 'It's the option,' he says, 'to be able to say to the other side, "Go f— yourself", and then walk out of the room.'

The whole time he was working to secure the Williams deal in France, he told the Bulldogs camp he had been to see some barristers and falsely assured them that the contract was 'better than Fort Knox . . . You can get out of Fort Knox: you can't get out of this.' The whole time I was thinking, "You arrogant f—s, I am going to f—you right up."'

'One of my favourite views in the world is when you fly into Sydney and those red terracotta tiles come into view,' Khoder tells me. 'I been all around the world and I wouldn't live anywhere else.'

Khoder says that he loves this country, as his migrant father does, but they view it differently.

'My dad's view is that Australia gave us everything and that we should just be grateful. When we were kids, if we ever got a hard time because of our ethnic background, he'd say, "Wake up. They invited us here. They gave us work here. We don't have any issues." That's not the way I see it.'

He sees a country still struggling with racism.

'It rears its ugly head all the time. Look at the Cronulla riots. Anthony is one of the people who can reveal the deep-seated hatred this country has towards indigenous people and people who are different—and that excites me.' (The next day news breaks that Parramatta centre Timana Tahu has left the NSW State of Origin camp after assistant coach Andrew Johns called Queensland centre Greg Inglis a 'black c—'.) Mundine converted to Islam after becoming friends with Nasser, a devout Muslim, and he also started to become more outspoken on Aboriginal issues. Was this your influence? I ask. 'Anthony has always known about the racism,' Khoder replies. 'Maybe he felt he had a better support system around him to speak out against it.'

Khoder's grandfather moved to the southern Sydney suburb of Hurstville from a poor farming village outside Tripoli in 1950. He worked in a factory for 11 years before he had enough money to bring his family out. His boys had been lucky enough to study at an English-language school in Lebanon and were good students. One was accepted into medicine at Sydney University while the other, Yasser—Khoder's father—enrolled as an electrical engineer. When the boys' father was killed in an industrial accident, they were forced to give up university to support the family. Yasser worked for most of his adult life at Australia Post, sorting mail. Eventually, he built an enormous 'wog palace' on his big block at Hurstville.

Khoder grew up playing cricket and football in the streets, climbing trees in his suburban backyard with his six brothers and sisters and watching the beloved Dragons at Kogarah Oval on the weekends. In many ways it was idyllic, but Khoder tells me that, even as a second-generation immigrant, he always felt like an outsider. 'I felt it from some of the teachers at school, too, but if I ever complained [to his father], I'd get shot down.'

As a child, Khoder was often in trouble, his father tells me, mainly because he was argumentative and had a fiercely independent streak. Having had his own studies interrupted, Yasser placed great emphasis on education and tells me proudly that all seven of his kids went to university. He's still disappointed, though, that Khoder never completed his studies (he eventually finished an arts degree at Wollongong University, majoring in economics and politics, but dropped out of a teaching master's degree at Sydney University).

'Khoder always had a drive and a desire to be something, to be successful,' Yasser explains. He just wishes that his son had made a different career choice. 'I don't like to see someone hitting someone else for no reason,' he says. Until a few years ago, he was still asking Khoder, 'When are you going to get a proper job?' Apart from being inspired by 'the knockers and the peddlers of mendacity' in the media, as Khoder puts it, you can't help but feel that proving his old man wrong is a potent, driving force behind his success.

Managing sportsmen was something he just stumbled into while trying to avoid finishing university. Nasser met Mundine one day when he sat next to him at the SCG in the late '90s. 'It was a pretty special day for me,' he remembers. 'It was the first proper conversation I'd had with an indigenous Australian—the rightful owners of the land. So I felt good. For the first time I didn't feel that I was an uninvited guest in this country.'

Over the next few years the two became close friends and would often meet to discuss life, sport and religion. One day Nasser was in the Dragons' dressing sheds after a game and a journalist asked Mundine a question about his playing future. 'I said, "Ask my manager",' Mundine recalls. 'And I pointed to Khoder, who answered the question. That's how it all began.' Mundine sacked his manager and hired Nasser, who hadn't a clue what he was doing. His previous jobs had been in a chemist's shop and a cafe.

His first business meeting was with the St George executive and former great Brian Johnston.

It lasted a minute. 'I asked him if he thought Anthony was the best player in the game. He said he did. I said, 'Good, come the end of the season we'll make him the highest-paid player in the game.' Nasser was 27.

That was in the relatively simple world of football; the switch to boxing is like moving from arithmetic to algebra. In boxing, managers seeking to secure the big bouts need to lobby and cajole the sanctioning body in Panama and Venezuela, purse money has to be found, promoters need paying off, boxers require quality sparring partners, television deals are essential and venues have to be booked at the right price.

On the night of a fight, the Mundine camp can include more than 100 people.

'When Khoder started out, he spoke to everyone he possibly could in the boxing game,' says boxing writer and commentator Paul Upham. 'He soaked it all up incredibly quickly and then he put his own twist on it. He's a very smart guy.'

But he also has a 'glass jaw'. Upham is one of a number of journalists to have been refused media accreditation at fights because Khoder disliked something he had written about Mundine. 'And I like both of 'em,' says Upham, a little exasperated.

Everyone I spoke to for this profile, even those who have had run-ins with Nasser, speak of his intelligence. Todd Greenberg—the chief executive of the Bulldogs when Sonny Bill Williams absconded—describes Khoder as a 'shrewd negotiator with a great business brain', even though he says he doesn't think much of him for lying.

'It is just what you stand for as a person,' says Greenberg. 'We were lied to time and time again.' Greenberg says they could have entered into a discussion to end Williams's contract peacefully, 'but we never had that discussion'.

Not long after Nasser became Mundine's manager, he met a beautiful 18-year-old Fijian–Australian woman at a barbecue. 'The first time he met me, he said, "I am going to marry you", Tatum Maybir, now 28, tells me. 'I fell madly in love. He's magnetic. There was strictly no sex before marriage; we just bonded.'

Maybir, who had been raised in a conservative Christian household, converted to Islam. 'Six months later, he just woke up one morning and said, "Let's get married", and so we did.' He is the only one of Yasser's seven children not to have married within the Lebanese-Australian circle.

He didn't tell his parents about the marriage until Maybir fell pregnant. One day, they went to the Hurstville house he'd grown up in. 'We walked into the house,' says Maybir, 'and Khoder said, "Mum, Dad, this is my wife." They just sort of stared at me. I hate reliving that moment: it was terrible.' Both her family and his consoled themselves by telling each other it would never last.

Ten years later, the couple have five children and what appears to be a loving relationship. He tells me that, every day, he thanks Allah for Maybir and his kids. 'I'm blessed,' he says with a smug grin. 'I'm blessed.'

Nasser's clients may like flashy clothes and Hummers, but he continues driving an old Corolla and wearing tracksuits. He lives in a modest two-storey house, a street away from his parents. So what drives him, I ask Maybir, if not money?

'His ego,' she says without hesitation. 'He's got an enormous ego. My gosh, he'll probably kill me for saying that. He's got a lot to prove, to himself and other people. He thrives on the controversy, too. We never get the *Telegraph* but when he's in that Bec & Buzz column, someone will point it out to him— he loves it.'

Mundine and Nasser own a cafe in Hurstville called Boxa, which serves as a de facto office. One day I visit the cafe as Nasser is preparing lunch—salmon and rice—for Mundine, Williams and their families and friends.

The sports agent is bouncing around the kitchen and gesticulating with a pair of tongs as the fish sizzles. He says the problem with most agents is they have too many clients and don't have enough invested in the success, or failure, of their individual athletes.

'You have got to actually feel what the other guy is feeling,' he says, moving around the kitchen as though he were in the ring. 'When he gets hit, you get hit. He gets sick, you're sick. In the Don King model, he sits there calmly. He owns both fighters, so whoever wins, who gives a shit?

'Whereas I sit on the edge of the ring, thinking 'F— there's a lot at stake here. One lucky punch and it could all be over.'

Nasser says it was during one of Mundine's darkest hours that he fell in love with his job. It was 2001 and Mundine had been a professional fighter for less than two years and was hungry for a world title. He managed to get a bout against the champion German fighter Sven Ottke, who was undefeated as a professional and was making his 10th straight world title defence. Nasser had advised Mundine against the fight on two grounds. First, he thought it was too early in his career, and second, he thought the business deal was a dud.

But, of course, Nasser and Tony were there, ringside in Germany as Anthony fought for a world title in only his 10th fight. For the first 10 rounds, according to the Associated Press report, Mundine was making Ottke, 'the man that respected US veteran trainer Don Turner called 'the most brilliant technical boxer in the world', look like a second-rate journeyman'.

Anthony was fighting the fight of his life. 'I turned around to Tony and said, "He'd better go for it. There are two more rounds. We can win this."' When he turned around, though, Anthony was on the canvas, knocked out cold. He looked dead. 'I jumped into the ring, terrified.'

It took an age for Mundine to come to. 'They wanted to take him out on a stretcher, but he refused and he hobbled to the dressing room. That's when all the talking began that his career was over—the media, everyone, even elements in the camp. I heard that back in the St George League's Club, people were dancing on the tables.

'But it was at this point that I got excited. It's when I thought, "Yeah, I love this. I see his dream now. I know what it means, the dream of becoming a world champion." It took me until then to work it out.'

Nasser met Don King—the US boxing promoter whom Mike Tyson claimed 'would kill his own mother for a dollar'—not long after Mundine began his boxing career. King wanted Mundine in his stable. 'He said to me, "Do you want a world title? You can walk, you can catch a train, or you can fly. With me, you will fly. But first, sign this contract." It was about this thick,' Nasser says, spreading his thumb and forefinger, 'and it dictated the brand of shoes Anthony could wear. I said, "Don, that'd be like locking us up and throwing away the key. Sorry, that's not our style."'

Instead, Mundine and Nasser have gone it alone. They've earned millions, promoting the fights themselves, but have drawn harsh criticism from some boxing writers and fight fans who claim that Mundine has often fought substandard opponents.

'Mundine has the potential to be known as one of the world's great fighters,' says the AAP boxing writer Adrian Warren, 'but he needs to fight some of the world's really great fighters to do that.' He adds that Nasser has managed Mundine for 'maximum return for minimum risk'.

Mundine admits that he is often in conflict with his manager over the quality of his opponents.

'There are certain fights that I want that he can't get,' he says. 'I want to rush, whereas he wants to build to a climax. I am ready now.'

Nasser bristles at these criticisms and says it's very difficult for an Australian boxer to secure big fights because there isn't the interest, internationally, in the television rights. 'Anthony sometimes doesn't understand that there has to be a build-up. Roger Federer doesn't play a Wimbledon final every week and not every fight can be for a world title.'

While Nasser has helped his clients earn millions for their sporting performance, they've never chased corporate sponsors. Mundine has no sponsors and SBW has few.

'Marketing is its own monster,' Nasser explains. 'Between you and me, I couldn't give two flying f—s about it. Marketing means that you are licking the arse of some corporation.

'They paint you on a billboard, make all the kids look up to you, while they are rorting every son-of-a-bitch $200 for a five-buck pair of shoes,' he says, laughing.

For him, it's all about 'balls'—having the balls to back yourself and go it alone. 'The boys, Sonny and Anthony, they've got elephant balls,' he says. 'They don't feel the heat. If you don't have balls, you don't have a manhood.'

Despite the bombast, Nasser is well read and enjoys books on history, philosophy, religion and great sportsmen. The book that's had the greatest influence on him, he says—apart from the Holy Koran—is Alex Haley's *The Autobiography of Malcolm X*.

'The lesson in that book is that you can be so small and be up against a massive system. That doesn't mean you're not going to get anywhere.

'He took a stance. Even though he knew he'd be killed, it didn't stop him and that's something to admire. He had balls, balls for a good cause.'

It's fight night in Brisbane. Anthony Mundine has an easy win against Carlos Jerez, a tough-as-nails Argentine who takes him to 12 rounds.

It's an entertaining display.

It's a different matter for Sonny Bill Williams.

Williams, cut like a Roman sculpture, steps into the ring with Ryan 'Hulk' Hogan—who looks as if he's just stepped off the set of *Little Britain*, where he's been playing Daffyd, the only gay in the village. He's more Sulk than Hulk. The fight is an embarrassment. Before the end of the first round, Hulk is on his knees, begging for things to end. Sonny mouths, 'F— me' at the pathetic capitulation and shakes his head.

The next day he's still fuming. 'What did you expect?' Nasser asks me. 'It was only his second fight; it was just a charity fight.' Not to worry though, he adds, 'He'll be picked for the All Blacks, he'll be a star.' No one will remember the debacle of Ryan 'Hulk' Hogan.

The dogs bark, the caravan rolls on.

27 July 2010

MY SPORTING HERO

Spiro Zavos

There is a photo of Keith Miller—apparently it was Sir Robert Menzies' favourite image of the cricketer—showing the great player finishing off a crisp cut with a pose that could have been carved on the Elgin marbles.

The bat has come through its arc after contact with the ball into a high flourish; Miller is leaning slightly forward but in perfect balance; there is a sheen in his hair and his face is as handsome as a Greek god's.

That photograph became my talisman as I grew up in Wellington, New Zealand, in the 1950s, the son of a migrant who owned a fish-and-chips shop. I carried it everywhere I went as a book marker. The image remained with me, too, well after the marker disappeared, as the epitome of excellence and beauty. It conveyed a formative and lasting message about how cricket should be played and life lived—as an adventure for the brave, the good and the chivalric.

Wonderment did not do justice to the emotions Miller evoked in me so far away from the fields of his triumphs. Only hero worship sufficed.

Children of migrants invariably seek to assimilate into the mainstream as quickly as possible. For a young boy in New Zealand, that meant becoming a fanatic about rugby and cricket.

Our national cricket team had several outstanding players—Martin Donnelly, Bert Sutcliffe and John Reid—but we tended to identify with the Australia XI as 'our team', for Australia was always capable of thrashing the real enemy, England.

Australian cricketers, through reports on them in the monthly magazines *Sporting Life* and *Sports Novels*, became our mentors. I read, for instance, that

Sid Barnes reckoned an opening batsman should never play forward until he reached 30. I spent a whole year following that advice and never playing a shot off the front foot through a dozen or so windblown afternoons.

Players such as Barnes, Arthur Morris, Neil Harvey and Lindsay Hassett were respected because they were the best players in the best cricket team in the world. There was the (misguided) feeling, though, that on a good day, for several shots perhaps, a person could emulate their style. But you cannot hero worship someone who you can hope to emulate.

Miller was clearly incomparable. He was out on his own. He played, as a dashing batsman and lethal fast bowler, in a manner ordinary mortals, especially a boy from Wellington, could only fantasise about.

It was said of Greta Garbo's beauty that what men saw in other women when they were drunk, they saw in Garbo when they were sober. It was the same for Miller. His talent was so prodigious, his play was so exciting, there was so much charisma in even the casual flick back of that mane of shiny black hair, that you knew—sober or drunk with fantasy—that imitation was not possible. Idolisation was the only reasonable response.

Even though I was a left-hander, I adopted Miller's rushing run to the wicket, with its torrential energy of a river in flood, that I had seen on the Movietone news clips. But a callow youth with no sense of propriety smacked my first five balls in the opening over of an inter-school game for fours. I decided that if I was going to be humiliated by being belted all over the park, I wouldn't waste too much energy in the exercise. So I converted to a finger spinner.

I followed Australia on my Bakelite portable radio, which had a battery the size of modern car batteries, through a tough tour of England in 1953. Through the dark watches of the night I listened to my hero claiming 10 wickets at Lord's and then throwing the ball into the crowd. It was gestures like these that endeared him to an obscure schoolboy.

Like the time in 1948, also, when Australia scored 721 runs against Essex in a day and Miller came out and made a deliberate duck. There was nothing of the flat-wicket bully in him. Nothing mean of spirit.

Fast forward several years. I'd been selected to play for a Wellington XI in a one-day match against the Governor-General's XI. The Governor-General was Lord Cobham, who as Charles Lyttleton had played county cricket in the 1930s. His XI comprised former New Zealand players and a star guest attraction, Keith Miller.

The magic of Miller's name, although he had been retired for some years, ensured a full house at the Basin Reserve as I went out to open the batting against my hero. There was the familiar (through film clips) bucking, tempting run, the last great stride, the heave of the shoulders, and the opening ball of the match was whistling past my shoulder, brushing the tip of my shirt collar on its way through to the wicketkeeper.

Looking back on the experience years later, I realise Miller was going through his bag of tricks to delight the crowd and not to embarrass me unduly with his obvious superiority in class. The bouncers he bowled were monsters, which were easier to play in the middle than it seemed from the outer. The crowd gasped but there was no danger to the batsman as the ball soared over his head. His swinging deliveries, too, beat the bat by comfortable margins, well away from my stumps.

Then he rushed in again and without changing his action bowled a curving, floating leg break. With the callowness of youth, I whacked the ball away to the boundary.

In hindsight, again, I realise this thuggish response ruined what should have been (and was intended to be) a talking point for the spectators for weeks to come. I should have contrived to have been befuddled by the change of pace and style so that the people at the ground could tell their friends later: 'You should have seen Keith Miller. He came into bowl and without changing his action bowled this perfect leg break. The batsman didn't have a clue about it.'

Arthur Mailey in his autobiography, 10 for 66 and All That, described how as a young man trying to make his name in Sydney grade cricket he once bowled to Victor Trumper. He bowled the great batsman several leg breaks and then slipped in a wrong'un, which beat Trumper completely, made him look ungainly, and bowled him. In a memorable sentence, Mailey summed his feelings as he watched Trumper make his way back to the pavilion: 'I felt like a boy who had killed a dove.'

Years later, I have the same feeling about my crass response to Miller's witty, improvised delivery.

Before we went out to field, our captain, Bob Vance, a man of style and tact, told us that under no account were we to appeal for LBW if we were bowling to Miller. And if we were offered a catch, we were to contrive to drop it. But not too obviously.

When Miller came out to bat, therefore, I had a swelling sympathy for the plight of my hero. He had been out of cricket for so long, please God don't let him make a fool of himself, I prayed.

Within moments, all these fears evaporated. We had an off-spin bowler, Alan Preston, who bowled flat and fairly quickly. He never landed a ball for about five overs. Miller was down the pitch to him, hitting the ball on the full, stroking it sweetly and powerfully to all parts of the ground. And when the ball was finally pitched so short he could not hit it on the full, Miller would lean back and cut.

For a fraction of a second, we could see the famous image before it dissolved into the champion waving his bat to acknowledge the applause of an enchanted crowd.

This was batsmanship of a class none of us had experienced before. And from a man who hadn't picked up a bat for many years. It was thrilling and humbling. We were in the presence of a cricketing talent that in its ancient condition made all us, even though we were in our primes, seem mediocre and mundane by comparison.

Thrilled by the triumph of my hero, I went up to Vance after Miller had reached 60 or so runs and asked innocently: 'Can we catch him now if he gives a catch?' The normally urbane Vance, now harassed over having to try and set a field that could not contain Miller's armoury of run-scoring shots, replied in what could be described as strong terms about getting rid of him any way we could. 'Run the blighter out, even, if you can,' he told me through gritted teeth.

A *Herald* interview in 1994 revealed Miller as suffering from hip problems that slowed him down, but retaining a presence that was larger than life: 'The handshake is still firm, the memory vivid, the laugh infectious, the eye and ear sharp.'

Reading the article, I was reminded of the old man in Hemingway's *The Old Man and the Sea*, who could be defeated but not destroyed. And of Hemingway's definition of style as 'grace under pressure'.

The two words, Keith Miller, still evoke in me a memory of the endless summers of youth, and an image of grace that provided a visual metaphor for how cricket should be played and the full life lived.

1 January 1997

TOUGH AS OLD BOOTS,
AND NOW HE'S A LIVING LEGEND

Michael Cockerill

There is a sepia-tinged photograph of Joe Marston which says it all. Ramrod straight. Chest puffed out. Hair parted perfectly. Arms to his side, feet together. The only thing missing is a salute. In front of him is the Queen Mother. Beside him, his teammates. It's Wembley, the old Wembley.

It's just before kick-off in the 1954 FA Cup final. Marston is about to play for Preston North End against West Bromwich Albion. The first Australian to play in an FA Cup final. And for a long time—until Craig Johnston scored on the same stage for Liverpool more than three decades later—the only Australian to play in football's most revered game.

What the photograph tells you about Marston is his sense of respect. Respect for authority, respect for his teammates, respect for the game. More than half a century later, the memory has dimmed, and appearances have changed. These days Marston is a grey-haired 86-year-old who walks with a limp. Three hip replacements will do that. Especially when you spent half of your career playing in heavy steel-capped boots, kicking a leather ball held together by stitches, a football that became a medicine ball as it soaked up moisture like a sponge. Marston's best years were spent playing in sleet and snow and driving rain, on cold, dreary, afternoons, when the lily-white shirt of one of England's most famous old clubs was usually caked in mud after the first clattering tackle. A man's game, in the most Corinthian way. Marston loved the honesty, because that's who he is. An avowedly honest man. Everything he's got out of life, he's earned. The most precious thing he's earned, the way he sees it, is respect.

Marston doesn't talk about himself easily. It's the way of his generation. But as the rain hits the roof on his townhouse in the back streets of Umina, and the kettle is boiled, the tray of biscuits presented, and he motions you to the two chairs sitting side-by-side in the study, there's an invitation to reminisce. If you're smart, and you don't ask too many questions, the answers will come at their own pace.

On the sideboard, a package from England containing the latest book about Preston North End. It arrived a few days earlier, but they still remember him at Deepdale. Until ill-health struck recently, Tom Finney, now Sir Tom Finney, would send his old teammate a Christmas card every year. A few years ago, Marston was included in Preston's official Team of the Century. He had arrived in England in 1950, after a four-day flight on a Lockheed Constellation. He came with his wife, Edie, because Preston had paid for two one-way tickets. It was officially a trial, but there was never any doubt about the outcome.

When Marston left five years later, the Lilywhites had risen from the second-tier to be a powerhouse in the old first division. He played 200 first-team games, including 196 straight. He also made a Football League XI and roomed with the boy wonder, Manchester United's Duncan Edwards.

In the end, Marston left not because the club wanted to lose him, but simply because he was homesick. Not rich, but rich with experience. A measure of the man is that he left on his terms. Which is why he's revered, to this day, in the blue-collar heartland of Lancashire.

There are photos and medals on his garage wall, and boxes full of newspaper clippings, to remind him of what used to be. But he carries another memento. On his left knee there's still a scar. He doesn't remember the game, or the opposition. But he does remember the pain. 'I got opened up from here to here,' he says. 'They took me inside, and poured whiskey into the wound. Then they put in six stitches, and sent me back out there. I had a little slug from the bottle myself. In those days you didn't have substitutes. And I remember how cold it was. That's why there wasn't a lot of blood.'

Tough as old boots, is Joe. It's how he was taught by 'Digger' Evans and Billy Orr when he came to first grade at Leichhardt–Annandale, aged 17, from a church team at Petersham. It was 1943. 'Those two blokes, they were hard as nails,' he says. 'You didn't answer back, you listened. And you bloody well did what you were told.' Joe met the love of his life, Edie, in the grandstand at Lambert Park. His other love was football. Blessedly, he's still married to both.

These days, Edie is in a nursing home 10 minutes away. Joe drives there every morning, and home every afternoon. He sometimes thinks about moving into the home, but there's shrubs to prune and the freedom of having his own television room. 'Besides, I'm not sure about the food,' he laughs.

It's good to see him laugh. The laughter comes easily, in truth. Maybe that's because, by his own reckoning, he's a lucky man. When he got back from England, he'd finally saved enough to buy his own home. Before he left, he made paintbrushes for a living. When he came back, he returned to his old job. He's never been back to England since, despite being invited many times. 'We couldn't really afford it,' he says, without rancour. Joe's first house was a fibro cottage in Lidcombe. He painted it himself, with his own paintbrushes. I ask him if he still has the shirt from his debut with the national team. He first wore that wonderful white jersey with the green and gold 'V' in 1947, against visiting South Africa. He's got the cap: No. 97. But the shirt? 'Oh, that. I used it to paint the house.' Laughing, again.

Marston went on to play 34 times for Australia over 12 years—either side of his spell in England. He also coached his country, once, in an unofficial match against the touring Italian side, AS Roma, in 1966. Only two others—Frank Farina and Graham Arnold—have captained and coached the national team. 'That Arnie, he's a good boy,' says Marston. 'He once asked me for advice. I told him, "Be your own man."'

So who was the best Australian player he ever played with, or against? 'Reggie Date, definitely,' he says. 'Great player. Great bloke. But boy he could drink. The selectors, they never liked Reggie. He was too much of a larrikin. They couldn't handle him.'

When Marston played for Australia, squads were picked by selectors, who then sat down with the captain to name the starting 11. That changed when Australia was re-admitted to FIFA in 1963, and Marston eventually tried his hand at coaching. He even had a brief spell in charge of Sydney Olympic in the early years of the NSL. But it wasn't his style. 'I'm not big on the politics,' he says. Authority, as he sees it, should be exactly that. Not to be undermined.

Which is not to say he's stuck in a time warp. He's informed, enthused and complimentary about the modern game. It took a while, but the nation finally began to recognise Marston about 30 years ago, first with an MBE, and then with a host of individual honours, the latest as one of Australia Post's 'Living Legends'.

Various functions have kept him in touch with the game, but lately he's driving less, and his bad hip makes it hard to get up stairs. It's why he hasn't been to too many matches in Gosford over the past few seasons, although he still loves watching his beloved Central Coast Mariners on the box. 'Don't worry, I still yell at the TV,' he says. Mariners skipper Alex Wilkinson is his favourite player. 'I love the way he can read the game,' says Marston.

It would be better if Edie was still at home, baking in the kitchen, or his hip didn't cause him grief, or his eyesight was a bit better. But he's got his two daughters, and his two grandkids, and he's got his wit. He makes a point of coming out to the driveway to bid farewell when you leave, and you notice that he's still well-groomed, and the military bearing is still there. A proud, dignified, man is Joe Marston. 'I've got nothing to complain about,' he says. 'Life's been good to me.'

6 April 2012

WE WUZ ROBBED

Sportswriting can sound glamorous, especially the allure of being paid to have the best seat in the house. Reality is different. It is often a tough, exasperating grind. At times you often have to resort to being a rottweiler to achieve the truth.

Two of the best in investigative sports writing are Roy Masters and Jacquelin Magnay, who understand the importance of persistence. Both boast impressive contact books, but more importantly know how to pursue a story relentlessly, even if confronted by brick wall after brick wall. Over the years, the pair have broken numerous major sports stories, many with international ramifications. And none of them was an easy task. Writing the story was probably the easiest part. Getting the information and making certain it was 100 per cent accurate is the tough part. It can lead good people to drink.

In this chapter are two solid examples. Masters delves into a serious Olympic boxing scandal, with the article nominated for a Walkley Award. Magnay's expertise in cycling enabled her to provide riveting details of what exactly goes on—years before the Lance Armstrong scandal broke. Both stories are tributes to what can come from painstaking hard work.

GG

THE RIGHTEOUS BROTHERS

Chris Barrett

'Hi,' says a surprisingly gentle but nonetheless self-assured voice over the phone. 'This is Tyler Winklevoss.' It is an introduction that requires little further explanation these days. *The Social Network*, last year's acclaimed film written by Aaron Sorkin and directed by David Fincher, made sure of that.

The 29-year-old is, of course, one half of 'the Winklevi', the cynical moniker attached, in the movie anyway, to twins Tyler and Cameron Winklevoss by Mark Zuckerberg, the 26-year-old billionaire who established Facebook. The brothers, sons of a rich New York academic, are known predominantly as the social networking giant's long-time adversaries: the chiselled, symmetrical duo who have been in and out of courtrooms and deposition hearings for the past seven years trying, as they say, to right the wrong of Facebook's founding.

They are also, as Fincher's film shows in a glimpse, world-class athletes. The juxtaposition of their pursuits is striking. There they are in the heady arena of corporate litigation, claiming Zuckerberg pinched their idea and suing for an estimated $US500 million.

At the same time, they are slaving for hours each day, chasing ultimate success in an age-old sporting discipline with effectively zero monetary return. The Winklevosses are deep in training for next year's London Olympics, where they hope to go several steps better than their sixth in the pairs in Beijing.

Tyler Winklevoss is calling the *Herald* from their rowing base in San Diego, California, where he and his brother spend their time on the water and in the gym between meeting lawyers and plotting their next legal move.

'Actually, a ton of the lessons I've learned in rowing carry over to the litigation, and kind of vice versa,' he says. 'In a lot of ways, the keys to success I've found to be very universal in all areas of life. But one is so much more public, and there's a lot of economics at stake. There's a movie, and people know me for that, whereas I spend the majority of my time actually training and rowing for a sport where there's no pay-off. It's simply the honour and satisfaction of winning a medal that doesn't have intrinsic value, and basically doing it unknown.'

The brothers had been budding rowing stars since about the time, in the American winter of 2003–04, they allege Zuckerberg stole their concept for a social networking site while they were all students at Harvard University. They claim they have seen electronic correspondence between Zuckerberg and others that, they say, proves he set out to defraud them after they and their Harvard classmate, Divya Narendra, asked him to write the programming code for their own website concept, ConnectU. It is the chief reason, as they continue to work towards the Olympics, they are appealing against a $US65 million settlement reached with Facebook in 2008.

'I already know that Mark is sitting in a place where he is today very much so because myself, Cameron and Divya Narendra approached him,' Winklevoss says. 'And Mark knows that. I'm satisfied to know that but Facebook hasn't admitted it. The thing is, Cameron and I hold a lot dearer to our hearts our becoming Olympians and that challenge because of what it took.

'It's a happier story . . . We set ourselves to a goal, we worked very hard, and 100 per cent through our own merit we achieved some height in sports. We came in sixth at the Olympics. What that taught us as people is much more dear to our hearts than the saga with Facebook.

'Even though the Facebook situation is highly publicised, there's a movie attached to it, it's just not the same thing. There's something about the Olympics, there's something about an Olympic medal, that is utterly priceless. You can't buy it, you can't steal it. There's something so pure about that, and it's very rare and unique in this world.'

The Winklevosses are sweep rowers but under the coaching of an Australian, the US team rowing coach Tim McLaren, they are also building on skills in sculling boats in an effort to make themselves viable contenders in more Olympic categories. Their association with McLaren is one of a few Australian connections—they idolised the original 'Oarsome Foursome' crew (Winklevoss mentions rowing royalty James Tomkins and Drew Ginn during the conversation, as well as another gold-medal winner, Duncan Free) and spent two months in 2006 training at the UTS Rowing Club at Haberfield alongside Beijing fours silver medallists Matt Ryan and Francis Hegerty.

Their opinion of their present coach is high. 'Tim's great,' Winklevoss says. 'He brings a really high level of technical expertise to American rowing, and what Australians have been good at is the very technical smaller boats, the coxless boats. In America, we have a big tradition in the eights, because that's our premier event in college. So when we come to the national team we don't have that coxless boat experience which Tim is definitely a master in.'

The masters-of-the-universe cockiness the film gives the brothers does not quite wash over into real life. They are, for sure, set on a medal, ideally gold, in London, but Tyler Winklevoss is quick to point out that the US team is a long way from being selected. The realisation of their lofty ambition at the 2012 Games would clearly bring unbridled satisfaction, but what of the other major challenge in their lives? What would be the gold-medal winning outcome in the Facebook feud?

'The best-case scenario is that Facebook and Mark Zuckerberg look in the mirror and have the courage to admit what they already know, and come to the table and resolve this in good faith,' Tyler says. 'It's not a question, did they know they did something wrong—they fully well know they did something wrong. But they're trying to get away with it, and that's really troubling.

'In 2002, myself and Cameron and Divya . . . we set out to start a website, and we'd been working on it a year. We approached a fellow student to include him, and we're stuck having our website, our source code, our ideas, not only sabotaged but taken. The only reason why we're still litigating is because Facebook refuses to act in good faith.

'It's one [thing] to do something bad to us as students at Harvard. It's another thing, and it's equally as disturbing, to be a $50 billion company and litigate this case the way they did by violating judicial rules and withholding evidence. We feel like we have no choice but to stand up for this.'

The Winklevosses and Zuckerberg, understandably, do not enjoy a particularly conciliatory relationship as the interminable battle over Facebook's intellectual property rights rages on.

Zuckerberg does not strike as a sports fan. Yet the question is too compelling: If these all-American brothers do go all the way and win gold in London, would he be watching? Winklevoss laughs. 'I don't know about that.'

18 December 2012

THE NEED FOR SPEED

Jacquelin Magnay

Cyclists are supposed to be super-human. They climb torturous mountains at a frenetic pace, day after day, month after month, or whip around the track at 70 km/h. There is the Giro d'Italia, the Tour de France, the Tour of Germany. The very reason for their lauded heroism is their hard-to-attain physical state. They are the gods of Europe and Japan.

In the past week there has been a collision of worlds: the cycling world's extreme measures and an unsuspecting public and its shock. There has long been a culture within road and track cycling to do nearly anything that will produce a better performance and help them conquer Mont Ventoux, Alp d'Huez or even Mt Hotham, or clock a super-slick time on the Dunc Gray velodrome.

Cyclists are determined control freaks. They strictly monitor their diet, they undergo intense training, sometimes for eight hours a day, they have intravenous fluid replacement, they pop and inject supplements, head for the Alps for altitude training and even shave their legs to make massages easier.

But Senator John Faulkner's claims that five elite cyclists used room 121 at the Australian Institute of Sport's Del Monte headquarters in Adelaide as a 'shooting gallery' set alarm bells ringing. Whether, and if so, just how a third of the institute's team were able to inject unknown substances into their veins and muscles for months on end without detection will be part of the urgent inquiry headed by the retired judge Robert Anderson, QC.

'Soon after moving to the AIS Del Monte I discovered a culture among athletes to inject vitamins and supplements as part of a regime of maintaining their general health in the course of extremely rigorous training,' the banned 19-year-old cyclist Mark French said this week.

He said the use of supplements was an 'open secret'. 'It is visible to those involved but hidden away from those who did not take part,' he said.

A family friend told the *Herald* that French was so terrified of needles, his father, David, had to drag him screaming to the dentist. Mark's older brother, Luke, had an illness which required intravenous drips and regular injections, which had left a mental scar on the young boy.

For decades cycling has been at the forefront of getting an edge, whether it be by legal means or illegal use of drugs, for the sport is surrounded by big money, the lure of superstardom and a professional climate. Illegal drug use among the professional trade teams is rife, with undetectable growth hormones, insulin and EPO (erythropoietin) most popular.

Cyclists are quickly introduced to the ideas of super-supplementation and massive vitamins as a legal way of helping recover from the rigours and demands of training. Whether they then progress to the illegal substances appears to depend on which team they become linked with. But even if the institute tries to quarantine itself from such murky practices, the cyclists are exposed to European ways from an early age. For several years the Australian junior road team (under-23) was based in Italy.

The trade teams in Europe all have medical personnel permanently attached to the team. A coach in another sport said nearly all of the distribution lines of drugs into international track and field and swimming came from cycling.

'Those guys [cyclists] were the guinea pigs because if it didn't kill them and it appeared to work, everybody else was trying to get some of the stuff,' he said.

As soon as new drugs were at the medical research stage, they nearly always found their way into the hands of cyclists, willing to try anything that is undetectable to gain a performance edge. In 1998 the red blood cell drug interleukin–3 was just being researched, yet sources claimed it was already being abused on the professional cycling circuit.

Back then, the Australian cycling head coach, Martin Barras, rated the success of drug testing worldwide at five or six out of 10, but that was 'compared to a zero a few years ago'.

And the institute team manager, Michael Flynn, said on the eve of the Commonwealth Games then: 'The Australians are clean—if one of ours are positive you can send me home butt naked. But I would be amazed if everyone felt that [international] cycling was relatively clean; it is naive to think that all sports here are clean.'

But French claims that he was so seduced by his role models at the institute, he overcame this terror in the pursuit of faster times, even though he said he nearly fainted when he was first injected with vitamin B by another cyclist. French, who was a four-time junior world champion and one of Australia's most exciting talents, has admitted to injecting carnitine (which aids in energy production), vitamin B and C and testicomp, which he claims he had been told by other cyclists, and he believed, was a legal homeopathic remedy.

Within cycling circles testicomp is touted as a substance to stimulate the production of testosterone—it was one of the 37 different substances found in the boot of the car owned by the disgraced and banned Lithuanian cyclist Raimondas Rumsas just after he finished third in the Tour de France in 2002. French's admission that he used testicomp was one of the doping breaches that resulted in his two-year ban from the sport and a life ban from Olympic competition.

But it is the existence of 13 empty vials of equine growth hormone found in the sharps container in the bottom of French's wardrobe by a cleaner that is at the heart of the drugs scandal. Somebody was using a banned poison designed for a horse in the strong belief that it helped performance. French claims anybody could have had access, in addition to the other cyclists he says used the room to inject vitamins—none of whom he has accused of using anything illegal.

The Adelaide manufacturer of the equine growth hormone, Bresagen, says one vial is enough for a 500 kg horse. It is a drug to promote growth. Institute staff say they are devastated at the French evidence.

Sources claim that the names French provided to the Court of Arbitration for Sport include several athletes very unlikely to take such a risk, and Del Monte cyclists are furious that 'a convicted drug-taker's evidence' is being used to slur their reputations. The Australian Olympic Committee is pressing the cyclists to reveal more to the Anderson inquiry, given that their Olympic selection is on the line.

There are clear processes at the institute for cyclists, particularly emerging ones like French, to obtain permission for injecting vitamins. Some cyclists have previously obtained official approval for injection of legal substances. The fallout from the French case resulted in two other cyclists being severely reprimanded by the institute for not notifying medical authorities that they were injecting vitamins.

French's evidence reveals his sheer trust of his peers.

'I accepted without question what I was told about these substances, that they were harmless and legal. I looked up to these other cyclists . . . as my role models; I had no reason to feel that I was being misled in any way . . . I wanted to learn from them.'

What does it take to be like them? These are elite athletes who train for six to eight hours a day at an intensity that sees super-fit athletes throw up. It is not unusual for cyclists around the world to wolf down substances like colostrum and creatine and lie in bed at night enveloped by an 'oxygen tent', which manipulates the oxygen levels of the air to encourage the body to produce more red blood cells.

The benefits can be financial. One of the reasons for the delay in the arbitration court's hearing in the French case, apart from the Australian Sports Commission wanting it to be heard after the Athens Olympics, was the unavailability of French. He spent 10 weeks in Japan in the lucrative keirin series, where cyclists are treated like greyhounds, shut away from the big-punting Japanese before competing at night. In each of five keirin races French was up against seven Japanese and he won the series overall. Sources claim he earned about $100,000 in that short time.

Defining the line between acceptable ethical practices and illegal cheating is not so easy.

Six years ago, the institute's cycling team was part of a university study to determine the effectiveness of colostrum, but one of the high-profile cyclists of the time, Lucy Tyler Sharman, refused to take part. Since then, research has shown that colostrum does produce elevated levels of a banned hormone, insulin growth factor-1, but it has not yet been banned. Now even one of the youngest members of the Australian Olympic team for Athens, swimmer Jessicah Schipper, regularly takes it, her coach believing it helps ward off colds and flu.

Nor is it easy for the athletes to comprehend the new world order in anti-doping. No longer is it sufficient for the drug testers to take urine samples, have them analysed and the laboratory uncover any murky goings-on. Nowadays the biggest drugs scandals around the world centre on circumstantial evidence and a new co-operation between law enforcers and sports bodies: the 1998 French border check of Festina manager Willy Voet uncovered a stash of growth hormone and EPO, both undetectable drugs at the time, and testosterone, which revealed how dramatic the systemised drug-taking of the elite road cyclists was on major tours.

Earlier this month, on the eve of attempting his sixth Tour de France victory, Lance Armstrong was implicated as a drug-taker in a book, *L.A. Confidential*, written by journalists David Walsh and Pierre Ballester. A former US Postal team official, Emma O'Reilly, claimed in the book that Armstrong used EPO; that he asked her to dispose of syringes at the 1998 Tour of Holland; and that she was sent to Spain to pick up drugs for him during his 1999 Pyrenees training camp. A furious Armstrong is suing the authors.

Lately there has been the Balco drugs controversy in the US, where evidence seized during a Federal Government raid has been turned over to the country's anti-doping agency. The computer files and calendar notations have resulted in drug charges laid against the world's fastest man, the 100 metres world record holder Tim Montgomery, as well as three others. They face a lifetime ban.

Evidence from that raid shows that being a sports cheat doesn't come cheaply—a five-month regime of a designer steroid THG, EPO, testosterone and growth hormone, with medical supervision and regular blood and urine screening, cost more than $US20,000 ($28,600).

At the moment the institute cyclists are preparing to move to Rockhampton for warm weather training. In Adelaide they have been assailed with comments from car drivers and questioned by family and friends. They are eager to escape the intense scrutiny to prepare for the Olympic Games.

'We are committed to competing drug-free and we are extremely disappointed and angry with ill-informed recent comments and innuendo, which have cast a slur on our sport and us as individuals,' seven of the cyclists said in a statement this week.

MORE THAN PEDAL POWER IN PLAY

'There is political warfare above our heads; we are the football being kicked around,' says a person closely connected to the Mark French drug allegations.

What is obvious is that the cyclists at the heart of the matter—those that have to prove their innocence before the Australian Olympic Committee president, John Coates, will ratify their selection for the Athens Olympics—feel they are being harshly treated. They say they are being singled out, not for any behaviour that has been looked at by two investigators already, but for political point-scoring.

And here is why. Coates is president of the AOC, but is also a board member of the Court of Arbitration for Sport and an International Olympic Committee member. He has long held strong anti-doping views and before the Sydney Olympics encouraged the toughening of the Customs Act to prohibit the trading of sports drugs. But Coates is at odds with Peter Bartels, chairman of the Australian Sports Commission, and Mark Peters, its chief executive. The ASC oversees and funds the Australian Institute of Sport.

Central to their power dispute is the $100 million the AOC accumulated as part of Sydney hosting the 2000 Olympics and its reluctance to use the money for anything other than sending away future Olympic teams. But there is debate about who should get credit for Australia's Olympic successes.

They have been taking pot shots at each other for quite a while—last year it was over childhood obesity and the Athens medal predictions. Now it is centred on how Senator John Faulkner got hold of a Court of Arbitration for Sport judgement into the French case.

Coates is linked to Faulkner through Labor Party associations, while Bartels is very much tied to the Liberal Party.

Coates says he just wants to protect the reputation of the Australian Olympic team, of which only fit and proper people should be members. Peters says there has been reckless use of information which appears to be driven by rumour and selective quotation out of context.

Coates's threat could lead to very ugly scenes. Observers think we are not even at half-time in this clash.

26 June 2004

OLYMPIC LOW BLOW

Roy Masters

The future of boxing as an Olympic sport is in jeopardy following a *Herald* investigation into claims of corruption at the Athens Games and reports of bribes and manipulation of the appointment of judges having led to an Australian heavyweight being robbed of a medal.

Australian Olympic Committee president John Coates passed on the material to Jacques Rogge when the IOC president visited Brisbane two weeks ago.

'I shared it with him,' Coates said ahead of an IOC meeting in Singapore in July, at which members will vote on sports to be included on the Olympic program after the Beijing Games. 'Allegations of corruption against a sport would not be timely. It would be a factor which would weigh heavily on the minds of IOC members.'

The man who chaired the body that appointed all judging officials in Athens was Egypt's Dr Ismail Osman. Egyptian boxers won two bronze medals and one silver, the country's best result. Egypt had previously won only one Olympic boxing medal—a bronze in Rome in 1960.

Egypt also had the highest level of protests against it in Athens, none of them upheld.

Australian heavyweight Adam Forsyth lost controversially to an Egyptian, Mohamed Elsayed, in a decision that still has fair-minded sportspeople who witnessed the bout, such as former Wallabies captain John Eales, dumbfounded. Elsayed, assured of a bronze medal, retired hurt before his next bout.

At an executive meeting of the sport's governing body, Association Internationale de Boxe Amateur in Liverpool, England, in late January, the *Herald*'s questions to Osman and his responses were tabled following a fierce exchange between him and the president of Boxing Australia, Sol Spitalnic. Six delegates of EABA, the powerful European division of AIBA, were given copies of the material and last month they met in Paris, resolving to remove those 'who were orchestrating the unfair results [in Athens]'.

The EABA meeting also petitioned AIBA to fall in line with an IOC request to change a rule barring officials who have attended one Olympics from refereeing or judging at the next Games.

'It is the most ridiculous rule I have heard in 60 years in the sport,' Arthur Tunstall, the former Australian Commonwealth Games Association chief and veteran top boxing official, said. The rule was introduced by AIBA president Professor Anwar Chowdhry, an 82-year-old retired Pakistani engineer who also invented the computer scoring system following the treachery of judges in Seoul, when American Roy Jones jnr, among other boxers cheated, was robbed of gold.

Chowdhry brought in the rule because he wanted unsullied officials in Athens, but, as Tunstall says: 'You can control them better when they are novices.'

Chowdhry's son-in-law, Pakistan's Shakeel Durani, is the secretary of the powerful Referees and Judges (R/J) Commission, chaired by Osman, and they, along with a Dominican, Domingo Solano, appointed all referees, judges and jurors in Athens. This was a radical departure from past Olympics, at which officials were selected by ballot or the R/J executive. Chowdhry was wheeled daily to ringside in Athens in a special cart and sat behind the chairman of the jury, whose function is to monitor the jurors, ostensibly there in case the electronic scoring system breaks down and the judges' scores can't be used.

Although infirm, Chowdhry is alert, with seasoned officials still talking about his drinking capacity when he celebrated his 80th birthday twice—in Turkey and Egypt—then chaired an AIBA meeting from 9 am to 5 pm.

He has anointed Durani as his successor but is intent on surviving to Beijing.

The worst decision in Athens came on August 25 when bottles were thrown into the ring, with angry fans storming the jury after it awarded a quarter-final light-heavyweight bout to Egypt's Ahmed Ismail over Greece's Elias Pavlidis.

The jury, which monitors the judges and scores the bout independent of them, was called in after the fight had been stopped because of injury and fled the angry Greek crowd like frightened forest creatures in the face of a bushfire.

It was a decision so violently in contempt of plausibility it provided yet another deckchair on the Titanic of Olympic boxing.

The referee, PKM Raja of India, stopped the bout in the third round with Pavlidis leading 19–12 on the judges' scoring. Pavlidis had a cut above his eye, caused by an elbow from the Egyptian in the second round.

Raja should have disqualified Ismail immediately, or at least deducted points. But he took Pavlidis to the ring doctor, who had no option but to stop the contest.

Asked how the Egyptian could have been declared the winner, Osman writes: 'A protest was presented from Greece concerning an unfair blow from the Egyptian boxer. The committee held a meeting and found the points for Greece were 19–12 but the jury results were 5–0 to Egypt.

'It also found no intention of the Egyptian boxer to injure the Greek boxer, so the committee rejected the protest.'

So Pavlidis's four years' hard slog, rising at 4 am to run road work in the freezing cold for his home Olympics, were all over because the five jurors unanimously had a totally different view of the fight from the judges, and the blow, although admittedly illegal, was ruled unintentional. And Ismail won a bronze medal.

When the *Herald* finally extracted answers from Osman he concentrated most of his response on Australian referee/judge Steve Donkin, whom he accused of 'incorrect and shameless behaviour'.

Donkin's crime? Osman claims 'Donkin was getting signals and instructions from some coaches and officials to score points according to whatever comes to him from outside, not according to what was happening in the ring'.

Donkin categorically rejects this, saying: 'I've never taken signals off anyone in my life. I'm not sorry for one thing I did at the Olympics. I judged it how I saw it. I was in the top five of officials for six days in a row and then was shafted.'

Donkin, a father of three, is reluctant to speak about Athens. He redirected questions to his roommate in Athens, Pat Fiacco, the mayor of Regina, Canada, who said he was so appalled by what he witnessed he promised Donkin he would take his complaints to the Prime Minister of Canada. Fiacco, when contacted by the *Herald*, would not comment on the record.

Referees/judges who attended the 16 daily meetings in Athens' Peristeri Stadium were gobsmacked at the presence of sinister-looking men with no official role and this has continued to produce an atmosphere of fear and intimidation eight months after the Games.

'They are trying to kick us out of Olympics, yet these blokes walk into our meetings and seminars and stand there,' one referee said. Asked why officials who had no designated duty were allowed in meetings in Athens, Osman said: 'No official attended where he had no job to do in our meetings.'

One referee insists he was initially offered $US1000, which was then increased to $US4000. Asked to comment on bribery and corruption in Athens, Osman, said: 'How could any bribery take place as long as no one knows who will officiate the bout? Only after the draw beside the ring and before the bout starts with few minutes [left] were the R/Js recognised.'

But, as one official said: 'The crooked ones knew who the appointments were going to be.'

Of the 10 protests lodged, three were against Egypt. Had the Australian camp protested against the Forsyth decision, it would have been four.

Asked at the time why Australia did not lodge the $US200 fee and protest, Australian manager Ron Pengelly said: 'It would have been a waste of money.'

Osman reports all 10 protests were dismissed because they 'were against the official results from the computer', a protocol not followed in the Ismail bout.

Referee Raja, also a judge in the Forsyth fight, was rated by Osman the third best official in Athens. Poland's Zbigniew Gorski, a judge in the Forsyth fight, was rated No. 1 official. China's Wang Jiabo, who refereed the Forsyth bout and was a judge in Ismail's earlier bout and the semi-final, was Osman's choice as No. 2 official. Osman wore headphones ringside in Athens, raising the question: to whom was he talking?

Asked the reason, Osman said: 'I am only allowed to speak to the organisers, not the R/Js, who sit around the ring separately, and it is forbidden to contact them.'

When told his response, one referee said: 'Strange. Dr Osman wasn't part of the Athens Organising Committee.'

Five months after the Olympics, the Liverpool Council Chamber was the scene of a heated exchange when the world body met to discuss the Athens Olympics.

The report on R/Js in Athens, usually distributed shortly after an Olympics, had not reached delegates, but Spitalnic had a copy of Osman's responses to the *Herald*'s questions.

After all, when Osman had ignored the *Herald*'s emailed questions for two months, it was Spitalnic who contacted Chowdhry and demanded Osman respond. On January 27, Spitalnic attempted to attend a meeting of the R and J Commission in his position as AIBA vice-president, hoping to gain some clarification of the bad report against Donkin and an explanation of the Forsyth decision. Osman barred his entry.

A day later, when the executive committee met, Spitalnic and Osman eyed each other, with the Egyptian saying provocatively: 'What do you think of my responses to the questions from Australia?'

Spitalnic, a Jewish businessman in Melbourne who sits comfortably in an essentially Muslim-run sport, warned Osman, saying: 'Don't take me on.'

However, the 17 executive members and nine vice-presidents sniffed something important and demanded to know the basis of the seething exchange.

Chowdhry adjourned the meeting while his son-in-law raced away and returned with printed copies of the *Herald*'s questions and Osman's responses.

'Everybody in the room knew what it was all about after that,' Spitalnic said.

However, Chowdhry did not allow debate on the matter because it was not on the agenda, although Europe's six delegates, including AIBA's secretary-general, Turkey's Caner Doganeli, left with copies of the document.

'The questions set the ball rolling,' Spitalnic said. 'The Europeans are crooked about the rorting that went on.'

The EABA met in Paris on March 6–7 and the report of the meeting is recorded on AIBA's website.

'Several members felt that the present system of judging did not serve its purpose anymore and was easily misused,' it says. 'A critic was [sic] lashed at the R/J Commission for their leniency in respect of the judges and of those who were orchestrating the unfair results [in Athens].

'Others [at the meeting] felt that the AIBA ruling not to allow R/Js to officiate at an Olympic boxing tournament should be abolished as demanded by the IOC.'

Doganeli, who has subsequently distanced himself from Chowdhry, was seen in Liverpool in discussion with IOC representatives and AIBA's legal representatives, fiddling with worry beads.

SCANDAL IN ATHENS

- Egyptian boxers won record number of medals after an Egyptian chaired the body that appointed all referees, judges and jurors.
- Two of the most controversial decisions went in favour of Egyptian fighters.
- Egyptian fighters attracted most protests—none upheld.
- Accusations of bribery and 'heavy' types at official meetings.
- Egyptian official attacks Australian judge/referee in retaliation to *Herald* allegations.

WHERE TO NOW

- Europeans have called for reform of scoring system and removal of corrupt officials.
- AOC chairman John Coates presents *Herald* findings to IOC president Jacques Rogge.
- IOC decides in September if boxing remains after 2008 Beijing Games.

OLYMPIC SCORING

- Referee controls boxers according to rules.
- Five judges press computer key when they think a punch has landed. If three hit the key within one second, a point is recorded.
- Five jurors watch the judges and adjudicate if system fails.

THE MAIN PLAYERS

Dr Ismail Osman

A seventy-something Egyptian sports administrator who was chairman of the R/J Commission that appointed referees and judging officials at the Athens Olympics.

Prof. Anwar Chowdhry

An 82-year-old retired Pakistani engineer who is president of the Association Internationale de Boxe Amateur, the world governing body for amateur boxing.

Steve Donkin

A 49-year-old Sydney butcher who was Australia's only referee and judge in Athens. He was the subject of an unsubstantiated verbal attack by Osman in retaliation to the *Herald*'s allegations.

Dr Jacques Rogge
A Belgian surgeon who is president of the International Olympic Committee and committed to reform. He has been passed the contents of a *Herald* investigation into allegations of corruption in boxing at the Athens Olympics.

16 April 2005

HEAD WILL ROLL OVER SCANDAL

Tom Reilly and Chris Roots

A leading harness racing driver has been allowed to continue competing despite admitting his involvement in a corruption scandal that threatens to destroy the sport.

The driver, who cannot be named for legal reasons, met the head of harness racing in NSW and confirmed his involvement in the fraud, in which it is alleged crooked stewards allowed horses to be doped as part of an elaborate betting sting.

Since that meeting, the driver, who is in his 20s, has won several races on tracks in the state.

The revelation comes as trotting—on which more than $2.2 billion a year is wagered—battles to restore its reputation amid fears that hundreds of races could have been fixed.

Parallel investigations are being conducted by police detectives and the head of integrity at Harness Racing NSW.

The *Herald* can also reveal that more than 40 trainers, drivers and owners have been asked to provide documents, including phone records, to the sport's authorities as they try to establish links among corrupt participants.

A source familiar with the investigation said some trainers and drivers had submitted incomplete phone records, and others had claimed not to own mobile phones despite having regularly been seen talking on handsets. No one under suspicion has yet lost their licence.

A racecourse insider said of the driver's meeting with the chief executive of Harness Racing NSW, Sam Nati: 'Driver X [name withheld by the *Herald*] met with Sam and took along his parents. He put his hands up to being involved in two races that were hot, but it became clear that Sam knew of more involvement and that this wasn't going to be something that could be hushed up.'

The driver has confirmed the meeting but denied making any admission of illegal activity. His father told the *Herald*: 'Yeah, I met Sam for a beer and my son came along. There's nothing unusual or illegal in that.'

Asked if they had discussed corruption, he replied: 'We didn't talk about nothing.'

Last night, Mr Nati said: 'We have had a number of informal discussions with various participants. But who those people are and what was discussed is confidential until such time as they are formally interviewed as part of the investigation.

'Some people have suggested that those suspected of being involved should have been stood down pending the outcome of the inquiry . . . but this inquiry is far-reaching and all-encompassing so we believe [it's right] to adopt the innocent until proven guilty edict.'

The *Herald* understands that harness racing officials have told participants that involvement in the scam cannot go unpunished but 'penalties will be mitigated' if those involved provide information that assists investigations.

The scandal erupted when the car belonging to the chief steward, Bill Cable, was firebombed on August 5. The next Monday, two stewards resigned after being confronted with evidence of alleged wrongdoing.

Authorities will allege both men were receiving payments—perhaps as much as $1000 a horse—not to test certain runners for drugs, thereby giving corrupt trainers, punters and drivers a huge advantage in orchestrating betting plunges. It is believed as many as 80 per cent of the doped horses won their races.

On Wednesday, Harness Racing NSW announced it would allocate up to $1 million for an integrity fund to cover costs from the scandal. The money will also be used to increase race day drug testing and provide greater security on the track.

'There's no doubt that, in terms of perception and ill feeling, we've hit rock bottom, but I believe we can bounce back,' Mr Nati said.

'I'm pleased the police have announced a task force so that people can have the confidence that it [the scandal] is being investigated properly.'

2 September 2011

TWO MORE ARRESTS IN DRUG SCANDAL

Chris Roots

The arrest count stands at five in the harness racing corruption scandal, and another stable has been implicated in the charges brought against former Harness Racing NSW steward Paul O'Toole.

Driver Cameron Fitzpatrick, the son of Harold Park stalwart Paul, and trainer Dean Atkinson joined premier driver Greg Bennett, Michael Russo and O'Toole in being charged yesterday. It was not the publicity harness racing needed in the lead-up to its biggest race, the Miracle Mile at Menangle tonight.

Police have not ruled out further charges being laid.

Twelve of the horses mentioned in the 38 races involving charges against O'Toole were prepared at the stables of Riverstone trainer Greg Sarina. Serene Major, which has since moved to another stable, scored four wins for Sarina in races mentioned in the corruption charges. The first three wins of stablemate Serene Jasper, which has won five of his seven, were all part of the charges against O'Toole. The Sarina stable had a winning treble at the Goulburn meeting on January 7 and all three also appeared on O'Toole's charge sheet.

The charges against O'Toole are that he corruptly received for himself and for Matthew Bentley, another former Harness Racing NSW steward, a benefit as a reward for not drug-testing horses.

Bentley has yet to be charged by police in relation to the corruption.

There are 34 counts of 'agent receive corrupt benefit' against O'Toole where the horses won, while the four counts of 'agent attempt receive corrupt benefit' were when the horses were beaten.

At Bankstown on July 1, O'Toole is alleged to have taken payment from connections of two horses in the same race. On that day, four horses were listed on the charge sheet.

Strike Force Tairora, which comprises detectives from the Casino and Racing Investigation Unit, executed search warrants at addresses near Goulburn and in Sydney's Camden area yesterday.

Police seized items relevant to the investigation and arrested two suspects during the searches.

Fitzpatrick was arrested in the Camden raid, while Atkinson was arrested during the raid near Goulburn. Both were charged [with] two counts of corruptly give agent benefit and one count of corruptly offer to give agent benefit.

Atkinson was to have had Im Dejazzman start in the Group 1 Trotters Mile at Menangle tonight. The horse has been scratched.

He and Fitzpatrick were stood down by Harness Racing NSW indefinitely under Australian Harness Racing Rule 183, which states a trainer or driver may be directed not [to] take part in a race 'pending the outcome of an inquiry, investigation or objection, or where a person has been charged with an offence'.

O'Toole faced court in Lithgow on Thursday where it was alleged he netted up to $400,000 from his role in the corruption scandal.

It is an amount O'Toole's solicitor, Ken Lambeth, indicated would be challenged. O'Toole's corruption charges extended over 19 months, starting with a horse at Penrith on January 21 last year, while the last race under suspicion was at Bathurst on July 20.

The charge sheet recorded the amount offered to not have horses swabbed was from $250 in lottery tickets to $1000 cash.

26 November 2011

BUNNY MONEY

WORDS: EARS McEVOY
ART: ROB DUONG

RABBITOHS OWNER RUSSELL CROWE DECIDES TO CALL IN HIS HOLLYWOOD CONTACTS TO SORT OUT SOME THIRD-PARTY DEALS TO GET GREG INGLIS AT SOUTH SYDNEY.

GI JOE. RISE OF THE RABBIT

INGLIS STARS AS A MEMBER OF AN ELITE PLAYERS' SPECIAL OPS UNIT TAKING ON A MYSTERIOUS SALARY CAP AUDITOR KNOWN AS 'THE SCHU'*.

*BONUS GAG. NOT SCHLOSSY'S.

THE INGLIS PATIENT

INGLIS NARRATES THE WORLD'S MOST BORING MEDICAL DOCUMENTARY COVERING ALL HIS AILMENTS FROM A BACK INJURY IN 2006 TO HIS 2010 HIP STRAIN.

A BEAUTIFUL MIND II

RUSSELL CROWE RETURNS IN HIS ROLE AS BRILLIANT MATHEMATICIAN JOHN NASH TRYING TO FIND A WAY TO BALANCE THE BOOKS AND FIT INGLIS UNDER THE SALARY CAP.

JABBA THE HUTT. THE ART OF THE DEAL

THE ART OF THE DEAL

INGLIS GOES ON THE SHANE RICHARDSON FISH FINGER DIET TO BULK UP FOR HIS ROLE AS JABBA IN THE STAR WARS SPIN-OFF.

DRAMA AND GREG

A HILARIOUS TV SITCOME WHERE INGLIS FACES AND OVERCOMES SALARY CAP SCANDALS, INJURIES, COURT CASES AND CONTRACT DISPUTES.

THE HEART OF
THE GAME

Australia has always attracted those from left field. Maybe it's because there's a touch of the last outpost before hell about this often forgotten country on the other side of the world. Maybe they look upon us as easy pickings.

Max Presnell, the *Sydney Morning Herald*'s esteemed racing writer, has seen plenty of these mysterious off-centre characters mooching their way around the betting rings at Australian racetracks, looking for a quick and easy earn. He has also seen them in action elsewhere—such as when Amarillo Slim was in town some years ago.

Amarillo Slim, who died in 2012, was something. He once took $30,000 off Jimmy the Greek by successfully rafting down the River of No Return in the United States, wearing a wetsuit designed by Jacques Cousteau. He played cards all over the world, including Colombia where he was kidnapped by agents of drug baron Pablo Escobar, who demanded to see him before he was released. He even bet on which sugar cube a fly would land on. And this all came after stints with the Navy and Army where he sold bootleg Mickey Mouse watches to foreign soldiers stationed in Europe.

Amarillo Slim was always at the heart of the game. He knew exactly where he sat, as does State of Origin original Gary Hambly, happy to reminisce about old league days in a completely different setting.

There are those who embrace everything about their sport and get miffed when people start to take it all too seriously, such as the shenanigans of part-time sub-district rugby players running around Australia causing merry hell, or the Queen of Goolma, who has her mind set on keeping bookies in the bush honest.

Or the moment can just take you away from reality. Such as was the case with Steve Waugh's last-gasp century at the Sydney Cricket Ground. And as usual we were there, trying to make sense of it all.

GG

OSCAR? RUSS WOULD PREFER NRL TITLE

Peter FitzSimons

But let's cut to the chase, Russell Crowe, as we sit on the balcony of your Woolloomooloo apartment, with the lights of the harbour twinkling to our right, and the soaring skyscrapers of the CBD right there in the palm of our hand in front of us. If, right now, you had to make a choice between getting an Oscar next year for your new film, *Robin Hood*, or having the club you part-own, Souths, win the NRL premiership this year, which would it be?

The response is immediate, as is the twinkle. 'I've already got an Oscar . . .'

And so he has, not to mention three nominations. If the implication of that answer, however, is that Souths winning the premiership is now the towering ambition of his life, he is equally quick to correct it. It's almost as if he has to rein in his passion.

'It is not about me,' he says. 'The groove is their groove, the players. I help build a platform for a group of young men to perform on the football field at the highest possible level they're able to. At that point, anything they achieve is about what they want to achieve. It is not a personal ambition. I have no control about that.'

Still, there must have been times in recent seasons when you have looked at the whole thing and thought, 'What the hell am I doing here? Why did I take this on?'

Crowe gives something of a deaths-head grin in reply: 'That's a recurring thing . . . that definitely comes up a number of times in a year. Because it is a very complex thing. And if you want something done to a certain level, you can only delegate a certain amount. You have still got to go and get your hands dirty. You don't have to do that all the time, but you do have to step in once a year and recalibrate . . . and then step back and get out of everybody's way.'

Again, there is a way Crowe recounts this, whereby one has the impression that the actor constantly has to remind himself to get out of the way of the professionals, and yet he still comes across as one who is well satisfied with the exercise.

'Push my button about South Sydney and I'll tell you a few things about South Sydney,' he laughs. 'Put 20 cents in the slot and I'll sing all night.'

All right, here's 20 cents, Russell. What is it about Souths that drives you?

'It started in the late 60s when I was four years old,' he recounts. 'My Dad had a muffler shop in Beaconsfield, the heart of Souths territory, in the last of the golden age of Souths, where the streets were decked in red and green week in, week out. Now, my Dad was a St George supporter and would talk to my brother and I about St George, and they just thought I would come along—a mistake I won't make with my boys—but he had a workmate, a Chinese Australian bloke, who would always talk to me about Souths. So by five years old, I'm a committed Souths supporter, and so from then on we were a fractured family that only came together when the All Blacks were playing . . .'

That passion for Souths remained with him through all of his incarnations, from nascent rock singer in New Zealand to starving busker in Sydney; from struggling actor to deeply successful actor, to internationally renowned acting icon and right up to the point where, in 2006, in the course of an interview, Channel Nine's Danny Weidler suggested to him that if he felt that passionate about it, he may as well buy it to save it, and Crowe thoughtfully replied he might do just that.

Next thing he knew, he and Peter Holmes à Court had laid out millions of dollars and taken control of the most famous club in the league. He went into it with his eyes wide open.

'[I said to Peter from the first], "There is no joy in this—this is not something we should be doing". Because regardless of whether it is successful or not, it is not something that is going to be attributed to you or I—and if it is, we have done it the wrong way.'

Another 20 cents for your trouble. Is it working? 'It would be fair to say that in terms of money outlay, we're still a long way behind. And yet the core business last year made a profit. There are other costs outside that core which still apply, because I like things done a certain way. But to go from a situation where the club is losing a couple of million dollars, year in, year out, to a situation where what we pay is what we earn [is great.] The core business is not dragging money from me.'

Interestingly, however, he draws a clear line between 'business' off the field, and how he approaches the Souths players. They are not 'employees' producing a 'product' that can be sold to the 'consumers'.

First and foremost he wants it to be 'sport', as that is what is in Crowe's blood—and not just because he grew up very tightly as the cousin of two of the most distinguished New Zealand cricketers of the modern generation, Martin and Jeff Crowe. He was also a good rugby union five-eighth at his New Zealand school; good enough that the famed All Black captain DJ Graham once said to him that he had 'a good rugby brain', a comment he treasures. From the first, thus, Crowe has had a personal touchstone belief—drawing on his own long experience both in sport and in acting.

'If it is not about passion,' he says, 'then what is it about? It has to be about passion when you get out on that field. It has to be about that total focus of mind and body . . . That goes with pretty much anything I do in my life. It has to be self-perpetuating. It can't just be about what I do that makes it work. You bring together people that share a common ambition, and a common work ethic—Shane Richardson, Errol Alcott, John Lang—all the way through the playing squad there's a lot of thought that goes into this team. And you step back, and look at it on paper, that is a very good-looking rugby league team.'

Sometimes, true, his own passion has spilled over into moments in which he has appeared vainglorious. Perhaps his most famous public moment with Souths came last year when the Rabbitohs were playing the Roosters and getting on top of them. The cameras flashed upon Crowe in the stands, just as he was mimicking a Roman emperor, giving the thumbs down signal to his player gladiators—as in 'put them to death'.

Now, Russell, did you come to regret that bit of footage, given how often it has played since, particularly in times when Souths haven't been going well?

'No,' Crowe says firmly. 'I regretted it the very minute I did it. There was still 56 minutes to go in the match, and I was very fearful that karma was going to come back and kick me in the arse, as the Roosters came back strongly. Fortunately, we held on.'

There is also the lovely yarn about the opening day's shoot of *Gladiator*, when Crowe met the great actor Sir Richard Harris for the first time. Now

Harris, who played the emperor Marcus Aurelius in the film, was a particular Irishman, and once famously said: 'I'll tell you this: two Golden Globes, one Grammy, five Grammy nominations, two American Academy Award nominations, two British Academy Award nominations, one Cannes Film Festival award, four gold records, one platinum record and so on. I am also a multimillionaire. And you know what? I'd give it all up tomorrow, the whole lot, for one Irish rugby cap. Just one.'

Crowe takes up the story from there. 'So I walk into this tent, and he's sitting on this chair, and he says, "Crowe, I hear that you were born in New Zealand, but you choose to live in Australia. Is that correct?" "That is right," I say. And Richard continues, "So, we can talk in hushed and respectful tones about the All Blacks, and I can yell abuse at you about the Wallabies! You're a good night out in one man, Crowe. I think I'm going to like you." That was the first thing he ever said to me.'

They remained firm friends until the day Sir Richard died.

One last question though, Russell, and you can have this one for free. Who do you support these days, the Wallabies or the All Blacks?

'I follow the All Blacks. That's the one residual New Zealand thing that I have. In any other sport, it's whoever wears the green and gold. Watching the All Blacks, though, represents late nights sitting up with my father. That black jersey . . . that haka . . . it's a primal thing.'

A primal man.

And very good for sport.

10 April 2010

THE SUBBIES STING

Greg Growden

For an organisation that almost self-destructed a few months ago, the feats of the Old Ignatians sub-district club this season are nothing short of exceptional.

Old Ignatians, who proudly stick to the edict of only one training session a week, will compete in the grand final of all five grades of the division one NSW Subbies competition at Wentworth Park tomorrow, where they will vie for the Kentwell, Burke, Whiddon, Judd and Sutherland cups. Their colts team has also made the grand final.

They have broken a bevy of Subbies records this year, including becoming the first team to pass 1000 club championship points, and the only club to have won all five grade minor premierships, before advancing straight from major semi-finals to the respective grand finals.

It has been the richest season in the club's 33-year history, but also the most eventful, considering that mid-season the club was facing a mass walkout of players, resignations of key figures, and an administrative coup all due to 'The Great Rugby Sting of 2002'.

The trigger for the drama was an item in the *SMH*'s Ruck & Maul column in June.

The item read: 'In the Old Ignatians' fifth grade team are several over-40s players who each year are involved in a try-scoring competition. The losers have to buy a case of beer for the winner. Last weekend against University of NSW, Tony Anderson scored early, to the annoyance of the others involved in this competition. In the second half, the ball was kicked clear and two players, Anderson and Rob Keogh, another in the over-40s bracket, were involved in the chase, both calling: "Mine." Anderson was first to the ball, and with a clear run to the line, was expecting try number two. However Keogh, just three metres from the line, tackled his teammate to stop him scoring. As both players continued to wrestle, they got over the line and the ball was forced. Both claimed the try. The referee ruled the move was illegal and neither scored.'

Several mischievous members of the Ignatians hierarchy decided the item was the vehicle they needed to play an elaborate practical joke on Keogh.

Ignatians president Paul Timmins, another fifth-grader, suggested to club secretary Domenic Lombardo: 'Let's see if we can suck Rob right in.'

Keogh was sent an official letter stating he had to attend a specially convened hearing with senior committee members for 'bringing the club into disrepute'.

The letter said the NSW Suburban Rugby Union had sent a 'please explain' after reading Ruck & Maul.

Keogh was contacted and, according to Timmins, didn't think the letter was serious.

'We then decided to go the whole hog, and deliberately leaked it out to certain people, knowing it would cause all sorts of dramas,' Timmins said.

Timmins sent an email to club members explaining: 'After discussions with the senior committee members we are struggling on what length of suspension to give Rob for this incident . . . Please be aware our actions are under the scrutiny of Subbies so the level of penalty will need to be rather severe.'

The whisper was that Keogh would get a six-month suspension, which caused a wave of protest among club members.

At this stage, the NSW Suburban Rugby Union was not in the loop. But executive officer Mark Green discovered something was afoot when he attended an Ignatians home game and was told: 'Whatever you do, don't go to the VIP tent because they'll lynch you.'

'I was then quietly told what was actually going on, decided to keep a low profile and play dumb,' Green said.

Timmins began receiving hate mail, and was told a large group of players were about to walk out in protest. His days as club president were also numbered. 'I thought "perfect . . . we've sucked everyone in",' he said.

On the night of the disciplinary hearing at the Gladesville Hotel, Keogh presented a written submission, which finished with: 'I challenge my accusers to choose well. I have no problem holding my head up with my name and actions being reported in the paper. Let those weasels in their brown cardigans come out and do the same.' After hearing Keogh's defence, the three-man disciplinary committee, headed by Timmins, told the player he had been suspended for three months.

'It may seem harsh, Rob, but we don't have much control over this,' Timmins explained.

'Subbies have been calling for a six-month suspension, but we've decided because of dedicated years of service, we'll halve that.'

Timmins recalled: 'When I said that, the faces of Keogh and clubmate Arum Duffy, who came to the meeting to defend Rob, went white. They were in a total state of shock.

'I let that sink in for a couple of minutes. There was total silence. Then I said: "But finally guys I should let you know that this has been just one big gee-up." With that the three of us on the committee burst out laughing.

'Rob and Duff kept glaring at us, asking: "What's so funny?" It obviously hadn't sunk in. I repeated: "Hey guys, it's a gee-up, it's a set-up . . . a bit of fun." It at last registered, and they also started laughing and cursing.'

Timmins suggested that they should continue 'The Sting'. Keogh and Duffy agreed. The next day, Timmins emailed everyone that Keogh had been suspended for three months, but that all would be revealed in a report to be released later that morning.

A half-hour later, Keogh phoned Timmins and said: 'You won't believe what's going on out there. There's guys wanting to resign, some reviewing our constitution and saying "you're dead" because they know how to kick you out as president. It's gone berserk.'

A concerned first-grade coach, Matt Perrignon, called Timmins and complained: 'What's going on? The whole club is falling on its head.' Timmins told the coach he had to be patient, as he was bound by a confidentiality clause because the pressure had come from the top office of Australian Rugby Union boss John O'Neill.

As protest meetings were being organised, Timmins eased everyone of their pain. The report was released and read:

'Official Report from the Rob Keogh Hearing. This whole affair was just ONE BIG GEE-UP !!!!!!!! Thank you for your interest and contributions. You can all line up with Rob Keogh for payback time. The Keogh case is now officially closed. Paul Timmins (The Sting).'

Peace was restored, and the club was once again one big, happy family.

13 September 2002

ORIGIN OF THE SPECIES

Jessica Halloran

Frank Sinatra is singing a love song on the radio, and the eggs on the grill are sizzling. Outside the Big Wheels cafe the sky is still thick with morning darkness, and the trucks are starting to pull up in front.

From inside, behind his coffee machine, Gary Hambly can see their trailer lights glowing orange.

Dressed in stubbies, old brown boots, apron and short-sleeved shirt, he's making strong coffee. As he does this, the former State of Origin player—one of the Origin originals—turns and says he doesn't like watching league.

'I find it boring, I don't watch the footy,' Hambly says. 'I was never really much of a footy fan, I'd rather go and read a book, do something different.

'I've been to two games, taken my kids to watch twice. I didn't see enough to go back.'

Hambly wore a NSW State of Origin jersey once. Just once. It was the first Origin game, in 1980, and it was his only game in the sky blue. Once was enough to write him into legend—not enough for him to follow the sport.

But that doesn't mean he didn't love to play the game. He played it solidly as a prop for South Sydney from 1978 to 1983. And he does look back fondly on that historic winter's evening at Lang Park.

As the first truckies start to drift in, he starts to talk about the intense atmosphere and the Queensland loyalists who packed the old stadium on July 8.

'They were everywhere,' he says. 'In the trees, sitting in the canteen roofs.'

Did he find it intimidating?

'No, it was wonderful, it was like a script,' he says. 'They were the heroes and we were the villains. It was like a role-play'.

Hambly starts loading the just-delivered newspapers into a stand. He says the game's changed, perhaps not for the best.

'It's a much more skilful game, a quicker game . . . I don't think it's a better game. It used to be a war of attrition,' he says. 'No replacements, you had to last the 80 minutes'.

Football no longer plays a huge part in Hambly's life. He arrives at his cafe, nestled in Botany, at four in the morning and leaves at seven in the evening. Apart from rugby league, Hambly has done many different things with his life—he's trained as a radiographer, been a fisheries inspector and a poker machine mechanic.

Hambly says that maybe he wouldn't be remembered if he had played his solitary Origin match in a different year.

'If it was the second one, who would remember? Who remembers the second man that walked on the moon?'

The man who captained Hambly in that game, Tommy Raudonikis, lives in enemy territory now, north of the border, and talks as if the game happened only yesterday. He talks about the beers the night before and that Lang Park crowd.

'I warned them. I thought something big was going to happen. The feel of the ground, the fans were crazy,' Raudonikis says.

'Then there was the big blue in the first five minutes. I just loved it. I got knocked out in the blue, but I finished the game, I don't sort of remember the first half.'

Like Hambly, he says the game has changed, but Raudonikis believes the fierce Origin intensity was back in game one of the current series.

'The atmosphere was terrific. We rarely get the big blues now, because of the TV and the do-gooders,' Raudonikis says.

'Now I can't knock that, but I think a bit of a stink doesn't hurt. With the introduction of TV and video, that fear factor has gone a bit. I played with a lot of teams [who] didn't like to play us, they knew we were going to give it to them. If you dished it out you had to cop it, too.

'But that's the way it works these days, that's the way it is. It's for the good of the game. I still think it's a great game of footy.'

Mick Cronin, who also played for the Blues in the 1980 Origin clash and is today running the family's pub in Gerringong, says there was always going to be a bit of biff with the players involved in that game.

He remembers the 'one-off' first game as new and exciting.

'For years NSW had been dominating the state games. In those early years Origin was more important to Queensland than NSW, they picked the squad early, we picked our team on the Sunday and played on the Tuesday,' Cronin says.

'NSW didn't give Origin the respect that Queensland did. We got complacent—we'd been dominant for so many years in state representative footy.'

Cronin says he'll probably watch Origin II on TV with the kids, while his old 1980 teammate Craig 'Fat Albert' Young says he will be sitting out at Telstra Stadium this Wednesday.

Young remembers the 1980 game as a very intense encounter.

'It was very special to Queensland . . . probably a few of my teammates were surprised by the intensity. I don't think any of players on that night imagined what the concept would turn into,' Young says.

He thinks the fight that erupted wasn't as tough as memory has it.

'It wasn't that bad, it was a long, long time ago. Arthur Beetson jabbed Mick. Mick was OK, Mick's a big bloke, he looked after himself,' he says.

'Arthur Beetson split my lip, I got some stitches in at half-time.'

Young is now helping coach St George while running his pub in Unanderra. And he will join his Origin originals at the second reunion of the 1980 side, in a charity golf day next Thursday at the Camden Lakeside course.

One of the initiators of the Origin series was former NSW rugby league boss Kevin Humphreys, who, like the players, didn't initially realise what great heights the series would reach. Nobody did, he says.

Humphreys says this year's opening Origin clash was one of the best in the series.

'I thought it was magnificent, a wonderful stadium, it was the best game of rugby league played within the rules,' Humphreys says.

So, what did those players do with their first Origin jersey?

Young thinks his is somewhere at his house, he's not too sure. Cronin thinks he may have raffled it, given it to charity . . . or one of his kids has it.

And Hambly?

'I just stuck it in a drawer. I think my daughter sometimes wears it to bed,' he says.

Hambly's started buttering bread rolls now, the cafe's busier and there's not much time to talk.

As he finishes telling his Origin story, Hambly seems quite content, happy, on reflection, with the experience.

After all, it was only a game.

21 June 2003

QUEEN OF GOOLMA RECKONS THE BEST HORSES RUN IN FAMILIES

Max Presnell

The boozers at the Goolma pub were expounding on how good they were at tennis. 'I'll beat any one of you using a frying pan,' Carol Burns, a contender for Australia's best horse player, challenged from behind the bar. One accepted and was beaten.

Without any hint of droppings of the bull, Burns, in all the best traditions of country women, serves straight from the shoulder.

According to bookmaker Ken Orbell, Burns has a 97 per cent winning strike rate around bush tracks and the streak has extended for decades. But obviously she doesn't fit the Hollywood George Edser (or George Freeman) profile of the high-rolling punter. Freeman was once tagged with '98 per cent' by chief magistrate Murray Farquhar.

'He had more help than I get,' Burns divulged this week. She hails from Goolma, a one-waterhole hamlet between Mudgee and Wellington. Burns is Goolma—she worked in the pub for 40 years, during which she also handled the exchange at the post office, toiled on nearby properties and was babysitter to just about every family in the district.

These days she has cut down for racing and is tending 2000 acres, where she runs first-cross ewes and Angus cattle.

'I drench 'em, tail 'em,' she explained. 'Do it all on me own. I might tail 800–1000 lambs. Not hard when you know what you're doing.

'Looked after my mother and father when I left school, and worked on this property for 20 years. And the two bachelors, they were gentlemen who had the property, looked after them. One died, then the other fellow got sick.

'I looked after him, and he left me the property.'

Let's get personal. Her age? It's 73. Gee, 1939 was a good vintage for foals. The secret of her eternal youth?

'Never drank, never smoked, never had much to do with men and nothing to do with women,' she said.

And the punt. Is the 97 per cent correct? 'No, more like 90 per cent,' she replied.

'Carol is a consistent winner and great for racing in the district,' her cousin, Brett Thompson, the Mudgee trainer whose family once owned the Goolma pub, declared.

Burns now travels with him to the meetings, three or four times a week, where she does battle with bookmakers including the Orbells (Ken and Peter), Noel Teys and Hilary Cohen.

'The Orbells don't bet overs, a bit stingy—and I used to go to the races with their father, Abby,' she declared. 'And Hilary gets very sour when he loses.'

Only last Monday at Dubbo, Burns backed the seven-event program following a successful visit to Rosehill to watch Classical Melody, a filly she part-owns, end up fourth in the Inglis Classic.

'I would have been satisfied if Classical Melody finished in the first seven. I had $10 each way on her but backed the winner [Cavalry Rose],' she added.

(Burns saw the Peter Nestor–trained Izababe during barrier trials at Dubbo and reports he looks ready to win.)

So how much does the Queen of Goolma outlay?

'If I think something is a good thing, I'll back big. Well four, five hundred dollars, a thousand on our horses when I think they can win,' she answered.

It started with Persian Puzzle, winner of the 1964 Doncaster. 'He's the first horse I remember being on. Wasn't any TAB then, but SP. I done a bit of that at the pub meself.

'I was lucky enough to be in a couple of good horses. I had a horse by Gunsynd called Gun Drift. Johnny Lundholm trained him. He won a lot of races.

'Cups around the bush. Went to all the races then. All the cups, the Coonamble Cup, the Gil (Gilgandra), the Galar (Galargambone), Warren and all them places.

'I like the greys, had a lot of luck with horses by Raffindale and Gunsynd. It doesn't make 'em win, but I go for nice-looking horses, well proportioned.' In the past 15 years, though, she has 'really started'.

Now she has shares in nine horses, including Thompson's Hewentwhoosh.

'Whenever I'm syndicating, people ask, "Is Carol in this one?" I say "yes" and they are in it too,' Thompson pointed out. 'She studies the books (the sales). Believes good horses come out of good families, more the mare line.'

And this is the key to her punting too. 'Back well-performed types and good jockeys,' Burns advised.

'Jockeys like Mathew Cahill, Greg Ryan and Kody (Nester). I don't like inconsistent horses and don't bet big in every race . . . I love it. Made a lot of friends in racing, trainers, owners, bookmakers.'

And they love her.

'Everyone out here knows Carol,' Thompson stressed. 'The young people go up to her for tips.

'A young bloke who works for me met Carol going to the races in the truck. She'll tip him one to have five bucks on and, after, ask him if he backed it.'

The kid will have his coat tugged in another direction and Burns will slip him 10 bucks.

'She's a real soft person, helps everyone out,' the trainer said. 'Mathew Cahill will tell you, whenever his father, Ossie, wanted a big paddock for a horse for six months, he would send it out to Carol and she wouldn't charge anything.' However, punting and race-going do not interfere with her toil at home. 'I make sure my work is done before I go,' she said. 'People say I should sell out and retire, but I'm lucky enough to be healthy.'

Horses on the property?

'Only ride a four-wheeled motor bike,' she concluded. 'Horses? You've got to catch 'em and saddle 'em. I just jump on the bike and go.'

Burns has got to save her revs for any drunk who wants to play her tennis. And she'll serve and return with a frying pan.

29 January 2012

SLIM PICKINGS WHEN THE TEXAN HIT SYDNEY TOWN

Max Presnell

'It's so quiet in here you could hear a mouse piss on silk,' declared the Texan wearing a Stetson that wasn't quite Bob Katter–large but still formidable.

The accent and hat triggered a siren of expectation for the City Tatts Club hard-heads, only too happy to accommodate the sporting activities of a lanky Yank.

Obviously, given the calm, the scene wasn't on settling day, which always fell on Monday in the Pitt Street, Sydney, club, a hub of gambling activity. On settling days bookmakers, both legal and SP, mingled with punters, squaring accounts for the previous Saturday. 'Melbourne Mick' Bartley once arrived carrying two David Jones carrier bags full of cash.

With the settling over, the action started. Games of cards and snooker carried side wagers galore. The rattle of the pokie handles could be heard at Railway Square.

Anyway, this uppity Texan was treading on dangerous ground and the vultures hovered for a kill. Do you fancy cards, he was asked. 'Yes, but poker is my game.' What about gin rummy? 'Never heard of it but I'll adapt.' Do you have coin of the realm? 'I think you'll find greenbacks will convert quite nicely,' he replied and referred all-comers to his bag man.

After this American polished off the also-rans, word got out that serious money was in the offing.

Amarillo Slim once said: 'They anticipate losing when they sit down and I try my darndest not to disappoint one of them.'

Thus the heavies were called in. Joe Taylor, as good as we've had, and

Eli Rose, with international experience, responded to the challenge. Taylor had a beautiful mind and applied it to the punt, particularly racing and gin rummy. He won the 1962 Golden Slipper with Birthday Card and plucked an estimated £50,000 off the bookies. Among Taylor's business interests was Thommo's (the floating two-up school) and assorted gambling and card clubs. Also, he was the patron saint of down-and-out punters.

Rose, born a Pom, blended in perfectly in the Sydney gaming scene. Alas, the circumstances of his departure from Manchester necessitated the Australian Jockey Club refusing the nomination of his horse, Lancashire Lad. But at the cards table City Tatts regulars regarded him as hard to beat.

'I never go looking for a sucker. I look for a champion and make a sucker of him.'—Amarillo Slim again.

The Texan confirmed his ability yet others shouldered to get on to the table. Nick Bodkin, as shrewd as they come—he launched plunges for Jack Denham—was keen to take him on. So, too, 'Booty Dick' Phillips, the shoe magnate immortalised by Ken Howard's radio voice-over for 'Dick's kickers'. Phillips was renowned for putting his orthopaedic slipper into inferior gin players at the club.

Well, the Texan cleaned 'em all out. Apart from the players, about 150 punters bet on the side. It was then suggested perhaps he could be tempted into a game of snooker. 'I play pool but I'll adapt,' he replied.

'It never hurts for potential opponents to think you're more than a little stupid and can hardly count all the money in your hip pocket, much less hold on to it.'—Amarillo Slim.

Thus Norman Squire and Warren Simpson, gelignite with the cue, answered the plea to rectify City Tatts' economy and reputation. Being professionals and the Texan having a pool style, different grip, they had to give a start and some national pride was restored. Simpson could only score off the yellow but still had a 63 break. '"If you live to be 100 you'll never see a break like that," Norman Squire told me,' John Simpson, the son of Warren, recalled at Rosehill recently. The Yank said 'no more' to Simpson.

'Nobody is always a winner, and anybody who says he is, is either a liar or doesn't play poker.'—Amarillo Slim.

Maybe the display was berley, because the Texan then cut loose on Squire. The final settling for the Texan has been compared with the safety-deposit-box robbery at City Tatts, an event after which bookies were hardly in a position to divulge their true losses. 'He came back a couple of years later and took out about $20,000, but that was hardly in the same category as his first visit,' said Kevin Young, an observer at the time.

And that's going back to the early 1970s. But we shouldn't feel too bad about it. The plunderer was, of course, Amarillo Slim himself.

'Growing up and living in Texas all of my life, I have heard tales and stories of the world's greatest gambler, Thomas "Amarillo Slim" Preston Jr,' he regales on his own website, amarilloslim.org. 'From beating Minnesota Fats at pool with a broom, to hitting a golf ball a mile across a frozen lake, or winning $300,000 from country music legend Willie Nelson playing dominoes, his journey to gambling greatness never fails to amaze me. He has played poker with presidents Lyndon Johnson and Richard Nixon, and drug lords Pablo Escobar and Jimmy Chagra, and of course a poker game with porn king Larry Flynt, in which Mr Flynt lost a whopping $1,700,000.'

But poker is Amarillo Slim's game and he has five World Series of Poker bracelets to prove it. He has fallen on hard times over indecency charges concerning his granddaughter. Plea bargaining came into play.

Asked as he was leaving City Tatts whether he would like a game of table tennis, he replied: 'Never picked up a bat but I'll adapt.' Still, he once made a killing against Bobby Riggs playing 'ping pong' with a skillet.

30 January 2011

SKIPPER'S CENTURY THE STUFF OF LEGEND

Peter Roebuck

Steve Waugh has done it. In an amazing, nerveless display typical of the game's foremost fighter, he waited till the last ball of a rollercoaster day to strike the boundary that brought the century a sporting nation and history itself had demanded.

Don Bradman and Doug Walters also hit boundaries off final deliveries to reach three figures, not bad company for an unpretentious young man from western Sydney. Now he sits alongside the Don with 29 Test centuries.

His extraordinary effort was acknowledged by opponents who answered their captain's call to gather outside the Australian pavilion to salute the warrior as he left the field. Perhaps they know something. If this was goodbye, it was not a bad way to go. Not that there seems to be any hurry. Spectators roared and sang their approval. It was a joyful day upon which men rose above themselves. You would not have missed it for quids.

Waugh's penultimate innings in Test cricket started with his team in trouble and fast bowlers pawing the ground. Has anyone heard this story before? Justin Langer had miscued a hook and a relieved Yorkshireman held on at fine leg as Australia sank to 3/56, a predicament commonplace years ago but unusual in these days of productive opening pairs.

No sooner had the chance been taken than a familiar figure began to thread his way through the crowd, a man who comes to life in a crisis. Nor did it take him long to reach the sunlight. Waugh has always hated a fuss and put on his gloves and started marching to the crease long before Langer's slow withdrawal had been completed. As far as Waugh was concerned, it was business as usual. He has played his cricket as a craftsman and a competitor, never as a romantic. It was 3.25 on a Friday afternoon and there was work to be done.

At Waugh's appearance, an ovation spread around the ground, for this was a moment of sporting significance, the last appearance of a respected warrior. At such times, crowds open their hearts in a way that can catch the hard-bitten player off guard. Don Bradman had a tear in his eye as he took guard for the final time in Test cricket, and he was not the sentimental sort. Sportsmen concentrate upon winning matches and inhabit a world insulated from daily discourse. Sometimes they see themselves through the harshnesses of newspapers, whose objectivity does not permit any show of affection. Only in parting can they sense the untapped warmth.

Not that Waugh showed the merest flicker as he strode to the crease. Long ago, he learnt to control his emotions, training himself so that mind and body found harmony. If he was nervous or dismayed, he did not betray the secret, for it is not his way to give comfort to an opponent. Instead, he practised a few shots—back defences mostly, the shot upon which his game has been built—as his partner faced the rest of the over. Damien Martyn survived those deliveries and then it was time for the long-awaited struggle between Waugh and fate.

Waugh took guard and settled into his stance, head low over the bat, staring defiantly down the pitch, eyes hooded like a buzzard's in the heat of the day. There is no grandeur in him and no gesture either, only the substance of the committed. England threw the ball to Steve Harmison, whose salvos caused a suffering Waugh such discomfort in their previous confrontation. Finding nothing to his liking or anything of menace, the Australian captain let the balls pass or pushed them back down a pitch now wan in colour. It seemed that Waugh might not break his duck before tea. An over remained and Matthew Hoggard was recalled to test Waugh with some frisky swingers.

Apart from 11 Englishmen, everyone wanted Waugh to score a few runs. After all, England had plenty to spare. Already it had been a fine day for old dogs, with Alec Stewart striking the ball around in his brisk way and Andrew Caddick taking wickets. At last, Waugh was underway with a characteristic crack through point, immediately followed by an efficient tuck off his pads. Viv Richards used to call out 'jam' as he played his favourite strokes, but Waugh has always preferred bread and butter. He retired for tea and bananas with eight runs to his name.

Afterwards, Waugh began to cut loose. His body seemed alive with the challenge of the moment, enjoying the surge that pressure brings. Runs came in bursts, boundaries taken off his pads, cuts dispatched through point. Although Caddick pushed him back, he looked in control, subduing the climbers and punishing anything off line. A roar for leg before rent the air and was rejected, a decision acclaimed by a crowded house. Waugh had higher ambitions than wearing down a limited attack, for he was on his toes, his recent flatness overcome.

Caddick strayed and Waugh pounced, sending the ball speeding away with late flicks of the wrist, three boundaries in an over, shots played with hidden power. Expecting to see the batsmen trotting a single, spectators were surprised to find long leg collecting a bruised ball from beyond the ropes. Waugh did not look like a tired old man ready to hang up his cap. He looked sharp. Contrastingly, Martyn did not settle, losing his wicket to a poor stroke. Nor could Martin Love outstare the moment. Waugh batted better than men either side of him in the batting order, a point worth considering.

Waugh continued an assault upon English bowling that has lasted 16 years. A withering off-drive took Waugh to 50, the crowd rose again and their cheers were acknowledged with a quiet raising of the bat. And then he went back to work. Like a barrister in court, Waugh was searching for the argument that could not be answered. Melbourne had not been enough, a dashing half-century before stumps and then faltering performances in the rest of the match. He bent low and drove through point, moving within sight of the runs required to reach 10,000 in Test cricket.

Minutes later, Waugh cut and put himself alongside Allan Border and Sunil Gavaskar in the record books, a wonderful achievement by an unpretentious young man from the western suburbs of the largest city on a remote, vast and mostly uninhabitable continent.

No less significantly, Waugh was playing the type of innings often seen over the years and sometimes taken for granted, the innings of a formidable competitor who has willed mighty deeds, feats that have played their part in his team's domination. Shane Warne and Glenn McGrath might be missing, but their captain was still there, trying to save the side, refusing to bow to the inevitable, wanting to win 5–0.

Not until a man is in a tight corner are his strengths properly understood. Waugh stood firm. If he goes or is pushed, he will be missed. And the beauty of it is he can resume this morning.

4 January 2003

OPEN LEGEND THOMSON CARDS AN 80 HE'S FINALLY HAPPY TO CELEBRATE

Peter Stone

Just twice in 30 British Open championships, Peter Thomson shot in the eighties. Well, 81 each time to be precise, and he wasn't too thrilled. Tomorrow he notches up a different 80, and it's cause for celebration.

His immediate family will gather to share his birthday with him, and on Monday his friends in golf will toast him at a party at his Melbourne golf design office, where more than 100 courses around the world have come off the drawing board.

'I'm quite proud of 80. It's a bit different to 80 strokes,' the five-time Open champion said yesterday. Unfortunately, 80 is a score he's shooting increasingly now, although just the other day he carded a 79 around his home course of Victoria GC playing off his handicap of six.

From 1952 to 1958, he virtually had a monopoly on The Open Championship, winning four times—in 1953, 1954, 1955 and 1956—and finishing runner-up in the other years. In 1965, he won a fifth, and although he has never admitted it publicly, there were surely dreams of eclipsing the legendary Harry Vardon's record of six titles.

Thomson sent a telegram to *The Age* office in 1969, just a couple of months after I'd been installed as chief golf writer, saying he thought he was in with a chance of a sixth going into the final round. He mused at the thought that, should he succeed, his portrait might be hung in clubhouses around the world alongside that of Vardon.

He finished tied third behind England's Tony Jacklin, and when reminded of that telegram yesterday he comments: 'I was a bad judge, wasn't I?'

Typical Thomson. He is whimsical, erudite and damn good company. But he is also forthright, even provocative. On course, he won more than 100 titles and, as mentioned, has created around the same number of courses. He was president of the Australian PGA from 1962 to 1994 and a quite superb golf columnist and television commentator.

About all he failed at was as a politician, but that wasn't really his fault. He stood for the Victorian Parliament in the seat of Prahran in 1982. 'I lost along with all the Liberal Party in a John Cain [Labor] landslide,' he laments.

Thomson was then invited to play a Legends of Golf event in the US, a tournament which preceded the US Senior Tour. In 1985, he won nine tournaments, and the Americans suddenly realised who Peter William Thomson was. He'd played there for seven years in the 1950s, but never embraced the scene. In 1985, he blitzed their ageing heroes.

'It was a very comfortable sojourn,' Thomson says.

He is not short of a dollar either, with homes in Melbourne's Toorak and in Scotland's St Andrews. He might have been megarich had he accepted an offer from the late Mark McCormack, who founded the International Management Group.

McCormack's first client was Arnold Palmer, who turns 80 on September 10, and then he added Jack Nicklaus and Gary Player.

'I had no interest in such a thing,' Thomson says. 'I had a revulsion of him [McCormack]. I didn't find him a nice character.'

Thomson doesn't mince words.

He admires Tiger Woods' skill as a golfer but turns the thumb down on what he calls Tiger's 'petulant' attitude on course.

'It might be time to get the whip out on Woods,' he says. 'He is taking an unnecessarily long time to make up his mind about some of his shots. I don't think it is very courteous to the fellow he is playing with. If everybody did the same thing, they'd never get through in one day.'

On the fourth occasion Thomson stood as a major champion—1956—he had to borrow a jacket for the presentation from the then captain of Royal Melbourne, Max Shaw. Months later when Shaw sent the jacket to the drycleaner, the winning cheque for £1200 was found in the pocket.

'I obviously didn't need the money,' Thomson says.

Now, Thomson believes his whole golfing life is completing the full circle. At age 14, he was hitting the ball 200 metres and was off 24. Now, he reckons the day is not that far away when it will be the same.

'I've been to the top of Mt Everest and now I'm on the slippery slide down the other side,' he says. 'I've got to this ripe old age in good health without too many enemies. That's all one can ask.'

22 August 2009

THE TURNING POINT

Sports identities can be so courageous, not just in their feats, but in what they say, often in difficult circumstances. The former Australian rugby union player Clyde Rathbone is a classic case.

After being a star schoolboy player in South Africa, Rathbone decided to leave for Australia. He was outspoken enough to repeatedly explain exactly why he had left his country of birth: it was a dangerous environment, which he didn't feel comfortable in.

That did not endear him to South Africans, and when he returned to Durban to play a Test for the Wallabies against the Springboks, he was subjected to an enormous amount of abuse. The South African media and public targeted him, often viciously. He grew accustomed to being described as a traitor.

But as always Rathbone was fearless, explaining a few days before that Test exactly why he was now in green-and-gold colours. I remember thinking as I interviewed Rathbone in the team's opulent hotel north of Durban that these quotes, which I was about to use in an extensive article on him, would inflame a nation. Sure enough they bounced back to South Africa, and Rathbone was confirmed as the country's public enemy no. 1.

There was an aftermath. Rathbone had a poor Test match, and his family, who were shortly after attacked during a robbery of their jewelry store, followed him to Australia.

Rathbone later suffered from bouts of depression, but was involved in an inspiring return to the football ranks, when he again played for the ACT Brumbies in 2013 after several years' absence.

Just as inspiring are the why and wherefores of a certain mark in a certain grand final which led to so much joy in Sydney. Richard Hinds does a stunning job in bringing it all together, much to the joy of his colleague Max Presnell, who in the same chapter makes the tough admission that a rugby league follower had been converted to the supposed enemy, AFL. For some that is the hardest admission of all.

GG

LEO'S LEAP OF FAITH FOR THE TRUE BELIEVERS

Richard Hinds

Leo Barry knew it would come back again. Even after he had thumped the ball clear of danger yet again. Even with 32 minutes gone in this interminably long quarter. Even as he turned back desperately looking for his opponent, Barry knew this undersized, undervalued Swans defence that had repelled wave after wave of Eagles attacks would face one more challenge.

Now the ball was in the air. Set in flight by the left boot of Eagles ruckman Dean Cox, it was tumbling toward a pack of players 15 metres from the West Coast goal. Barry was just to the side and his opponent Michael Gardiner was, well, where was he?

Barry had lost contact but Nic Fosdike knew where he was. Gardiner was standing beside him. The 179-centimetre Fosdike had played the game of his life. Coming off the bench, he had run straight and relentlessly, like the brilliant middle-distance athlete he had been in his youth. Now, for a split second, it looked like he would have to compete in the air with a man 20 cm taller, the fate of the premiership on the line. Just one thought crossed his mind: 'Oh shit!'

Tadhg Kennelly was standing in front of Fosdike. In the first 10 minutes of the match he had gasped desperately for air, overcome by the enormity of the occasion. Now, having composed himself on a stage he didn't know existed just six years ago, Kennelly knew his time had come. He could see young West Coast ruckman Mark Seaby preparing to take his leap. He would have to throw himself into the pack and somehow try to get a hand on the ball.

At the front of the pack Amon Buchanan had quickly worked out the ball was going to clear his head and threw himself backwards into the oncoming traffic. 'Just didn't think, just didn't think,' Buchanan would recall later of what was merely one of several moments of bloody-minded bravery he had performed in a heroic final quarter. 'You just don't in this team.'

Through the minds of others further from the scene came exhortations. Even prayers. Jude Bolton, his head covered with the bandages and helmet that have become de rigueur for any self-respecting 'Blood', was 30 metres from the pack. Two words kept rushing through his head: 'Spoil it! Spoil it! Spoil it!'

Brett Kirk, the world's most fearless Buddhist, was practising faith of a different kind. Earlier in the quarter, Kirk had thrown his body recklessly into a collision with Eagle Ben Cousins, a moment of sheer abandon that sent shivers up spines. Now, as the ball hung in the air, he hoped—no, he knew—someone would make a similar sacrifice. 'When it's on the line you stick your head over the footy,' he would say. 'That's the Bloods.'

For those who could no longer control their own destiny, that ball seemed to hang forever. Sitting on the interchange bench for the final 10 minutes of the match, Luke Ablett had composed the apology he would issue his coach and teammates for his calamitous error that had gifted Cousins a goal. Ablett was preparing for a change of identity. He would no longer be known as the nephew of the great Gary Ablett. Now he would be the man who cost the Swans a premiership.

Behind Ablett sat football operations manager Andrew Ireland. He was still wearing the headphones. The messages from the coaches' box kept coming. But he knew nothing could be done. All he could do was watch to see if all that time spent attempting to replicate the success he had achieved as chief executive in Brisbane would bear fruit. Or would he suffer that same gut-wrenching disappointment he knew three times as a member of losing Collingwood grand final teams?

Others are too callow to let fate dictate their moods. Adam Schneider was still up near the interchange area, bouncing up and down and hoping to get the coaches' attention. Craving the spotlight. Desperate to be in on the fun, he watched without fear.

Some could not watch at all. Rick Quade was the first man to coach the Swans in Sydney. He is now a member of the board. When the ball hit Cox's boot he lowered his head, closed his eyes and braced himself for the worst.

Beside him, Swans chairman Richard Colless was having what he would call a 'Zen moment'. Few had worked harder to get the Swans this far. Few knew what was hanging on the outcome of this impending contest. 'After all this time, after all this work . . .' he thought. But with introspection, not panic.

In the umpires' race, old South Melbourne warriors Bob Skilton and Barry Round stood holding their breath. Skilton had played in just one final in his brilliant career. Round had won a pre-season title for the Swans in their first year in Sydney but not the real thing. Both Skilton and Round were the type of 'old Bloods' on whom these Swans have modelled themselves.

Now, throughout an epic grand final, this team had filled Skilton and Round with pride. Whatever happened when that ball came down, they were going to sprint onto the ground and embrace the club's new heroes. But for the moment, they stood transfixed.

Paul Kelly was standing near the two old-timers. If the Swans won, he would present the premiership cup to the winners. All day his body had twitched and contorted, the instincts of a man used to shaping such contests with his own will. Now he could not throw that small frame in front of the charging pack, but merely hope someone would meet the challenge. Someone like Buchanan.

Amid all these thoughts and emotions and the deafening noise of the crowd, the mental calculator in Barry's head had plotted his flight path. The ball was turning perfectly. He was beside the pack. He had a few steps to propel himself. There would be a couple of players blocking his way, but he would roll the dice. He would back his famous leap to propel him over the pack and his strong hands to grip the ball. He would ignore the mantra of all stout defenders—always punch from behind.

As Barry took off, in the crowd of 91,898, there was probably only one man who had no doubt what would happen next. Leo Barry snr is a big country bloke with a broad smile, a firm handshake and a nice way of making what would be one of the greatest moments in the history of grand finals seem as inconsequential as Leo jnr climbing a particularly tall tree on the family farm. 'He loves a challenge, my boy,' Leo snr would say later. 'He just loves a challenge.'

After Barry took that challenge, a split second of confusion. Bodies colliding. A pack crumbling. The ball disappears.

In the coaches' box, Paul Roos thought it had been marked by the Eagles. But Roos had also thought Nick Davis's matchwinner against Geelong was a point. For a man who lives such a charmed life, the AFL's new supercoach is a born pessimist.

Kennelly looked around and saw Barry's hands on the ball. Seconds later he heard the siren but Barry did not. He did not know it was over until he was being hugged and kissed by Kennelly, then Buchanan. Fosdike, who had seen the No. 21 rise up before him and pluck the ball away, slumped over in elation and relief.

Quade heard a roar and thought the worst until he was thumped by Colless. The old-timers ran onto the ground as fast as their arthritic joints could carry them. The rest was mayhem. And history that will be retold for as long as they wear red and white. The mark that saved the flag.

26 September 2005

MY JOURNEY FROM SOUTHS DIEHARD TO SWANS TRAGIC

Max Presnell

Conversion to the Swans, emphasised by the red-and-white tie—the only pleasing feature of the picture byline on this page—was the equal of Richard The Lionheart switching to an Eastern religion.

The light was seen because of the late Graeme Pash, a big punter in a golden age, great racing administrator and Swans director. He was accomplished at tilting at windmills and old-guard thinking, rusted with tradition. Rosehill's acclaimed Grand Pavilion, originally set wrong, not giving the best view of the straight, was righted thanks to his engineer's eye. But converting a South Sydney diehard to aerial ping pong was his finest achievement.

Earlier, Ken Williams, originally from Port Melbourne and now long-time lead singer, mascot and motivator for the Swans, tried and failed before I was a teenager.

Now in his 80s, Kenso Ken, with the signature grey mop, came to Sydney when only a young strapper around racing stables and the wise guys at the Doncaster pub, where we both spent formative years, figured the Yarra waters had sent another around the twist considering his taste in football. At that stage, even with the assistance of lubrication, he was closer to tone deaf than Pavarotti, showing no sign of his future role.

Later, my mother, Stella, who hailed from Caulfield, asked me to take her to see the Swans. 'I'll get the best seat at the SCG for you and your friends, waiter service, and will shout an after-party at a club with poker machines of your choice, but don't ask me to go when there's a rugby league match on and that includes the juniors,' she was told.

Mum was followed by my wife, Colleena, from Perth. Alf Neeson, two seasons with Hawthorn, later to leave his mark for East Perth, where Pash cut his teeth, and finally a legend in Kalgoorlie, figures in her bloodlines. Pressure was intense to get me to the game she grew up with as a kid, yelling 'Kick the ball Sheedy (Jack, not Kevin).' Enter Pash. No politician shook more hands— nor did so with such sincerity than the former Sydney Turf Club chairman. The smile beamed and the grip was loaded with camaraderie.

Yet he went on higher beam at the mention of Micky O. So intense was he about the team, I had to see how he would react if they went down to a bad umpiring decision. Under his enlightenment, the skill and team spirit of the Swans flourished under my eye.

Micky O was a revelation, Adam Goodes would have been a great lock for the Rabbits and is one of the best in any code I've seen. Barry Hall was also an instant hit. For one who had been blooded by John Sattler, Big Bad Barry was a knuckle man of worth. When he dished out a lesson in manners and left rips to some West Coast Eagle, the applause in our lounge room lifted the roof.

With such a cohesive outfit, to name a few seems unjust to those left out, particularly after such a great season, but the staying ability of Jude Bolton, the development of speed and direction of Lewis Jetta are features. And the steadying influence of Ted Richards? What a player. Shane Mumford and Mike Pyke have had great seasons. Racing NSW chief steward Ray Murrihy, originally from Warrnambool so he should know better, was a member of the Pyke naysayers.

Still, some of us were amiss with Lewis Roberts-Thomson; hardly up to the standard of a BLT (with half-cooked bacon). 'What's he doing there,' Steve Brassel, then the PR man for the Swans, was asked a few seasons back. Brassel gained polish and a considerable thirst under my tuition at *The Sun*, the long-gone Sydney afternoon newspaper. LRT is RBG. Real bloody good.

Ironically, I could never get Kenso Ken to Redfern Oval to see the little master, Clive Churchill, or Big Macca and Ron Coote. Perhaps it was because red-and-white was his favourite colour, and a feature of his time with trainer Fil Allotta.

'If Cabochon had won the 1967 Doncaster it would have changed my life,' Williams recalled. Trained by Allotta, Cabochon (66–1) had the Doncaster won before the mighty Tobin Bronze swamped him by a short head. Allotta had three other winners on the same day. Williams had backed them all-up. They were owned by the Tait family, whose silks were red and white.

Had Cabochon got home, Kenso Ken would have had enough to outbid Geoffrey Edelsten to buy the Swans. Not that he would have been any happier than his present role.

'Gee I've had a good time with them,' he enthused.

Ditto.

30 September 2012

THE TROUBLE WITH PARADISE

Greg Growden

There are certainly less appealing places to live in South Africa. Drive about 35 kilometres down the south coast road from Durban, head past Wild Boys Surf Shop, left before The Biltong Man, Buddy's Pub and Tavern and Rathbone Jewellers, and right in front of you, just beyond the High Tide Fishing and Tackle Shop, is the ultimate beachfront.

Fishermen are catching plenty off the rocks, surfers are attempting to tame a sloppy beach-break, a family, perched under a large umbrella on the sand, is hoeing into the sosaties and samoosas, and, at the cafe backpackers are suntanning their legs. Warner Beach is one of those pleasant, out-of-the-way coastal villages where everyone knows everyone, but you can still hide away and enjoy a more generous pace of life.

As Clyde Rathbone explains: 'We'd walk out our front door, head through the garden and you're on the beach. You could throw a golf ball into the sea from our place. It was a great place to grow up.' A few kilometres back towards Durban, Geoff Harrison, headmaster of Kingsway High School, shows off the honour board in the foyer. AC Rathbone appears in a long list of head prefects, showing that he was the school's head boy in 1999. He also appears twice, in 1998 and 1999, in the rugby captain list.

No sighting of his name under the dux-of-the-school list though.

A teacher advises us to move on. In the main hall, senior students are undergoing an exam and we are making too much noise. Was C Rathbone a performer in the main hall? Was he an excellent student? 'That was not his strength,' headmaster Harrison replies. 'His focus was rugger. He was so single-minded. He just wanted to get his Natal rugby colours. He was so engrossed by that. And he did it.'

Harrison says that with immense pride. Kingsway High is a good, functional, co-educational school with 1080 black, coloured and white students from a community that comprises affluent coastal areas, middle-class suburbs and nearby black townships. But it is not a prestige school, and definitely not a renowned breeding ground for Springboks, or Wallabies for that matter.

The upmarket schools are in Durban, and the people at Kingsway High are still chuffed that Rathbone stuck with them and resisted the lure of a rugby scholarship. He was loyal. He just wanted to stick with his mates.

'We had some good rugby seasons when Clyde was here. And what was so delightful was that he didn't get poached by any of the bigger schools in the area,' Harrison said.

His school rugby coach, Daryl Vorster, offers a guided tour of the school oval where, for several years, Rathbone was the standout. This is not exactly Joeys or Riverview. At one end a tractor, manicuring the playing fields, kicks up a cloud of dust. A freeway skirts one side. Deep bushes the other. It's rudimentary. If you want to watch, you stand on the sideline, not in some elegant private school grandstand. The surface of the main ground appears very hard. Unprotected heads and footballs bounce high off the surface.

It was here that Rathbone was first noticed.

'Right from the start, Clyde had this vision for the game,' Vorster said. 'Out on this field, he could see the gaps. And he would just love to run at opponents and bounce off them. He had such a rugby brain. You can't teach that. It's just a natural talent.

'But what was most rewarding about his involvement here is that it showed that someone could make it to the top from a smaller school. Very rewarding.'

Why, in the end, did Rathbone leave? Not to a bigger school but to a different country, from an idyllic, alluring coastline where he was gaining special status as the victorious South African captain at the 2002 under-21 World Cup.

It all centred on opportunities.

'Leaving here will always be the hardest decision that I'll make in my life,' Rathbone said on Friday [August 2004]. 'But it was also the best decision that I will make . . . for my future and my family's future. In terms of opportunity, Australia is probably the best country in the world.' Rathbone said his fiancée, Carrie-Ann Leeson, who hails from the same part of Durban, was the 'perfect example'.

'Carrie-Ann finished her degree in marketing here, and then spent seven months trying to find a job. We then went to Australia. By the end of the first week, she could choose between five or six different jobs,' he said. 'That is just mind-blowing for a South African. That's why so many South Africans who move to Australia have such a great work ethic, because they have seen the other side of the coin. Living in South Africa, you just don't get those opportunities. Unemployment here is 40 per cent.'

Then there are the safety issues.

'I was immediately blown away by Australia and how everything works. There are a lot of things Australians take for granted. But here it is difficult to find work. You also worry about where your family and friends are all the time. My fiancée came in and saw me at the team hotel last night with a mate of mine from school. She had to drive home and I made certain she rang me when she got home so I knew she had got there all right. Driving on South African roads is very dangerous. That's the reality of it. We have something like a couple of thousand road deaths just over the Christmas period . . . Then there's 20,000 people murdered in South Africa last year.'

Rathbone was the victim of petty crime during his Durban days: the family home broken into once, his car stolen twice.

'But we were lucky because we haven't been involved in any violent crime,' he said. 'At the end of the day I think most people can live with high levels of crime. But what sets South Africa apart is the violent crime. If someone is going to shoot you for your mobile phone that is a completely different issue. But that is the reality of what's happening in some places here. They'll literally take your life for 50 rand in your wallet.'

Since moving to Australia, Rathbone has not held back on his thoughts about South Africa. Rathbone's pointed comments about his land of birth have seen him castigated in the South African media, with even Springboks players screaming at him during the Perth Test last month that he was a 'f—ing traitor'. He is bemused by it all.

'I really can't understand a lot of what is printed over here. A lot of what I say is misconstrued in the South African media. They take what I say, twist it around to say that I'm bashing South Africa, or bad-mouthing South Africa. My view is that I made a decision, and I'm going to be honest about it, in particular the issues in South Africa. If that is going to make me unpopular here, then so be it. I'm not going to stop saying what I believe in.'

And his views on where South African rugby has gone wrong are certain not to improve the fragile relationship he has with his former countrymen. 'I just don't believe the quota system here works. I don't believe it is fair for anyone. I believe in transformation, but that's another issue. The way SARFU has gone about transformation is completely wrong . . . You don't start at the top and say we want five black players in a team. You instead start at primary schools and get kids from disadvantaged communities into the best schools, where they are exposed to proper nutrition, coaching and that sort of thing. Then the process takes care of itself.

'South Africa has so much potential but it has to get the right structures in place. There are 45 million people here, but there are only about 10 million who would have what you would consider a decent standard of living. What people don't see is how the quota system is affecting the lower levels of rugby. I've seen mates miss out on teams because they were white. That's just wrong.'

Back at Kingsway High, his old rugby coach is in two minds. He wants his star player to do well on Saturday, but not that well. Mr Vorster, a small, stocky, committed rugby man, cannot get a ticket for the Test but will watch the game at home on television, cheering one Wallaby and 15 Springboks.

'I do want Clyde to do well. It's a pity he's playing for Australia.'

In the background, the tractor kicks up a bigger cloud of dust.

21 August 2004

IT'S NOT WHETHER YOU WIN OR LOSE

Sometimes how a story is written can be as intriguing as the story itself. In this chapter, Jamie Pandaram's piece on Nader Hamdan is of the highest calibre. How it appeared on the written page is as interesting. Pandaram recalls: 'This was the first time I had been given access to a fighter's dressing room for a world title fight. Hamdan and I developed a strong relationship and I spent the day of the fight with him. What I will never forget was the atmosphere in his dressing room before the fight. Few outside of Hamdan's camp expected him to defeat Mundine, but as the fight came closer I got an ugly sense that even Hamdan's crew, and the fighter himself, had serious doubts. There was an overwhelming silent panic weighing heavy in the room. When he was called, I followed behind Hamdan. Just before he made his entrance, Hamdan suddenly rushed off to the side, and nobody knew what was going on. He later revealed he had "a moment", he was on the verge of tears and needed to scream before biting down on his mouthguard and forcing himself into the packed arena. Hamdan was outmatched in speed and skill by Mundine but showed a warrior's heart to go 12 brutal rounds. Mundine was a convincing winner on the judges' cards. As Hamdan re-entered his dressing room, a defeated man, he received loud applause from his family and friends. A brief interaction between his father and his son formed the underlying basis of my piece, which almost never saw the light of day. I had my uncle's wedding on, but had promised my sports editor, Ben Coady, that I would file the piece in the morning before the ceremony. I had my wife drive to the church as I typed out the story in the passenger seat, but I was in such a rush that I forgot to save the document. With the piece finished, I went to send it but somehow lost the entire copy, and could not retrieve it. We had just pulled up to the venue, so I had to jump out in a state of panic and try to enjoy the wedding. Immediately after, I called Coady to tell him what had happened, and he told me not to worry about writing it again—early deadlines! But I was adamant, so he gave me 30 minutes to send it. I took my laptop to the hotel foyer where the reception was about to start. I sat in a corner, and while the other wedding guests were toasting champagne and celebrating, I furiously typed out from memory what I had written that morning. I saved it this time, and managed to file it just before deadline. I really enjoyed the wedding reception.'

STICKING WITH IT

Michael Cowley

Gabriel Vallejos couldn't sleep. He tossed and turned in his bed on Wednesday night but just could not manage to nod off and get the rest which an athlete requires when competing the following morning.

His mind was abuzz. Thinking of that next event, of how he would swim the 100 m freestyle, but, above all, thinking about his experiences here in Sydney at the Paralympics.

So the 32-year-old sat up in bed, picked up a pen and paper, and jotted down a few words he felt he needed to say.

'Ladies and gentleman,' his letter to the Australian public began. 'I came here with the hope and aspirations, perhaps a little ambitious, of winning a medal. I wanted to do it. But, with the love you have given me, it has made me feel I am a triumph. I will always carry you in my heart.

'If there is a paradise, this is where it is.'

It was a heartfelt letter but in reality it is the Australian public who should be grateful. For anyone who had the privilege of watching him swim would want to say thank you to Vallejos for opening their eyes to what the Paralympics are really about.

We quite often get overcome rightly or wrongly by the pursuit of gold. Sometimes even silver and bronze barely rate in comparison.

Vallejos has not won a medal at these Games. He hasn't really even come close. But while he has no jewellery, he has won the hearts of everyone who witnessed his performances in the pool.

It has nothing to do with pity when one watches the S3 swimmer, who was born with just one leg and neither arm fully formed. To watch the courage of Vallejos can only be described as inspirational.

The Australian public got their first taste of him in action on Monday night when he contested the 200 m freestyle final.

He took 4 min 42.84 s to complete the four laps of the pool doing backstroke, with his arms rotating at a furious rate, but after watching for almost five minutes, the large crowd stood and cheered when he reached the wall. They did it again when he contested the 50 m breaststroke, and again yesterday in the 100 m freestyle.

And no doubt the cheers will be boisterous today when he swims in the 50 m freestyle.

He's not the slowest swimmer in the pool, over the short distances he would give Equatorial Guinea's Eric 'the Eel' Moussambani a competitive race, but there was something about Vallejos's effort which had a hypnotic effect on everyone.

'I have really enjoyed taking part and sharing it with the people,' he said. 'That I am involved in sport is just a coincidence. What is not a coincidence is my desire to keep living and enjoying life.

'Swimming is my life. It is like a drug. For me it is an important way to enrich myself.

'I have always been given much love from people wherever I have been competing, and what has been shown here touched me deeply.'

Vallejos has been swimming for 22 years. He also tried other sports such as shot-put, javelin, discus and table tennis, but his sport of choice was swimming.

It has taken him to three Paralympic Games, and although he is yet to win a medal, it has not diminished his enthusiasm or will to win.

'Winning is important,' he said. 'Those who say they come to the Paralympics and don't care about winning would be lying. I would love to win a medal, and God willing I will one day. But overcoming one's limitation is very important. That is someone's triumph.'

Vallejos lives with his parents and a total of eight brothers, sisters, nephews and nieces in Santiago. He works as an accountant and auditor, specialising in tax law.

He is Chile's only swimmer at the Games, and one of just four athletes competing for the nation at these Paralympics.

He said he had received a lot of recognition in his home country as one of the leading Paralympic athletes, and although he was not a regular visitor to the dais, he felt he had achieved many things.

'I think I have achieved something regarding the opinion people have of disabled sport,' he explained.

'Around 10 or 15 years ago, people looked at a disabled person and thought, "Should I give them money, should I move away, should I smother them with more help than they need?"

'I think I have contributed to change that mentality.'

Vallejos will leave Sydney without a medal when the Games finish.

He will, however, leave enriched by his experience, and so, too, will anyone fortunate enough to have watched him swim and realise they have witnessed a triumph not only of sport, but of life.

Thank you, Gabriel.

27 October 2000

HAMADOU THE HIPPO ON THE THAMES IN HIS JOURNEY OF DISCOVERY

Rupert Guinness

'You're an absolute inspiration,' yelled the American woman from the banks of the Thames as we rowed towards Hammersmith Bridge.

Tempting as it was to thank her, it was not me she was yelling at but the man sitting behind me in the bow seat of a double scull—Hamadou Djibo Issaka of Niger, the cult figure of the 2012 Olympic Games.

Issaka, who rowed at the Olympic regatta courtesy of a wildcard for developing nations, finished stone, motherless last in each of the races he contested in the men's single scull. But it was the manner in which he lost, his determination to finish despite some obvious technical deficiencies, that earned him first the affection, then the respect, of the crowd at Eton Dorney.

He was soon given the nickname 'Hamadou the Hippo', a nod to swimmer Eric 'the Eel' Moussambani Malonga from Equatorial Guinea who brought crowds to their feet at the 2000 Olympics in Sydney as he struggled to finish the 100 metres freestyle. He has also been likened to Great Britain's Eddie 'The Eagle' Edwards, who soared to fame because of his lack of skill in the ski jump of the 1988 winter Olympics.

Apart from the British crews that won a swag of medals, no rower at Dorney Lake received greater cheers from the 26,000 crowd than Issaka, a 35-year-old father and former swimmer who took up rowing seriously only three months ago and came to London with just 500 kilometres on the water under his belt to race against the top rowers, who notch about 5000 kilometres in training a year. His entry to the sport began last November when he showed his potential as a novice by finishing his races in the African zone qualification regatta at

Alexandria in Egypt. That led to the Niger Olympic Committee requesting a wildcard to the Olympics under a development initiative of rowing's world body, FISA, and then to Issaka being urged to give it a go.

Three months after training under Tunisia's head coach Faysal Soula, Issaka became the first from his country to row at the Games.

The day after the Olympic rowing regatta finished, Issaka was back on the water—on the Thames starting at the London Rowing Club in Putney—with one eye on the 2016 Olympics to be held in Rio.

It was Issaka's first outing on the Thames and a long way from the Niger River, which passes through his home in the Niger capital, Niamey, and where the biggest danger is territorial hippopotamuses and crocodiles.

As we rowed down the famous old river, Issaka told of how he had loved the roar of the 26,0000 crowd at Dorney Lake, inside the confines of Eton College. 'I was very, very happy that they encouraged me to finish the race as fast as I could,' Issaka says. 'I was very happy that they encouraged me because when someone encourages you, neither him or you alone is enough to finish the race.'

No matter where he placed in the single scull, Issaka is an Olympian and will be for life. He is what most of us never will be.

Issaka also has his own sense of achievement. He will forever cherish that in his first of four races he finished last and one minute, 35.9 seconds behind, as he more or less did in his next three races. His main objective, though, had been to honour the wildcard he received by finishing all his races. 'I feel good. I finished all four of my races. It was a good reference as I leave. I put everything into my four races. I am so happy about that. I finished well, and in good health,' he says.

Just finishing seems an easy enough goal but there were the dangers of crashing into the lane markers or tipping out of his flimsy craft. Issaka smiles and says: 'I finished all four of them well and in good health. I was afraid. It was my first time to compete—especially in London—in wet conditions, and I respected the lanes well. So it went well.'

As we continue rowing, it is clear that strength is on the Hippo's side.

Issaka knows his technique needs work. But he is confident he can improve now that he has four years to do it, rather than the fast-tracked three-month program with the Tunisian squad that included a three-week training camp at Hazelwinkel in Belgium where he rubbed shoulders with the crack New Zealand squad, whose training regime and systems opened his eyes to how the top rowing nations go about their business.

Issaka comes from a country where heavily subsidised training programs don't exist.

One of four children whose deceased father was a chauffeur in the public service, his life in Niger consists of 15-hour working days on various jobs—from working his family's vegetable farm to attending a children's swimming pool. 'We don't have just one job. We do anything that pays money. I don't rest from six o'clock or seven o'clock on,' Issaka says.

He says he is determined to fit his rowing into his life. 'It is from rowing that I have just raced in the championships of the 2012 Olympics in London. It's for that, that I want to continue it,' he says.

But rowing won't be the only change to his life. He has become a national star that he says his son Abdoukarime, 6, and daughter Ziada, 4, have followed from Niamey. 'They saw me on the television, in the newspapers, everywhere on the internet and on Facebook. There are a lot of people who are so happy for me,' he says. 'My life has changed.'

7 August 2012

HAMDAN'S TITLE SHOT NO MISFIRE

Jamie Pandaram

Bruised and disfigured, with glue holding his left cheek together, Nader Hamdan looked at his three sons yesterday and said: 'It doesn't matter if you win or lose, what matters is how you conduct yourself. If you work hard you will always be a winner.'

Hamdan gave Anthony Mundine a fight for his World Boxing Association super-middleweight world title and was beaten, but not defeated.

In the days after the brutal encounter he has not moped—far from it. The 34-year-old has celebrated what he calls 'the best fight of my career'.

'If I retire now, I will walk away a happy man,' he said.

'I gave it my all, everyone is proud of me. If this fight is my last I'm glad my family, friends and supporters were there to share it with me, and I'm glad it was against a great fighter, champion and person.

'Anthony Mundine can go as high or as far as he wishes—Muhammad Ali was hated through his career but now is loved and respected, and I'm sure Anthony will be the same.'

The fight was the greatest experience in his 46-fight professional career, Hamdan said.

'What a fight, what a preparation, what an atmosphere—I'll never forget it,' he said. 'My body is aching, my face is swollen and sore, but I'm glad I could make my father proud and my family proud.'

Hamdan walked into a Chinese restaurant two hours after the fight and received an ovation, a practice he has been growing used to in the past few days.

Wednesday started with a ritualistic 5 am prayer, and later that day he met his close friends for a late lunch at an Italian restaurant in Leichhardt.

A shirt-less Hamdan relaxed at the table as those in his team, trainer Haytham Jouni, strength man Hassan Balagi, and joker Bilal Mshaourab— inadvertently responsible for relaxing the fighter with his wit—gather around and talk about 'destiny'.

Pizza and pasta eaten, Hamdan heads home at 5 pm for an hour's sleep, and as the car drives through Marrickville he says: 'Who would have thought 16 years ago when I was hanging here and terrorising these streets that I would be fighting for a world title?'

By 7.55 pm, Hamdan is sitting in the dressing room at the Sydney Entertainment Centre, surrounded by his crew and friends. World-rated boxer and friend Hussein Hussein is among them.

'It's when they start taping you up that you really feel it, you know it's happening,' he said.

In the split second before a driver smashes his car, the stomach knots and a jolt of panic shoots through the body. Take that feeling and multiply it every minute for an hour—that's what a boxer experiences before a fight.

As another Hamdan trainer Billy Hussein began strapping his hands an hour after his arrival, the demeanour of the fighter shifted from relaxed to edgy.

At times, Hamdan's eyes seemed to plead for help. His foot tapped, he rested his head on his arms, and the few times he spoke his voice was barely audible.

Beside him was long-time friend Jimmy Barakat, a huge tattooed man likely capable of staring down an agitated gorilla.

The two spent juvenile detention together after a fight with police in which Hamdan grabbed an officer's pistol. Barakat has survived gunshots, comas and jail, but hopped from one foot to the other like a nervous child.

'It's like I'm fighting,' he said.

There is a terrible moment in dressing rooms before a fighter walks out when the silence is deafening and people put on uneasy smiles to disguise their torment.

Reflecting on that build-up later, Hamdan said: 'I had to stop myself from crying.'

Hamdan was at the entrance of the arena, his music was blaring and the audience screaming, when he walked back inside to an adjoining corridor. Wild glances were exchanged among his team.

'I had to compose myself, I was shitting myself. I took some deep breaths, bit down on my mouthguard and said, "This is it."'

He walked in to raucous cheering and thousands chanted his name for 12 rounds. Hamdan received and delivered thunderous punches, his cheek opened up, he was hurt and staggered yet continued to swing until the final bell.

Back in the rooms, there is only respect and satisfaction.

'That was the effort of the century,' Billy Hussein said. 'I am so proud of him. It is an absolute honour and pleasure to train a guy like him.'

Jouni added: 'No one gave him a chance and he showed tonight he has a ton of heart and deserved a [title] shot.'

Hamdan's other trainer, Mick Akkaway, said: 'I wouldn't call it a total success. We came for the belt and we didn't get it, but Nader gave it everything and you can't ask for more.'

Rising star Zac Awad described Hamdan as his 'inspiration'.

Hamdan knelt to kiss his son Ali, and at the same time the boxer's father, Hassan, looked down on him with eyes swelling in pride.

Hamdan searched his swirling mind for the words that would comfort a boy whose hero had fallen short, but could not find them. Yet as young Ali gazed up at his father's battered face, and the dressing-room crowd cheered and applauded, he seemed to recognise that courage is the most admired of qualities.

1 March 2008

KID WITH NO TALENT PROVED MAJOR SURPRISE

Peter Stone

Peter McWhinney, whose golfing career was done and dusted years ago, still laughs about the day he wondered what all the fuss was about with a young bloke called Tiger Woods. Sure, he was a pleasant enough kid, but without much talent. He would never win a major.

History shows that McWhinney was a poor judge with modest credentials. He won in Japan and was twice runner-up in the Australian Open.

It was November 21, 1996, and McWhinney and his Queensland mate, Peter Senior, were drawn to play with the 20-year-old Woods in the opening two rounds of the Australian Open at The Australian Golf Club. The build-up was all about Woods, who was paid, just days after he turned professional in August that year, a $300,000 appearance fee. He won twice on the US PGA Tour before heading our way.

It was front and back page news, and will be again this week when Woods returns to Sydney for the first time since 1996 in his second appearance in our national championship.

I was watching Greg Norman and Bill Clinton have a round, so I can't fill you in on Woods's first round. But McWhinney can. He, Woods and Senior played in the afternoon.

'I thought I was going to be paired with Norman, and I was actually pissed off that I was going out there with Woods in the zoo,' McWhinney says. 'There had been so much hype, and thousands turned up who knew little about golf. It had been an unwritten rule that the champion of the previous year and the runner-up [which he was] would be paired together.

'You put one Tiger on the southern shores of Sydney, and it turns into a zoo. But I had to cop it, I was playing with Pete, and it's always fun with him. Tiger seemed a nice young guy, a pleasant guy, but he was 10 over after 12 holes. I said to Pete, "I don't know mate, but this guy doesn't impress me one bit. I don't think he can play." People were saying he'd win a major. No chance, I thought. I was two over in the howling southerly, around 35 knots it was, and playing like Ben Hogan, and kicking his arse.'

Three young blokes, dressed in Tiger suits were in the gallery taking turns to wheel the buggy carrying an esky full of grog— 'Tiger! Tiger! Tiger!' They chanted any time he did anything. But, by the 13th, the guys were turning a bit nasty saying, 'The guy can't play, he's a pussycat, he's not a tiger,' McWhinney recalls.

Woods himself said the same thing in his interview, as reported by my colleague Michael Cowley: 'I'm not going to say anything. I think some of them might have had a few [beers].'

McWhinney continues: 'I can honestly say he was really enjoyable company out there. He was a young guy enjoying what he was doing—well not so much with his score at the time—and why wouldn't you be; he'd just signed for $10 million or whatever it was from Nike and Titleist. We waited on one tee, and he told a couple of jokes. He stood on the tee rubbing the toe of one foot down the sock of the other. "What's that," he asked. Pete and I just shook our heads. He said, "A black man taking his condom off."'

He used it again, once in front of four women at an official function in the US around 1997 before his management lowered the cone of silence.

But, without a hint of modesty, McWhinney says he 'made Woods's career'. Through nine holes, Woods was hitting iron off the tee when driver should have been the club around the Jack Nicklaus–designed Australian layout. 'The crowd was getting a bit ugly, and I said to him, "You've got to understand the Australian mentality, Tiger. You're 10-over par after 12 holes so just grab your driver and smash it. All they want in this country is that, it doesn't matter how crooked it goes, it's how far it goes."

'He stood on the 13th tee and took driver. I'm standing there thinking, "Not this hole [a par four of 349 metres with a dogleg right], please not this hole." He fired it down the 12th, pin-high to the 13th green and chipped over for birdie, and then hit driver, driver on the [par five] 14th where Pete hit driver, driver, seven-iron. Another birdie. By telling him to hit driver, I saved his career.'

McWhinney will dine out on the story for years. 'At the time, he wasn't the tiger. It was just a pleasant few days in the paddock with a kid I thought had no talent, one who'd never win a major,' he says.

For the record, McWhinney fell apart on the back nine, shooting nine-over 81 and then missed the cut; Woods had 79 and went on to make the cut and finished tied fifth behind Norman.

Maybe Woods will look across from The Lakes this week to the adjacent Australian course and he, too, will have his memories of 1996.

5 November 2011

THE MAN WHO MADE BRETT KIRK

Michael Cowley

You never tire of the Brett Kirk story. Not quite good conquering evil, but an uplifting, inspirational tale of a country boy's iron will, steely determination, his refusal to be told he couldn't be an AFL footballer, and how he became an icon in the game. But this isn't that Brett Kirk story.

That he bares his soul every week on the football field is not news. But in the lead-up to his final game in Sydney, the Swans leader agreed to tell the untold Brett Kirk story. It is a story of the man, not the just footballer—of how having 'sleepwalked through a large chunk' of his life because of his drive to play AFL, he developed a sudden awareness of life and people.

Not only does he consider 'that day' in December 2002 'a really big turning point in my life,' it was also 'the day my heart opened'.

Jay McNeil was in his early 30s when he joined the North Albury footy club, and immediately he and Kirk, then a teenager at that club, were drawn to one another.

'We just struck up this amazing relationship,' Kirk recalled. 'I went around there for dinner one night and met his family, his wife and his two young kids, and from that point on I spent many a night and afternoon around there at the dinner table, on their lounge, out on their back verandah.

'Jay was ahead of his time in terms of footy. He had a lot of talent but for some reason he got missed in terms of playing AFL football, but he was well respected and had a really distinguished career in the Ovens and Murray [league]. He taught me so much from a young age and I've pretty much taken that, and I'm still doing exactly the same things now that Jay and I sat down and spoke about at length all those years ago.

'We spoke about everything in life. He gave me a really good balance and I think being at that age, sometimes you need a bit of a guide in your life and he was one who came out of the blue, and basically took me under his wing. I'm not sure if he meant to do that, it's just the way it happened. He had an amazing mental strength which I really admired and I really tried to look at the way he looked at different things.

'And also as a dad, and how much affection he gave his kids, that meant a lot to me.

'It was great to be able to share it with him when I did finally make it, because throughout my life there has been people who have had big influences over me. I think as a kid it's your parents who guide you in terms of the values they instil, and then Jay was the next one who was a guide in terms of footy and life balance, and then I met Hayley [Kirk's wife] after that.'

Kirk moved to Sydney in 1999 when the Swans gave him a second chance, but he remained in constant contact with his mentor back home. He can't remember exactly when it was, but he recalls when McNeil told him he had been diagnosed with leukaemia.

'I was pretty naive. I knew how mentally strong he was and the type of person he was, I just never thought of him actually dying,' Kirk said.

'In December 2002, Hayley and I had got engaged, and I asked him to be one of my groomsmen. I remember him saying to me he was going to get himself fit. He was pretty crook at the time, but he said he would start walking from his front door to his mail box, then extend it to across the road and down the street.

'Later that month we were at Hayley's grandma's and I got a phone call from his wife Chrissy telling me Jay had passed on. It just hit me like a ton of bricks. Hayley found me in the bathroom at her nan's, bawling my eyes out, with blood all over me because I had got myself worked up so much I got a bloody nose.

'That was a really big turning point in my life. Up until then I hadn't really lost anyone close to me. I just started to question a lot of things about life and I think it opened up my spirituality in terms of questioning life and meaning.

'I gave the eulogy at his funeral—one of the toughest things I've had to do—and I remember sitting at the funeral thinking: "I don't think I told Jay that I loved him", and it dawned on me then that I was a young bloke who probably struggled to express my emotions and wasn't overly affectionate.

'I just changed from that point. I can remember walking out of the church after the funeral and I was really upset and I remember giving James, his son, a big hug and it was from there—just in terms of the way I expressed myself, the way I was around people—something in me changed.

'Jay passing on really opened up my awareness to life and what was going on around me, and to people. I think I sleepwalked through a good chunk of that life because I was so driven to play AFL and so focused and probably really selfish at times. What I wanted to give to people changed and it's changed dynamics in my own family and the way I express myself to them.

'As a teenager and in my early 20s I struggled to show that. I bottled up a lot of emotion, good, bad or indifferent, and it wasn't until I had a few drinks that I found myself a bit vulnerable at times.

'I don't really see myself as a religious person. I'm a spiritual person and I think I was drawn to Buddhism when I started to ask questions of life: why are we here, why am I here, why do good people die . . . Jay, with a young family, a great person? I started to read about different ways to look at life and I read about Buddhism and something resonated inside of me.'

Kirk was close to Jay's wife Chrissy, and their children James and Ellen, and although he was now in Sydney, he wanted to be there for the kids, who were now growing up without a father. He wanted them to know he would be there if they needed him. Later that year, James filled the role which was to be his father's, as groomsman at Brett and Hayley's wedding.

In the summer of 2008, James, a talented cricket all-rounder, received a scholarship to join the University of NSW. He spent the first three months in Sydney living with the Kirks, and it is still a weekly ritual that he dines with them each Tuesday night.

'I'm really close with James and Ellen, and they are really close with my kids now,' Kirk said.

'It's funny, but there was an age difference between Jay and myself of 14 years, which is the same as me to James, and then James to Indhi [Kirk's son].

'I want to be there for them, and if James or Ellen need me I'm there. They are both at a time in their lives now where you probably do need a bit of guidance, you're discovering where you are going or what you are doing or creating who you are and I hope I can give them the support and guidance, like their father did to me.'

'James comes to the footy a lot. He comes down the rooms and I really enjoy spending time with him. I know Jay would be really proud of the way his kids have grown up.'

Jay is never far from Kirk's thoughts, even during games, most recently when he played his final game at the SCG two weeks ago.

'I just wish he could be here now to share in what I've been able to do because he's had a massive influence on me as a person and as a footballer, but I know deep down, he's somewhere and he knows,' Kirk said.

4 September 2010

THE BIGGER PICTURE

Pursuing a yarn can take odd turns, as Jamie Pandaram discovered when he decided to write about Lopini Paea.

'This is a great example of how a story can take a life of its own and move in completely unexpected directions,' Pandaram said. 'The Roosters media manager at the time, Jodie Hawkins, pitched the idea of writing a feature on Paea given he had just become a regular starter and little was known about him. She mentioned he was interested in producing music, so this was an interesting angle I explored with Paea during an interview in his bedroom. He showed me some of his work on his computer, using software to produce hip-hop beats. It was a decent story, I thought. As I wound up the interview, I asked Paea about any experiences he believed had shaped his character. After a pause, he said that beating cancer was his greatest achievement. I literally lost my breath. Paea detailed his battle with the disease, the despair of his family, and his long road back to rugby league.

'All of a sudden I had an incredible story on my hands, but Paea was determined that if I were to write it, I had to understand the passion of his faith. He had started a prayer group for troubled youths in western Sydney and asked if I would come to a meeting. I held the story for a week so I could attend a meeting, and when I did I met Paea's teammate Charlie Tonga. Paea identified Tonga as the catalyst for his newfound faith, so after the meeting I chatted to Tonga about his own journey. What he divulged was astounding, openly admitting to have nearly murdered a man.

It struck me in that carpark, as both Paea and Tonga spoke to me in the dark, that they overcame very different struggles to be at this place with the same vision. What started as a story about a league player/wannabe music producer had become a tale of two, of recovery and redemption, united by religion.'

Other interesting discoveries are revealed in this chapter, as fellow sportswriters embarked on similar journeys.

GG

MAN FROM UNCLE: HOW TOUGH LOVE TURNED BENJI INTO A TIGER

Glenn Jackson

Benji Marshall, stoic and brash as ever, says he doesn't care. Does he wish to know his paternal father, whom he has never met? Why wish to know one father when you already have many? 'Growing up without a father, I don't know any different,' Marshall says.

It's impossible to miss what you don't know. What Marshall does know might not be a father in the strictest sense of the word, the dictionary definition, but there is no shortage of father figures—a band of uncles, all hardened men with tattoos and black belts, who taught and tamed him.

'I never even thought about knowing my father because they've all been fathers to me, and they realise that,' Marshall says. 'To tell you the truth, I don't really care [about knowing my father]. All of my uncles . . . took me in at some point in my life, took me in and looked after me, whether it be for a week or a month. I stayed with a couple of them for a couple of years. They were all like fathers to me. They used their own money to help raise me, and help my mum out. I've got about 10 or 11 fathers . . . which is not a bad thing.'

To know why this is the case, it's necessary to first ask how. Lydia Marshall gave birth to Benjamin Quentin when she was just 15 and still at school. Subsequently, the child who would become Benji spent significant time with grandparents, uncles and aunts, as well as the couple—not blood relatives— whom he came to describe as Mum and Dad, Annalie and Michael Doherty, the parents-in-law of one of Benji's uncles.

'Mick', who died in December, is the only man Benji calls Dad, but it is impossible to overstate the influence of his mother's brothers, his mother's keepers.

'There was a time I lived with four of my uncles, and they never really had any money,' he says. 'I just used to rock up to anyone's place and sleep on the floor or sleep on the couch.'

Says one of Marshall's men, his Uncle Phil: 'Sometimes I wouldn't even know he was there, and then I'd find out he'd been there for a week.'

Benji roughed it with them indoors and he roughed it with them in other ways, outdoors. While Marshall says on the whole he is a bit of a softie— 'I think I slept with my mum until I was about 11'—he was given a hard crust by those uncles.

Before he had even left his mother's bed, he was playing touch football one day with them, the men who were intent on hardening him. One, in particular, picked on him this day, and Marshall was left on the grass crying. His uncle had no mercy, telling him: 'This is what you get when you play with men. F— off home and come back when you're ready to play.'

They all thought that would end Benji's involvement for the day, but 10 minutes later he returned.

'I'm ready to play now,' the 10-year-old said.

His bones and joints have been brittle in the past but few have ever doubted his heart.

'When I was young, they used to make me cry, pick on me, but it made me stronger,' he says. 'It taught me about everything, playing with pain, having to overcome a lot of things.'

To understand Marshall, you have to first understand these men who made him. All sons of Toby Marshall, the family patriarch, they were themselves forced to grow up quicker than most. They were all brought up in the four-bedroom house, which was built by their father, a carpenter by trade, in Whakatane, in New Zealand's Bay of Plenty. The region's name was a misnomer; the only thing they had plenty of were rivals for a bed. The house was built sturdily enough but it was regularly stretched at the cladding.

'There were three or four of us sharing the bed sometimes,' Phil says.

The family had little money. Some of the children went to school without shoes. So they threw themselves into things that required little of either: touch football and martial arts.

'It was either that or bloody ending up in jail,' Phil says. 'It allowed us to do things without having to get arrested. We weren't lily-white when we were youngsters. We were sort of gangsters. We thought we were tough blokes when we were 16, bulletproof. We stuck together as a family. If one of the brothers got hurt, the other ones would feel a bit of pain. Most of us moved out of the family home by the time we were 16. We grew up really fast.'

Years later, Benji was no different, terrorising the neighbourhood ('storm troopers', as his cousin, Tu Umaga-Marshall, recalls), but at the same time showing enough talent that he could have more success terrorising athletes.

'It was a similar thing for me as it was for my uncles,' Benji says. 'A lot of my mates who I went to primary school with, they grew up and went the other way.'

While some of his friends' lives went south, Benji's went west, to the Gold Coast via Brisbane, travelling to Australia officially for a tourism course but unofficially trialling to play rugby union. Subsequently, he was spotted by a league scout, signed to a scholarship with Keebra Park State High School and plonked on the path towards a career with Wests Tigers.

'My mum couldn't pack my bag fast enough to get there,' he laughs. 'I didn't want to leave, because I didn't want to miss my brothers growing up, and leave her, but she packed my bags for me and said I had no choice, really. "Get on the plane." Once she spoke, that was it.'

Marshall describes his mother as 'one of the strongest women I know'.

'I remember when I was 15, I couldn't imagine having to look after a kid,' he says. 'Our family doesn't have the most money—sometimes you'd have Weet-Bix for breakfast and dinner, or you'd go to school and have tomato sauce sandwiches. What we lacked in money, we made up for with love.'

While his uncles gave him bloodied noses on the footy field, Lydia taught him bloody-mindedness.

'If someone tells me I can't do something, I do it,' he says. 'I guess that's why Mum always told me not to do the dishes. I like it when people say bad things about me or try to put me down.'

The biggest influence was the man who carries the same name, the uncle he was named after, who said to his sister as a joke 'Benji's a good name' before seeing it printed on the birth certificate.

'Growing up, he was my rock,' the younger Benji said. 'If Mum couldn't look after me, he'd look after me. He treated me like a son. He really has been like a father to me. When times were hard, he was always there.'

It was uncle Benji whom he asked to move to Sydney at the start of 2005 to help keep him on the straight and narrow. His uncle Benji still lives in

Westmead, with his wife, Michelle, and son Michael, as well as a grand final ring, a World Cup medal, every Kiwis jersey his nephew has worn, his first Tigers jersey, framed grand final photos—all ready to find their way back to their rightful owner when young Benji is older and nostalgic.

Who knows what the footballer will eventually want back from the father figure, and when? When it comes to the man and the men who helped raise him, Benji says he wouldn't have any of those luxuries, the jewellery or the jerseys, without them.

8 January 2010

POWER AND THE PASSION OF PAEA

Jamie Pandaram

Cancer's ghastly grip couldn't hold Lopini Paea from realising his ambition to play elite rugby league. The unforgiving walls of a jail cell failed to close in on Charlie Tonga before he emerged to reach the same destination, after taking many wrong turns.

They made it. The satisfaction, admiration and money that comes with breaking through to the NRL make for a lovely reflection with feet up.

But this isn't the time. The worn feet of Sydney Rooster Paea and former Bulldog and Rooster Tonga, having climbed separate mountains of adversity before meeting on the same path, are not done walking.

The purpose of their religious journey is to help those around them, particularly the Pacific Islander youth of south-western Sydney vulnerable to gangs and crime.

'We don't believe in coincidences,' says Paea, who will play against Wests Tigers tonight. He is referring to all the circumstances that conspired to bring him and Tonga together.

They could have—and should have—missed each other.

Ten years ago, Paea was lying in a hospital bed believing 'leukaemia is just when you lose all your hair', while in the hallway his family was breaking down.

'I was only 13, I didn't really understand what was happening to me,' says Paea, who now sports an afro.

Seven years ago, Tonga nearly beat a man to death in a drunken rage. With wrists handcuffed, he was sentenced to two years' jail at Queensland's highest security prison, Woodford Correctional Centre.

'I was an alcoholic, a drug addict,' Tonga says. 'I never had a mum or dad, I was looking for love in all the wrong places.'

Yet here they stand, in this warehouse-turned-church tucked away in the corner of an industrial estate near Campbelltown, singing the praises of a higher being in full voice. Arms rise, tears fall.

Among the 50 or so believers gathered on this still night, you can play 'spot the lower-grade Rooster': Paea's younger brother Mickey on drums, Steve Meredith on the microphone, and Frank-Paul Nuuausala and George Ndaira seated near the stage where people get up to sing a mixture of karaoke and gospel tunes.

This is Power Up, a class set up by Tonga, the Paeas and Meredith primarily to steer Islander teens from the Campbelltown–Minto area towards life in accordance with the Bible. The players—all members of the Hillsong Church—are driven by a mission to reduce the increasing rate of crime committed by that demographic.

'We hold it on a Thursday night to keep the kids away from the shopping malls because it's late-night shopping,' Paea says. 'We thought it's better for them to come to Power Up than be hanging around the streets causing trouble. It's a place they can come to hang out, talk about their feelings, sing, rap, just have fun.

'We empower kids to go out and make something of their lives. A lot of kids use the excuse that they're from the rough part of Minto, they don't have opportunities, but we tell them, "I grew up next door to you. We're from the same crappy neighbourhood, we come from the same streets, and we made something of ourselves so you can reach your goals."'

The goal of playing in the NRL, so common among their targets, was an impossible dream for Paea as he endured two years of treatment to cure acute lymphoblastic leukaemia.

He recalls the day he found out. 'It was in 1997—the last week of November. I woke up and my mouth was bleeding on the inside.'

The diagnosis was followed by pain. 'We decided against radiation treatment. But the drugs I was taking make you really sick.

'I was throwing up every day. I gained 35 kilos. I didn't have the energy to do one lap of an oval . . . I never thought I would play again.'

To the contrary, Paea recovered and returned to the field at 16, dramatically regaining form to catch the eye of Roosters talent scouts, who quickly signed him and Mickey.

Paea wears a constant reminder of what he has overcome on his chest; the scar from the Port-a-cath intravenous device used during treatment.

Tonga's scars are buried in his conscience. In jail, his transformation from wrong to righteous occurred after some harsh realisations.

'I was broken, my friends deserted me, nobody came to see me. Only Christ,' Tonga says.

Another prisoner had urged Tonga to read the Bible, telling the Queensland Cup footballer it was his only hope if he did not want to return for a longer stint. While Tonga's prosecutors had fought to incarcerate him for five years, he served nine months before walking out a changed man.

'I used to sit in jail and wonder what would happen when I came out,' he says. 'God gave me an opportunity with the Bulldogs, and I changed my whole lifestyle.'

At 28, when most first-grade players are thinking of signing their last contract, Tonga signed his first and moved to Canterbury. After one season, he joined the Roosters where he met the Paeas and Meredith. One night he invited them to play cards, told his life story and convinced them to take the holy walk with him.

'When you do trust in God, you get that peace,' Paea says. 'It doesn't happen overnight, it is a work in progress—it took me a couple of months to give up drinking.'

The singing voices, powerful in unison, flow out of this church door and cut through the night air, but there's no one else around to hear it.

One of the young members of the gathering, Korey Johnson-Too, tells the *Herald*: 'I used to try to slit my throat and cut my wrists—I tried to commit suicide eight times.'

In his 17 years, he has moved from one foster home to another, but is now settled with a family affiliated with the Hillsong Church and Power Up group.

'I haven't smoked or taken drugs for two years,' he says.

Professionally, Paea and Tonga are moving in different directions: Paea has established himself as an NRL player in the past month; the Roosters released Tonga two weeks ago.

Spiritually, they move together. The view is nice up here, but they feel it'd be better shared with people still climbing their own mountains.

10 August 2007

A FORCE FOR UNITY,
DOGGED DETERMINATION PROVES THE
POWER OF ONE SKINNY LAD

Peter Roebuck

As Shivnarine Chanderpaul, a waif with a pixie's face, was stroking his way to 62 on a Test debut made in 1994 on his home pitch in Georgetown, Guyana, a female voice cried out across the ground: 'If dis Chanderpaul think he marry a foreigner, he don think again.'

Another woman, selling biscuits and sweets by the side of a potholed road, said: 'I like dis boy, he so young and he play all the shots.' And it was the Afro-Caribbeans who invaded the pitch as the frail teenager, of Indian descent, reached his 50. Guyana had immediately taken Chanderpaul to its heart.

He is a local lad, born into a fisherman's family in a village called Unity, an hour's drive from Georgetown along the coast of a country whose population hugs the seas, the interior being thick with forest. Unity is a subsistence village; its wooden houses are built on stilts and its hospital and leper colony closed long ago, times having been hard in Guyana. Apart from a small field, it has no sports facilities. Yet Unity has produced two Test cricketers, Colin Croft and Chanderpaul.

The latter's cricketing pedigree was promising. Kemraj, his father, played good cricket and kept wicket to Croft, who lives a sand wedge away. Both uncles played for strong clubs and Davi, his sister, wielded a fine bat. 'They could pelt it as hard as they like and she stand up. But her shoulders slim and there no ladies' cricket round here,' recalled Kemraj.

From the start, Chanderpaul was a cricketer. 'When he was in his mother's belly she bowl to me,' says his father, whereupon uncle Martin adds: 'When he was a boy, I soak the bat and he drink the oil.' Thereafter, it seems, a life in cricket was inevitable.

At the age of eight he started practising in the local community hall, which is not as posh as it sounds. 'I start he inside,' says Kemraj. 'I heard Kanhai practised on concrete. It's the same idea. We got our own calculations here. Finally, we had to stop because damage to de balls got expensive. So I took he outside.'

But outside there were no nets, no pitch, just a small field of rough grass upon which goats and cows periodically grazed. Undeterred, they rolled and cut a pitch and sewed a net from the ones Kemraj used every day to catch bottle fish for the overseas market. The wicket remained muddy and bumpy.

By then Chanderpaul was batting three or four hours a day. He'd go to school with his bags and bat and ball, throw his bags away and run to the nets. 'The teacher wasn't pleased,' Kemraj recalled, 'but he pleased now.'

At 13, the boy left school. 'He play cricket all the time anyhow,' says his father. The entire village was behind him, volunteers bowling morning, noon or night, the boy practising in rain or shine. On match days, they'd crowd around him so that he hardly had room to breathe. Long ago, he learnt to live with pressure.

Kemraj used to talk to his son late into the night. 'I tell he to watch the footwork of Kallicharran. I tell he Gavaskar never go out in the 90s. I tell he, if you afraid get hit, stop playing the game. Little children go out and play all kinds of things. I tell he marbles never carry you nowhere.'

Taking his father's advice, Chanderpaul decided to aim for the top. His father said he must try to play for Guyana while still a youth and then to 'knock down the door of the West Indies so he can go in'.

Chanderpaul rose quickly, joined the prestigious Georgetown Cricket Club, scored 117 on debut and left saying 'something is wrong with my batting'. He did not like club practices because he could bat for only 10 minutes, compared with three hours at home. But he persisted, and word of him soon spread.

By that stage we'd drunk lots of coconut water and talked for hours and it was time for lunch. Then Chanderpaul wandered in, for it was the rest day during his debut Test. He had come home on one of the mini-buses upon which all except the rich travel, but he had not had to pay his fare.

Chanderpaul proved shy but ready to smile. He was a little embarrassed that his relatives were displaying an exercise book with cuttings glued in. He confirmed he didn't like getting out, saying: 'If the ball hit me, nothing wrong. I can't get out.' He added: 'When I get mad, I hook off the front foot.'

He slept in a small room with a mosquito net, a chest expander and lots of cricket bats. He had not expected to play in the Test and thought: 'Reaching the side is one thing, staying in it is the main thing.' He'd been pleased to score 62 but was vexed to fall short of three figures. The sigh of disappointment when he lost his wicket to a long hop could be heard across Georgetown. The boy was furious, his father understanding.

Already he had achieved much. Chanderpaul knew his selection was controversial. He also knew an entire village and half a country were watching, expecting him to do well, for as his father said, 'Since he small the whole island know he'. The thin boy with a gentle smile had taken it all, and scored 62 in his first Test. He was determined and level-headed and more would be heard of him.

17 November 2005

WE CAN'T FORGET BUT WE CAN FORGIVE: CAMPBELL

Brad Walter

On the eve of his greatest achievement, Indigenous All Stars captain Preston Campbell has revealed his biggest fear and a key reason for him organising tonight's historic match at Skilled Park.

'I'm scared,' Campbell told the *Herald* in an extensive interview at the team's Gold Coast hotel, where his emotions ranged from pride at the quality of the Aboriginal team to despair and sadness over the centuries of suffering still being felt by his race.

'A lot of us indigenous people are dying at a young age. The average life expectancy these days for an adult indigenous male is in the fifties [53], which is pretty scary. Even though I am a fit person or a fit man, I'm likely to keel over just like that. The indigenous life expectancy for a man is much shorter than for the normal Australian male [78] and that scares me.'

Campbell stressed repeatedly during the interview that he was not trying to make a political statement.

But through his upbringing in Tingha and the hours of community work he does each week, the Titans fullback knows first-hand the devastating impact the British invasion in 1788 and racist government policies since, such as assimilation and the White Australia policy, have had.

'They talk about the great wars of the world but there was a war pretty much here in Australia and so many people died,' Campbell said. 'When I was playing [for] Penrith, the local people down there talked about how they fought for nearly 40 years for their land.

'It takes a long time to get over things like that and some people haven't got over it and maybe they never will. People lost family, they lost friends and then there is the Stolen Generation.

'A lot of people really couldn't do anything about stopping them from taking their kids away and whether they feel bad about not being able to do enough to save their kids from being taken away or whether they just felt helpless or whether they felt like they weren't there for their kids . . . There is just so much missing and whether they missed out on their child's first words or first footsteps, those are things you can't get back.'

Among the stories Campbell recounted was that of the Myall Creek Massacre, a racially motivated mass murder in northern NSW in 1838 in which a group of 12 white men killed 28 Aborigines, most of who were women and children. After initially being found not guilty, seven of the settlers were convicted of murder in a retrial and hanged.

'That happened not far from where I grew up [Tingha] and I know that it is really hard for the people back home to get past that,' he said.

'It's not like someone has come and stolen their car or their money. They killed their families and their friends and they took their kids away but I think the only way we can get past that is to work together, and as human beings we need to do that to see the future out.'

One giant step towards the healing process, Campbell believes, will be the match tonight.

Coinciding with the second anniversary of Prime Minister Kevin Rudd's national apology for the stolen generation, the public's reaction to the idea of a full-strength indigenous team playing an NRL All Stars line-up has filled him and the other players in the side with great pride and hope for the future.

'This is part of the healing process,' Campbell said. 'It's a football game but it's about a lot more than just football. Football is a big part of a lot of indigenous people's lives and I don't think people realise how important it is for us to be able to put this game on.

'So many devastating things have happened, people are finding it hard to get over that and the consequences of what happened are still around. It is something we can't forget but maybe there is a chance we can forgive. I think the only way we can move forward as a country and as human beings is to work together and that is what this game is about.'

The more than $1.5 million raised from the match will be used to fund

Australia with Anthony [Mundine] and Gabi by my side. Reality says things may not go that way. My heart is in my relationship.

'I could give football away and be with Gabi and be happy. I may be able to get back into it one day.'

As Richens was indulging in a facial and other luxury treatments, Haumono was looking anything but destructive as he tried to sidestep Sydney's media.

The plan of the Men in Black—the close friends shared by Haumono and Anthony 'The Man' Mundine—was in turmoil.

Abs, Fedi, Claude and Ross were Mundine and Haumono's crew on this job and just plain good mates every other day.

'We wanted to make a clean getaway, but this Channel 9 situation got in the way,' said Abs. And Fedi, owner of the appropriately named Spy cafe in the city, said: 'The media circus was out of control.

'Even the police were questioning us. We wanted to get Choc [Mundine] to training and then get Sol back to headquarters [the cafe] so he could chill with the boys.'

The boys knew Richens was coming to town before the media did. Mundine had tipped them off on a stopover. They knew Channel 9 was paying the way via a small sum of cash and accommodation.

But they didn't realise how seriously Nine was treating its investment. From the airport to the hotel, Haumono was accompanied by a Nine producer and from then on by a bodyguard.

'They weren't letting Sol out of their sights,' said Abs. 'It was like something out of a movie.'

Outside Haumono's room were two other guards.

'Solomon couldn't believe it,' said Abs. 'They checked him and his parents in and gave them all these rooms.'

The family was booked in under the name Smith.

The Men in Black weren't excluded, but they couldn't run the show as they had up to that point, including putting Haumono in touch with Mundine when they were both in England.

'I had to ring back to HQ to try to find Sol,' Mundine said.

'I couldn't get in touch with him so I got the boys to ring him. He was supposed to meet me at the airport, but I knew why he couldn't. Eventually our paths crossed.'

community programs supported by the NRL's 16 clubs and, at Campbell's urging, the Titans have allocated their share to a health initiative aimed at closing the gap between the mortality rates of indigenous Australians and the general population.

Campbell said he also hoped the match would encourage young indigenous people to aspire to greater achievements.

'We've got people drinking, sniffing petrol, doing drugs and we know that's in all walks of life but it's more so in indigenous communities,' he said.

'Maybe something like this here can inspire or show indigenous people that there is more to life than sniffing petrol, there is more to life than smoking drugs and there is more to life than drinking. If you put your mind to it you can pretty much be anything you want.

'I know the footballers in this team come from different walks of life but we're all footballers and we've all had to do the same things to get here and we've all had to work really hard to get here. We just want kids and people in the indigenous community to know that if we can do it so can you.'

13 February 2010

PLEASURE HUNT

Danny Weidler

Gabrielle Richens was in a pleasure zone, lying back in a five-star Sydney hotel getting a facial.

She had beaten lover Solomon Haumono and his rescuer, Anthony Mundine, into town on Thursday and was unwinding.

'My life has been turned upside down since Solomon arrived on my doorstep,' said Richens, who has no problem with her 'Pleasure Machine' tag, which originated from her role in an advertisement for British airline Virgin.

The passion play starring league's Romeo and Juliet is set for a long run.

'It's been such a strange week. I know he loves me so much and I love him. I can see a happy ending.

'Don't worry, we are not going to end up like Romeo and Juliet. We won't kill each other off.'

The long-distance romance will face another challenge this week when Richens is due to fly home.

'If I can get work in Australia I'll stay, but otherwise I have to go,' she told *The Sun-Herald*.

If Haumono had his way he would follow his heart and fly out with her. That would open up a new chapter in the love story, but most likely would be the final sentence for Haumono's Australian career.

He is prepared to give everything up for Richens, who admits to knowing next to nothing about league, which she calls 'rugby'.

'I don't even know how many players are on the field, but I do know that Solomon is one of the most destructive players on the field,' she said.

'If it was an ideal world,' Haumono begins, 'I would be playing league in

Mundine walked into Richens' life a few days after Haumono made his great escape.

'Solomon just called me and said "Babe, what are you doing for the next week?"' and he asked "Can you get some time off?"' she said.

'He knew not to say to me what he was doing because I would have freaked out. It was nice to see him, but I was worried.

'He's only young. I wish I could get through to him.'

But on the subject of Richens, not even Mundine, his buddy of more than 20 years, can get through. Mundine chooses his words carefully when asked what Solomon Haumono means to him.

'I never had a brother,' he said. 'Solomon is just like my brother. I'd die for him. The reason I went was because I love him. I don't like seeing him hurting. I also don't want him to waste his talent and I'm sure he won't.

'I told him Canterbury could hurt his career and that he could go down if he didn't come back.

'I didn't go there to try and sign him to St George. I could have done that plenty of other times. He has a talent and I want to make sure he doesn't waste it.'

Mundine said outsiders did not realise the relationship and the emotional connection between the pair. 'It extends to our families,' he said. 'Our relationship is priceless.

'In our cultures, it's all about bonding. When I greeted him in a cafe in London I just gave him a hug.

'I told him how women all over Australia would think he is a Romeo. I'd have done the same thing for my woman and he'd have done the same thing for me.

'That's why mainstream Australia is freaking out. They don't understand our link.'

Haumono simply says of Richens: 'She's my woman, she's my life, she's my everything.'

He hadn't seen Richens for nearly a year, and his monthly phone bills were about $1,500. He is hurting enough to seriously consider quitting football, as he feels he is no longer fully committed to the game.

Richens said: 'I worry about him a lot when I know he is down. When I was with him we had some ups and downs, but that is part of a relationship.

'I thought I'd go back to England and see how he went on his own.

'But then he got fined by Canterbury just before Christmas and now with him coming over, I really think that I should be in Australia. If something [came] up I'd definitely settle in Sydney.'

Richens said Haumono's quiet manner was an instant attraction.

'He is polite beyond belief,' she said. 'He lets me get my own way all the time and he spoils me rotten.

'When we lived together, he'd get up before me and go to McDonald's and get me breakfast because he knows I love it and he'd bring it to me in bed.'

Sitting together, Mundine was listening carefully to everything Haumono was saying in his interview with *The Sun-Herald*—especially when he spoke of the possibility of quitting.

'That's not what you're going to do, Sol, is it?' interrupted Mundine. 'It's too soon to say. You'll talk to your family first and then decide.'

Haumono thought for a moment, then answered quietly but firmly.

'Whatever I do, my parents will support . . . but I'm my own man,' he said.

14 June 1998

WANTING IT ALL

Kathryn Wicks

As a netballer, Mo'onia Gerrard is the ultimate don't-mess-with-me, white-line-fever girl. But sitting in a Kensington cafe, she's just Mon, a confident yet relaxed young woman faced with the same career-versus-life dilemma that occupies the thoughts of many 31-year-olds.

Here's the dilemma. At present she is the co-captain of the NSW Swifts netball team, which begins its 2012 season on Saturday.

She hasn't played in a Commonwealth Games gold-medal winning team because of an awful knee injury in 2006, so she would really like to have a crack in Glasgow in 2014. And the next netball world championships will be held in Sydney, her home town, in 2015.

She'd really like to try her hand at rugby—her brother, Mark, and her boyfriend, Dave Dennis, both play in the Super Rugby competition—and represent Australia ('or, if they don't want me, Tonga') in rugby sevens at the Rio Olympics in 2016.

'I just get itchy,' she says. 'I think it's from my dad. I just want to have a crack. Maybe it is a risk, but whatever.'

In her spare time she is heavily involved in developing netball in Tonga, and runs her own active-wear fashion business, MonStar.

Oh, and she wants to have six kids.

'The kids are coming!' she says. 'I'll probably have kids in between.'

In between what I can't quite figure, and she had better get busy if she wants six.

Previously a bit of a taboo subject—few Australian women have returned to international netball after having children—the matter is now in the open under new Australian coach Lisa Alexander.

'Lisa has been pretty good,' Gerrard says. 'She's expressed that we're a ladies sport, a female sport, and we have to encourage these girls to be females.

'It's never been put out there before, women having babies and playing sport. It's always been one or the other and that's how I always had perceived it from when I was a kid. I didn't know anyone who had a kid while they were playing.'

That has not been the experience in New Zealand though, where many players have had children at a relatively young age then returned to the court. The New Zealand goal shooter Irene van Dyk, 39, has a 13-year-old daughter.

'And they're still playing. It's cool. If they can do it, why can't we? Lisa has put it out there, and says if you want one I'm not going to discourage you. We are females and that is what we are supposed to do.'

But did Alexander really mean six?

'I want six. I want half a netball squad. My mum is from a massive family, she is one of eight. But it is just me and my brother. I used to say 'Mum, this is boring.' So my brother is about to have his fourth. He's way ahead of me.'

There is no doubt [having] children is something she wants, the question remains when. She is serious about rugby but acknowledges she cannot play netball and rugby for Australia at the same time if she wants to succeed at rugby.

'The hardest thing is we have got the [netball] World Cup 2015 in Sydney and Lisa Alexander says, "What are you going to do?" And I say, "Well, there's a few things."

'The Australian Rugby Union has been pretty cool with it. They are willing to help me whichever way I want to pursue it. I was training with them at the end of last year so I'm interested. I just have to find the time to throw it all together and if I have to sacrifice my Aussie [netball] stuff to play sevens rugby then so be it.

'But I'm looking at all that next year.'

For now, this netball season brings new challenges for Gerrard as captain for the first time. She feels no pressure around the job and believes that actions speak louder than words.

'I don't feel any pressure whatsoever,' she says. 'If I go out there and play my own game and get that right everything will fall into place. And I know that the girls will look at that and think "Mon's doing it, why can't I do it?" That's how I see myself on the court leading the team.'

Her toughness, she says, comes from the backyard, playing footy with her brother and cousins. She didn't play Barbies. 'I had one but I wasn't into it. I was more into constructing the house than putting clothes on the Barbie.'

She is most proud of her work in Tonga, where she has helped establish Mo'onia's Cup, a netball tournament for young women.

If there is one thing that gets her motivated it is helping young people achieve their dreams. 'I'm just trying to encourage them to get out there and get active and get healthy because they're not really looked upon to be active or achieve certain things in sport. It's always been male dominated.

'I have got two great aunties who have helped enormously to get the word out there. So netball in Tonga, the association, is starting to get some people on board to help develop the game and introduce it to high schools. That's my biggest passion at the moment, to develop a team.'

Just how she accomplishes everything she wants to remains to be seen. But you get the feeling that for Gerrard it isn't impossible.

'I think women are good at juggling a few things at the same time,' she says. 'I've got no qualms about that.'

26 March 2012

MEARES GEARS UP FOR FINAL STOUSH

Georgina Robinson

While British golden girl Victoria Pendleton's face and body lit up screens and billboards all over London in the lead-up to the Olympic Games, Anna Meares trained in anonymity in northern Italy.

When every English newspaper splashed with Pendleton's take on the most hyped rivalry in track cycling and how it might play out in London, no one could get to Meares.

The 28-year-old from Central Queensland was holed up with the Australian sprint cycling team in Montichiari, a small town in scenic Lombardy, preparing quietly for what could be the final showdown between the two undisputed queens of the velodrome. Decamping to mainland Europe allowed the team to escape winter in Adelaide. But it also removed Meares from the spotlight—first in Australia and then in London, where Pendleton is 'Queen Victoria' and Meares is portrayed as some sort of athletic wicked witch, the fly in 'Our Vicky's' ointment and the biggest obstacle to the 31-year-old's perfect Olympic swansong.

Today, the games begin. The pair meet in the first of three events they will both contest, the team sprint. 'I am relaxed and confident that I have done all the work that I could have possibly done,' Meares said from Montichiari shortly before she left for London. 'I don't believe there is anything more or anything that I could have done better . . . I am in the form of my career.'

She will need to be. Though favourite to win the individual sprint and the keirin, Meares learnt four months ago, when she was pushed into disqualification at the track cycling world championships in Melbourne, how badly Pendleton wants to finish her career on top.

It was the latest, extraordinary twist in their rivalry. Before Beijing, where Meares took silver—behind Pendleton—seven months after breaking her neck in a cycling accident, the Australian was used to playing second fiddle in the sprint.

It took Meares another three years to crack a victory—an emotional win at the world championships in Holland—and she maintained the upper hand with a semi-final win over Pendleton in the Olympic test event in February. The Melbourne race in April has given Sunday's sprint showdown a deliciously uncertain edge.

'There are so many components you have to get right to end up on top,' Meares said of her favourite event. 'You can be the fastest and lose, you can have all the skill and technique yet lose. This race is about who can compile all the qualities and components required to win, who can perform under pressure, [who's] done their homework, who knows their opponent's strengths and weaknesses, who can confront another and outwit them. It is the most difficult and challenging race I have ever had to ride . . . it tests me to the max.'

Pendleton has made it clear she wants a normal life after London. No more soul-baring documentaries, no more glamorous fashion shoots, no more pressure to win, win, win. From her training base across the channel, Meares followed a lot of the commentary on their rivalry but didn't think she stood to benefit from Pendleton's sky-high profile.

'If Vicky can keep herself grounded and not allow the many distractions of being a home Games and of being a face of the Games to a minimum then no, it is of no help to me, the spotlight she is under,' Meares said. 'She has proven many times in the past she can handle it, I am not expecting any different. She is a good competitor, as are all the other girls.'

Two weeks ago, Meares stopped posting on Twitter. The usually relaxed and bubbly voice on social media fell silent. 'Thanks for the support. See u all after its all been run,' she posted in her farewell.

'The build-up has been long and the excitement hard to control,' Meares said from Montichiari around the same time. 'Nerves are there but under control ... I hope I can do something great and all I want is that chance. The rest is up to me to get over the line—first.'

2 August 2012

THE FORCE IS WITH HER

Carlie Ikonomou

Dual international Ellyse Perry remains virtually anonymous among her university peers. To many, she is just the girl in daggy tracksuit pants who often runs late for class.

During summer, the fast bowler and agile right-winger juggles her demanding international football and cricket duties with university commitments. 'Everyone is quite trendy at university, so I sometimes feel embarrassed turning up in my training gear,' Perry said. 'At times I cringe, but in those kind of situations, it is nice that not many people recognise you.'

Perry is one of the fastest female bowlers in the world, has nearly 5000 fans on Facebook and possesses a lethal right foot that would unsettle even the most seasoned goalkeepers. Yet, she remains the same down-to-earth, disciplined young woman who her friends and family knew as a 12-year-old aspiring to play for Australia.

It is Perry's relaxed sense of humour, humble disposition and composure on and off the field that has elevated her to almost cult-like status in women's football and cricket.

Perry ventured into uncharted sporting territory at 16, when she became the youngest athlete, male or female, to represent Australia in cricket and football. Since then, she has exponentially driven the profile of women's sport.

'The most exciting thing about women's sport in Australia is the improvement and steps forward that have been made—it is fantastic,' Perry said. 'There is more and more coverage of women's sport and girls now see it as an opportunity to develop a professional career.'

When asked how she felt about being such a role model for young athletes,

Perry said she felt privileged. 'I don't know if I do that,' she said. 'But it is certainly nice to be in the position that I am — to meet so many people from different walks of life, to know that your experiences can help others in their pursuits and that you might have had an impact.'

The phenomenal athlete developed her passion for both sports as a young girl playing backyard cricket and football with her father. She continues to attribute her success to the pivotal role her parents have played in advocating the importance of a healthy and active lifestyle.

'From my earliest memories, my parents always emphasised the physical outdoors. I developed a huge affinity and love for doing all those things because of them,' Perry said. 'Dad was always there to help me learn and develop my skills — he still is my main coach for cricket. My parents have always been extremely supportive of anything I do.'

Earlier this year, Perry was given an ultimatum by Canberra United chief executive Heather Reid and coach Jitka Klimkova that amounted to 'quit cricket to play football or leave the club'.

It prompted several supporters to voice their concerns for the athlete who had so admirably balanced her commitments between the two. Others supported Canberra's move towards greater professionalism.

Yet Perry accepted the decision and harbours no animosity. 'I completely understand where they are coming from in terms of wanting to progress and develop a culture and philosophy around the club — that is coach Jitka Klimkova's prerogative and I accept that,' Perry said. 'I absolutely loved the three seasons I played for Canberra. I still have a good relationship with everyone there and if it had worked out my first choice would always be to play for Canberra.'

The ultimatum has not deterred the Australian representative away from football — rather, it has reinforced her passion and desire to excel in both sports.

'I still love playing both cricket and football, and for as long as that is possible I would like to continue,' Perry said. 'I have been fortunate enough to have some other opportunities and I am fairly confident that I will be playing in the W-League this year.'

Perry is preparing for the Women's Twenty20 World Cup, which will be held in Sri Lanka this September. Having narrowly defeated New Zealand in the 2010 final, Perry is hoping to defend Australia's coveted title.

Shortly after returning from the tournament, she will continue her juggling act, dividing her commitments between the W-League and the Women's National Cricket League. It is certainly not your typical sedentary summer, but Perry relishes the challenge. 'It is actually a lot of fun,' she said.

'During the summer season I train twice a day, I go to university two or three days a week. I play my cricket matches on Friday and Sunday, but will miss one game a week when I play for my W-league team.'

As for downtime? Perry laughs. 'I am lucky that some of my closest friends still live nearby; I really enjoy just catching up with them — it helps me to unwind.'

In the long term, Perry hopes to continue to play a pivotal role in both national squads, with an ultimate goal of winning the FIFA Women's World Cup. 'Football is so globally oriented, so it would be incredible to win a World Cup,' she said. 'It would be wonderful for women's football in Australia and women's sport in general if we were to achieve that result.'

But she is under no illusions that Australia will easily slide into Olympic or World Cup final contention. 'Being in the Asian Confederation has been an exceptionally competitive thing,' she said. 'We have come ahead in leaps and bounds, having been in constant competition against a host of countries. But we now have to earn our right to qualify for world competition.'

But for now, think twice before you raise an eyebrow at the young woman wearing tracksuit pants and training gear around the university campus. It is probably Ellyse Perry.

28 July 2012

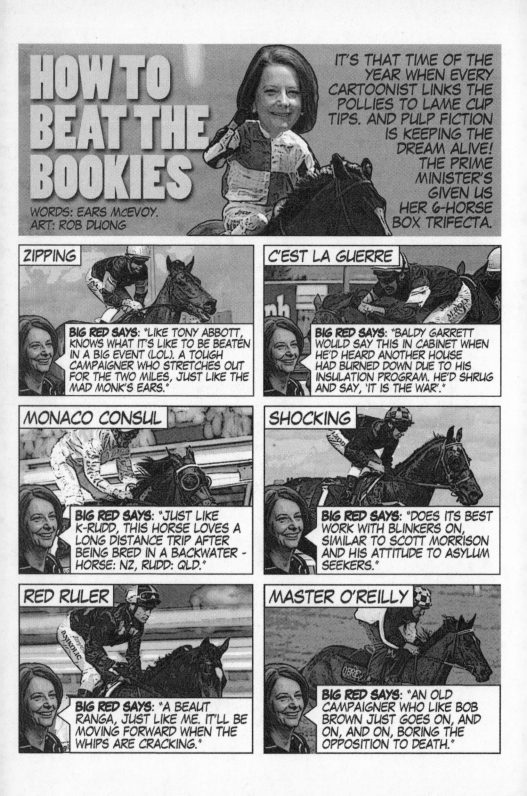

LEFT FIELD

Sportswriters are always searching for the ultimate last line, the classic punch line. Evan Whitton, one of Australia's most renowned investigative reporters and a provocative rugby union columnist, once provided me with the advice: 'Make certain there is one joke in your story. They'll soon forget the story, but they'll remember the joke.' Good advice, even if many readers fail to understand irony.

You often hear sportswriters on the phone trying to calm down agitated readers with the line: 'No, no, no it's a joke.' The good jokes don't get the phone calls. Instead they are remembered.

In this chapter, Paul Kent, who loves a good yarn and a good joke, shows how you can grip the reader with something from left field. His piece on Joe Louis revolves around the last line, and his greyhound story revolves around something different about the dog's anatomy. Proper Tears indeed.

Kent has moved on to News Limited and made a name for himself on television—using the same philosophy, make your point, but never lose sight of the humour. After all most people pursue sport as it is an escape. Never forget that, and the good writers work on that theory, ensuring that they not only enlighten but also entertain.

GG

MONDAY MAUL

Greg Growden

In response to the 100 reasons why we love rugby league in Saturday's *Sydney Morning Herald*, here's 100 reasons why *Monday Maul* loves rah-rah:

Dave Brockhoff. Test matches actually mean something. No one has written: 'Rugby was the winner'—until now. The Rat pies at Rat Park. No Kings Cross shootings. The World Cup is an old soccer trophy. Field goals mean something. The haka. Conversations with Ben Perkins. The gibberish before NSW–Queensland games. Buddha Handy and his wrestling singlet.

Lunch with Nick Farr-Jones at the Nippon Club. Being in New Zealand when the All Blacks lose. Bomber the kicking-tee dog. Fort Fumble. Players calling referees 'Sir'. George Ayoub. The green frogs at the Millner Field canteen. Vikings v Shamrocks. No one actually wears leather patches. Campo. Campo's quotes. Campo upsetting everyone. Campo laughing it off. Bordeaux oysters.

Tussling with Phil Wilkins for the lead in the *SMH* tips panel. Scott Johnson when doing the New Zealand poxy island routine. The craic of Dublin. It never claims to be the greatest game of all. Nick Farr-Jones meeting Ringo Starr in Monaco (ask NFJ). What other sport produces the Hammer from Kiama? The laws don't make sense. Tah Man.

Wristy le Roux's peek-a-boo photographs. Eddie Jones press conferences. Watching Fast Eddie give someone the 'stink eye'. Murray Mexted's bizarre commentating. Nooky Tindall. Tonga beating Australia in 1973. Spike Milligan's a big fan. Long lunches with Mark Ella. Short lunches with Ella. Any lunch with Ella. No one in Australia really caring when the Wallabies lose. Campo's 'Hail Mary' pass to Tim Horan in 1991. Fab Fenton.

The steak sandwiches at Southern Districts. The SFS pies. Tom Richards.

The lunatics on the mike at University Oval. Buddha Handy lighting up his face with Chartreuse. Dave Brockhoff (the legend deserves a second mention). The Bledisloe Cup disappearing for a decade. The Bledisloe Cup being named after someone who had no interest in the game. Knowing what physical acts have occurred with the cup used as a prop.

The pre-Test function at Dunedin's Speights Brewery. Waking next morning still in the brewery. Bluff oysters. Players have two-syllable-plus vocabularies. Coaches too—sometimes. 4am Chippy Lane in Cardiff—chips with curry sauce a specialty. Hearing *The Land of My Fathers* in Cardiff. *La Marseillaise* in Paris. *Scotland the Brave* in Edinburgh. The south of France. The luge at Rotorua (pre helmets). Stan Pilecki. John Eales complaining that nobody calls him by the nickname 'nobody.' The game being a nonsense, but a serious nonsense. Tony Shaw. Shaw's 50th birthday invitation, which included 'Wrestling togs are optional'. Robin Williams meeting Jonah Lomu and telling onlookers: 'Quickly! Tell the other villagers we go now!' Being there for the 1991 and 1999 World Cup triumphs. Bob Dwyer giving it to a referee. 'Wallaby Bob' McMaster—wrestling's greatest ref. A Chinese-Midori lunch with Jeffrey Sayle. Sayle's kookaburra laugh. Nude Penrith training sessions. Australia v France, 1987, Concord. Flip Westhuizen. Subbies footy.

The mascot of the first Wallabies in 1908 being a carpet snake called Bertie. Australia almost originally called 'The Rabbits'. Steve Merrick. Kings Bar, Le Grande Motte, French Riviera, ask for Christy. Nugget May. It produced the worst hospital pass in history—Peter FitzSimons to Phil Scarr, NSW v Auckland, Eden Park, 1990. Classic player–coach conversations such as between Penrith coach Fab Fenton (impressed with the fitness work of his first-grade prop): 'You obviously know the difference between fat and cholesterol' and the prop's response: 'Don't know about that, coach, I've never woken up with a cholesterol.'

ARU chief 'Smokin' Joe French conducting press conferences in his pyjamas. Nelson Mandela in a Springbok jersey. Wallaby tours provide an opportunity to visit Mandela's cell on Robben Island. Watching Springbok fans hand their guns in at Johannesburg Airport. The *Herald* Cup flattened by a fruit truck on Parramatta Road. A night out with Dan Crowley on the Riviera. Actually remembering it. Watching Clive Woodward lose the plot. Ken Elphick. Concord Oval. Meeting more than 7000 All Black trialists in the past 20 years.

And finally, a Wallabies tour doesn't mean six weeks in Leeds.

10 March 2008

A ROLLERCOASTER RIDE FOR A FLASHING GREYHOUND ROMEO

Paul Kent

When Joe Corte tells you the name of his dog, he says, without the slightest hint of irony, his name is Proper Tears. And his tale is enough to make you weep.

It begins on the Gold Coast last year when Proper Tears was entered in the Gold Coast Cup, a 457 m race with a $35,000 first prize.

By the end of his heat, Proper Tears, a white and black dog blessed with explosive early speed, had run a sizzling 25.08 s which left those in the know standing solid with mouths agape.

It was a world record. Corte leashed his dog in the catching pen and walked him back to the kennels, washing him down before heading off to give a urine sample.

All was right until a fortnight after the final, which Proper Tears also won, when stewards went to Corte to tell him there was an irregularity in the sample. Proper Tears had tested positive to lignocaine, a painkiller used in horses and dogs alike to get them running freely.

Joe Corte disputed the decision but stewards disqualified Proper Tears and with it went the cheque and the world record.

Corte hired a Sydney lawyer to fight the disqualification in court. He claimed if lignocaine was present then it would be only a minor amount and only because he had been feeding the dog horse meat.

Slow thoroughbreds make fine dining, and in court the trainer Corte tried to have the amount of lignocaine present revealed, as if to justify his claim it was not purposely administered.

'If there was anything in him it would only be a minor, minor amount,' Corte says.

But stewards, Corte says, would not reveal the quantity of lignocaine, only confirming its presence as they were required to do. After spending $15,000 to fight the decision, Corte finally dropped off.

Meanwhile, Proper Tears was racing. From 24 starts he had 16 wins and six placings.

He broke track records. Then he broke down. During a race at Wentworth Park Proper Tears tore his hip support muscle, severely crippling him.

Aware of his stud value, and not wanting to run it down by running an injured dog, Corte retired the dog to stud. The world record was gone but you can't disqualify speed.

Corte immediately put him to work, serving 14 bitches straight up. He was working harder than a miner, the workload tougher than average because Proper Tears, bless him, was born with only one testicle.

'That doesn't affect his fertility,' Corte says.

Yet something was wrong. Proper Tears was failing at the job. More than half his bitches failed to take.

Significantly, though, while he worked like a dog all day, Proper Tears' lame hip muscle was getting just the exercise it needed.

Soon, it was as strong as ever.

Corte put him back in work and Proper Tears was soon back at the track. If he sniffed past a bitch Corte would rouse on him, to keep his mind on the job. He remained content the old speed was still there.

At a trial at Singleton, Proper Tears blitzed the field and pulled up in the catching pen. He had broken the track record but had broken his toe as well.

He ran a couple more times but Corte 'knew something was wrong'. X-rays showed bone chips in the toe.

Corte would have to retire him or remove the toe to continue racing the dog.

That's when things started to brighten for Proper Tears. Corte let him keep his toe and put him back to stud, ringing a vet for advice.

He told the vet Proper Tears wasn't firing live rounds. That his equipment worked sometimes but not others.

He [had] retired him once before, he said, put 14 bitches to him and came up with nothing.

Fourteen bitches! Man oh man, said the vet.

You got to start the dog slow. Work him up to it, let him learn what it's all about.

'I put too many bitches in front of him the first time,' Corte says. 'It was my fault. The problem was me.'

Seems poor old Proper Tears didn't have enough time to recover before he was asked to go to war again, a situation any man can understand.

So Corte started him easily. The toe healed slowly, and even more slowly, Proper Tears served only two or three bitches the first three months.

In October last year he had his first litter. And just last Wednesday he sired 11 pups, a time to shed proper tears.

1 September 1997

RECALLING THE PORKY
AND JOE SHOW

Paul Kent

The scene was Chicago last week and Tiger Woods was in town to do Oprah. Across town, Michael Jordan was making it tough for the Indiana Pacers in their play-off series, and on this day, Jordan had a rare day off and was acting mortal again.

Now, when he is acting mortal, Jordan is like many men with too much time and a wife, and he dreams of being something of a golf pro.

He plays off a single-handicap himself, and with Woods in town, it was always going to happen that they would get together for 18 holes. The place was the Merit Club in Libertyville, Illinois.

With his handicap being put to use, it was reported that the pair played 18 holes and at the end Jordan's wallet was somewhat lighter than when he made his way to the course.

Apparently Jordan's handicap couldn't overhaul Woods's course-record 65.

The story recalls a long-ago incident, one that has certainly been told before and should be told again and forever.

It is repeated here not through laziness or absence of ideas, but because it is one worth remembering and the recent matchplay in the State of Illinois seems as good a reason as any to run it.

The story concerned a man named Ed Oliver, a golf pro disqualified from the 1940 US Open because he began the three-way play-off against Lawson Little and Gene Sarazen ahead of schedule. In 1946 he lost the US PGA championship to Ben Hogan, beaten in the final match.

He was runner-up in the 1952 Open and equalled the tournament record of 279 at Augusta in 1953. The only problem was, that was the year Hogan shot 274 for victory.

That's how things pretty much were for Oliver, nicknamed Porky and described as a jolly fat man by the great American sportswriter Red Smith.

Anyway, to that story.

It was during the war and Porky Oliver was assigned to camp somewhere in the south. Smith thought it might have been Fort Bragg.

Heavyweight boxing champion Joe Louis was drafted into the forces and, in between bringing down his handicap, was travelling American bases putting on boxing exhibitions.

Louis worked almost as hard on his golf as he did on his boxing, though, like Jordan, one was considerably more profitable than the other.

Louis went through Fort Bragg on an exhibition and, what do you know, he ran into his mate, Porky Oliver.

'What you doin' way down here, Porky?' Louis asked. 'Whyn't you come up to Camp Shanks where we could play some golf together?'

Things were easier in the forces for Louis, being a celebrity and all.

So Porky Oliver told how he didn't think the idea would sit well with General Marshall, Fort Bragg's chief of staff.

'Hell,' Joe said, 'I know the guy. I'll fix it.'

So a few days later Porky Oliver was transferred, and to Camp Shanks of all places.

Soon Louis was on to Porky about taking a day off, so they could go to New York, or Wilmington, or anywhere they could play golf.

'Look, Joe,' Porky said finally, 'there's a war on, or hadn't you heard? I've just got here and I've got no pass.'

'I'll give you a pass,' Louis said. 'I'm the sergeant.'

So they got to playing golf, and one day Louis, the heavyweight champion of the world who loved nothing better than a hit of golf, cornered Porky Oliver and put it on him for a quick eight holes.

That's all they had time for.

'But you gotta start me two-up,' Joe said.

This sent Porky Oliver into a mad rant, Porky not believing a guy could ask to start two-up in an eight-hole match. 'You gotta,' Joe said, 'I'm the sergeant.'

You've got to understand Porky wasn't too happy when, unlike Tiger

Woods, he was unable to come up with anything like a course record. With Louis's two-stroke handicap, Porky paid up, begrudgingly.

Joe, too, liked to have a bet with his golf.

Almost immediately, something of a conscience developed in Louis.

'Tell you what, Porky,' Joe said. 'Now we'll box four rounds. I'll give you the first three.'

25 May 1998

HARK THE HOOFSTEPS
OF A LITTLE CAVIAR

Andrew Wu

What if Frankel and Black Caviar were to breed?

A race between the king and queen of world racing may be out of the question, but a tryst between the champion pair could produce a $5 million baby with near impossible standards to maintain.

As one prominent breeder, Darley's Henry Plumptre, put it: 'It would be a bit like the firstborn of Prince William and Kate Middleton—there'd be high expectations.'

As Australia's wonder mare prepares to chase her 22nd win from 22 starts, at Royal Ascot early tomorrow, England's unbeaten champion confirmed himself as the best racehorse since 1948, according to one agency, with his stunning, 11-length victory at the famous course on Tuesday. It was his 11th win from as many starts.

When Black Caviar's heroics on the track are done, her lucky owners will decide if she has a date with Frankel—a union welcomed by breeding experts despite their similar pedigrees. The pair have bloodlines from one of the most influential sires in history, Northern Dancer, on both sides of their family trees.

John Messara, the chairman of Arrowfield stud, said horses on the Northern Dancer line can be more susceptible to airway issues and can bleed internally. But in Frankel's and Black Caviar's cases, his presence was from sufficient generations back to accommodate any proposed dalliance.

'It doesn't make it a super-ideal mating but, wow . . . who's to know what might come out of a joining like that,' Messara said.

The offspring of the pair, breeders predict, would most likely be a sprinter-miler that would be most adept up to 1600 m, ruling out any tilt at Australia's most famous race—the Melbourne Cup—but that would not hurt its value.

'Two exceptional athletes, if they were to throw a sound athletic foal, it's the sort of thing dreams are made of,' Messara said.

And how much would it cost to turn that dream into reality? Messara estimated a price tag as high as $5 million at a yearling sale, while Plumptre was a touch more conservative.

A half-brother to three-time Melbourne Cup winner Makybe Diva last year fetched $1.2 million, but 'this would be by a world champion out of a world champion', said Plumptre, who estimated a cost around $4 million. That would still be well short of the record $US13.1 million required in the mid 1980s to buy Seattle Dancer.

But just as timing ruled out any chance of a racetrack meeting between Black Caviar and Frankel, it could also deny a match made in heaven.

Juddmonte Farms stud, which owns Frankel, is unlikely to send such an important stallion to the other side of the world, which means Black Caviar would have to be served during the northern hemisphere breeding season.

Unfortunately for racing fans, the $5 million baby may never become more than a twinkle in Frankel's eye.

22 June 2012

THE VIEW ON VIEWED

Phil Wilkins

Viewed's win in the Melbourne Cup had its annual reverberations across the thoroughbred industry, not least for a mare named Decency, now found at Woodwinds Farm in the mountains behind the Gold Coast, having been rescued two days before she was to be slaughtered in a dogger's yard in Brisbane.

Early last year, the powerful brown mare—who has a terrible scar extending from mid-belly to her flank after she was impaled on a stake while squeezing through a gate with other horses—was discovered in abattoirs by an astute young woman named Rebecca Bates, who was searching for a riding horse for a friend.

There was something about the doleful animal standing at death's door that attracted Rebecca's attention, something that caught her horse lover's eye.

She returned home and told husband Shannon: 'I can't get this mare out of my head. She's so lovely, so quiet, so nice to ride. We have to save her. I've got a feeling there's something good about her pedigree.'

They purchased her. Normally, a sale of her dubious circumstances would cost $400, but she was such a big mare, she cost $600. For want of a better name, they called the unknown, unnamed acquisition Mary, as in mare, mare Mary. They took her back to Woodwinds Farm, a fertile, 40-hectare stud—formerly a dairy farm until deregulation of the industry and drought forced the family to close down the bails—in the picturesque Numinbah Valley on the northern side of the range wrapping around Mt Warning.

Pursuing Rebecca's hunch, they began research. The mare's brands made her traceable through the Australian stud book, and to their delight they discovered she was New Zealand born and bred from a reputable stud farm, that she came to Australia as a yearling and was, in fact, the daughter of the well-credentialled stallion Defensive Play from an obscure mare named Lovers Knot. The word was around about her abattoir fate. 'Mary' was listed as dead.

Further research authenticated Mary as the thoroughbred mare Decency, leaving unanswered the reason for her sad decline to the point she had been about to be put down for dogs' meat. The suspicion was she had a history of slipping foals, further complicated by her terrible belly wound. The Bates basically discounted her for breeding purposes and regarded her as a sale proposition to a nearby riding school.

The day before Decency was to be inspected for purchase by the trail farm operators in July last year, a quail burst out of the grass, startling her and sending her tumbling down a bank, leaving the mare with a fractured wither.

'She was so sore it put paid to her becoming a riding horse,' Rebecca said. 'We nursed her through the injury, and I looked at her and said, "You don't want to leave us, do you? You just want to stay here. But that's all right. You're a lovely, big girl."'

In August last year, equine influenza struck, slamming shut all property gates, preventing movement of horses in Queensland and NSW, with Numin-bah Valley classified as a buffer zone, further delaying the normalisation of horse transport.

The family's ambitions of utilising the new stud's two stallions for servicing mares flew out the window.

In desperation, they covered Decency with Tanabota, their Redoute's Choice–sired stallion.

Shortly after servicing, Rebecca took the mare for a short ride and came back, declaring to her mother-in-law Erica: 'I've had a talk to Mary. She's going into foal. We'll be all right.'

By October of last year, Decency was confirmed in foal. The following month, Efficient won the Melbourne Cup. Efficient was foaled by a mare of Defensive Play, the stallion that sired Decency. Now Decency has her own strapping brown filly foal, nicknamed Tyra, bouncing at her side.

'Decency could not be a better name for her,' Rebecca said. 'She has a wonderful temperament. She's a wonderful dam, everything about her. She's a totally decent mare.'

Browsing through the weights for this year's Melbourne Cup, Shannon Bates spied the nomination of the five-year-old stallion Viewed, trained by

Bart Cummings. Glancing at his breeding, he saw something that made his head spin. Viewed was out of Lovers Knot, the same mare that threw Decency.

So, if cheering was prolonged as Viewed and Bauer duelled along the Flemington straight, and joyous for Lovers Knot's canny owner–breeder Ian Johnson from Finch's Crossing Stud on the Hawkesbury River when Viewed muzzled his way to the Cup, it was even more thunderous in the community hall at Numinbah Valley as locals celebrated their 'connection' with Viewed in the Cup sweep. 'Having Defensive Play as her sire was our first payback for saving Decency, and then learning she was from the same dam as Viewed was our second payback,' Erica said, still glowing in the reflected glory of the Cup, and brandishing a $5 each-way betting ticket that returned her $239.

So, the $600 rescue fee has been more than justified. How much more? One bloodstock agent suggested the broodmare value of Decency, now 11 years old, at about $100,000. Her foal, he thought, depending on her soundness, was also in the vicinity of $100,000. Such is life in the horse breeding game.

14 November 2008

STUMPS

The death of an important sporting identity is a sad moment. But it does give those who knew them well in the journalistic trade the chance to provide insights into and observations of a rich life.

To do this right is a demanding task. Due to the demands of newspapers, there is not the chance to spend days mulling over someone's life. There is no opportunity to revise, re-edit, and let it breathe: the sports editor wants it now. So the writer, usually emotional about the departure of a close friend, has to quickly regain composure, revert to being objective, and, under a demanding deadline—usually minutes or at best hours—come up with perfect prose to get into perspective someone else's life and their impact on others.

Here are five of the best.

GG

THE RIDDLE OF ROEBUCK, WHO GAVE US SO MUCH YET GAVE SO LITTLE AWAY

PETER ROEBUCK

Malcolm Knox

Peter Roebuck worked with dozens of young cricket journalists. If he thought highly of them, he would say: 'Don't get bogged down in this. The world is bigger than cricket, and you should see more of it.'

Of course, many stayed. Journalism is a profession and the true professionals stayed because they enjoyed being good at what they did. Those who took Roebuck's advice, on the other hand, were left with a question. If this man of such intellectual depth and curiosity and the erudition to convert it into a luminous body of work thought that he knows nothing who knows nothing but cricket, what was he still doing in it?

This was the riddle of Roebuck. He was a born mentor who counselled as he wrote, with wisdom and an unimpeded view into the core of your being; yet it was impossible to know what he saw when he turned those eyes on himself.

A few months ago, I met the Somerset writer Stephen Chalke, one of the few to write in the same league as Roebuck. We were agreeing that Roebuck, like the great champions, was enjoying an Indian summer in the past three years. Chalke said: 'Peter could have been anything, a professor of literature or a High Court judge or a political leader.'

Roebuck came down from Cambridge as a lawyer, but became a teacher, a writer, a broadcaster and a cricketer. He played 335 first-class games for Somerset, 298 one-day matches, and more than 100 in a lively second career at

Devon; many Australians first came across him when he began writing cricket articles in *The Age* and *The Sydney Morning Herald* while coaching and teaching at Sydney's Cranbrook School in the mid-1980s. He still played, and for a young cricketer, he was a revelation.

You met batsmen who ended up in Sheffield Shield and Test cricket, but no Waugh or Taylor could teach you as much as Roebuck. We had a gifted outswing bowler who got ball after ball pitching on the stumps and swinging late past the off-bail. Yet first slip might as well have kept his hands in his pockets. Roebuck didn't touch a thing. His discipline opened a window into how real first-class cricketers batted. He had no off-stump, really, because the moment the bowler had one going at top of off, Roebuck would tuck it behind square leg. He didn't make his runs fast, but you could bowl for a week and the only person who decided when Roebuck got out would be Roebuck.

As a writer he cleaved more to the amateur tradition than the professional, a Ranji or Fry when his colleagues were wage-earning Shrewsburys. He didn't use a computer until recently. Once he had given it an amused look, as he might a front-loading washing machine, and went back to his old wringer. He believed something of his daydreamer's art was captured in the process of scribbling on a pad and dictating, with unflappable patience and courtesy, to the Fairfax copytakers. But he wasn't a dogmatist. Getting into strife when a copytaker once misheard 'deceit' for 'defeat' did not convert him to keyboards. He didn't want to put the copytakers out of work.

But when the company was phasing them out anyway, and when he discovered that typing didn't dissolve his ideas, but even enabled him to refine them, he became a wry late adopter. He even had a personal website, never updated, in fact one of the internet's least helpful, but still, he liked to mention it.

Roebuck was as great a broadcaster as he was a writer. Radio returned him to that immediacy between thought and expression. Cricket has been lucky with broadcasters, but never luckier than when Roebuck was painting play from the inside out.

He got inside without trying to court players' company. This could make him frustrating to work with, because News Limited's cricket reporters had comments men such as Mike Coward, Ron Reed and Robert Craddock who were good for a news tip. Roebuck had little idea what news was. The way he saw cricket transcended the day's cut and thrust. Getting close to players was not his focal length: he could see all he needed from the boundary, and what he lost in being outside the loop he more than made up for through intelligence. From a distance, he was more spot-on than anyone.

Did he know himself as clearly? His taste in cricketers tended to the solipsistic: he detested the showy, the shallow, the lazy, the smug. He saw no glamour in wasted talent. Having suffered from class snobbery, he absolutely detested it, and nothing could rile him more, after he became an Australian citizen, than to be described as an Englishman of any kind, even a former one. No reader doubted his pet hates, but they had a consistency. He could put Marylebone and the Zimbabwe Cricket Board in the same category because, no matter the superficial differences, Roebuck saw a unifying class prejudice and political toadyism.

You knew, when he extolled the astringencies of early mornings, cold showers, hard runs and practice, his words were shaped by his battles with Ian Botham, Viv Richards and Joel Garner at Somerset in the 1980s. For many years he and Botham were like a long-divorced couple, exaggerating each other's failings, projecting them on to others. Roebuck's frustration with jazzed-up players like Chris Gayle and Brian Lara seemed to be displaced feelings for Botham. But did Roebuck know he was writing about himself? Hard to say.

It was always hard to say, because there was a carapace of Roebuckness that not even his best friends could get through. It was the one remnant of his English upbringing that he couldn't shake off. He was instinctively generous through counsel or guidance or financial aid, or more formally through friends in coaching or the LBW Trust, a global charity for which Roebuck was a driving force. When he knew he was needed, generosity was his reflex. He helped more than he knew. Yet he was embarrassed by emotions and a hard man to convince of his own good deeds. He made us laugh very much more often than we could make him laugh. Sometimes, as he said, he forgot.

As a cricket writer, he was sui generis. He fitted neither the professional nor the amateur tradition. He was an educator who would have hated to be seen as a pedagogue, an artist who was more comfortable in the audience than on the stage. Was cricket not a big enough world for him? I think for Roebuck, cricket was akin to a religion, not as a system of belief but as a series of texts that, if studied closely enough, could reveal some of life's secrets.

The game had no importance as a vehicle for celebrity or career, but it could offer a portal into a greater world that he had the gift of sharing with his readers, full of magic and mystery, liable to change from black to white and back again in a moment. Chalke thought Roebuck could have been a professor or a judge, but concluded: 'I'm glad he does what he does, because we're the ones who've benefited.'

Peter Roebuck's writing on cricket was unparalleled and contained a remarkable combination of perception and poetry.

14 November 2011

The following gems from Roebuck were compiled by Patrick Smithers

HAROLD LARWOOD
At 85, sprightly, humble, and still speaking in a broad Nottingham accent, Harold Larwood, scourge of Australia, is alive and well and living in Sydney.

Somewhat short-sighted, he potters around home in his slippers, listening to Harry Secombe and brass band records, polishing his mementos, sipping tea with Lois, his 'missus' of 63 years, chatting to such children and grandchildren as pop by.

An old man in repose, his battles lost and won, Larwood lives in a small and comfortable house with nothing grand about it, simply a house in a row of like-minded houses. He lives without pretension and fuss, in his own way and on his own terms, happy with his lot and determined to live on his merits, not on his name. It is this which makes him the most impressive former cricketer I have met.

ALLAN BORDER
A glint-eyed toughie, black hat and stubbled chin, the fellow who plays poker and spits in the spittoon.

MERV HUGHES
Watching from the safety of the press box, it was sometimes difficult to see how Mervyn Hughes took his wickets. Facing him on a slow pitch cleared the matter up.

SHANE WARNE
At the academy, Warne was a brazen dumpling. He did not look much like a cricketer for the supposedly modern era. From the start, though, he was

fascinated with the intricacies and possibilities of spin bowling. Nonetheless, it was impossible to tell him apart from other promising youngsters. But Warne kept improving. He just did not stop. He relished the limelight and was fiercely competitive. Warne is full of bluff. His annual discovery of a new ball is proof enough of that. He understands the value of theatre and the rewards that await a man prepared to lead his life in public.

VIV RICHARDS

He talks about the ability of boxers to destroy an opponent before a fight. He describes the way each boxer stares, forcing lesser men into unsettling introspection. Richards studied the disdainful glares, the upright, confident appearance of champion boxers, and realised that they betrayed not a glimmer of doubt, not a hint of vulnerability.

That is why Richards will not wear a helmet; he will not give the bowler that much credit. It is not that he is immodest—he rarely mentions his achievements, even in private—it is simply that he recognises that, to be the best, he must dominate.

IAN BOTHAM

At school, Ian Botham ran with a gang that beat up other kids if they did not surrender half-a-crown. He failed his 11-plus exams deliberately because he didn't want to go to grammar school, where they played rugby, but instead went to Bucklers Mead secondary with his mates.

He didn't think mathematics would be of any use to him and he was right.

At 17 not one of his friends took his cricket seriously, yet at 19 he was a champion.

PONTING AS A TEENAGER

Ricky Ponting may be the best thing since thick-cut marmalade. He is 17, wears a tiny, defiant goatee beard, a shadow of a moustache, has a pale face and feet that fairly skim across the turf.

Already he is a batsman of intuition, power and confidence, one with a sense of stillness and space and a glint in his eye that belies his calf country, Launceston, the country cousin of a country cousin.

THE AUSTRALIAN GAME

Australian cricket might remain frustratingly Anglo-Saxon in some ways, but it does not exclude anyone and its heroes are down-to-earth characters. Beer is drunk at the matches, and working-men's clothes are worn. A man who scores runs or takes wickets rises through the ranks. A fellow in a bad patch falls back. At practices, players bat in order of arrival and never mind that a first-grader must wait his turn. Crucially, the culture is strong. Even the sixth team plays competitively, with short legs and team talks and so forth.

ZIMBABWE

A letter has arrived from a rising young cricketer in Zimbabwe, a well-educated black player eager to serve his country. It is also a letter from the betrayed, from a cricketing community let down by greedy, arrogant, hate-filled elders.

Of course it is idle to suppose that the opportunists running Zimbabwe Cricket might care about anything except themselves. But their paymasters, the Board of Control for Cricket in India, ought to rethink a close relationship that brings shame on their house. Perhaps, too, obedient television commentators with international voices will remember they are responsible for confronting tyranny.

THE PRESS BOX

The press box in Australia had no pretension or pecking order and this newcomer was treated on his merits, and never mind that he was from the Old Dart, had been to Cambridge and had spent most of his cricket career blocking furiously. By and large, the English cricket writers were unpleasant and miserable.

CORRUPTION

Never forget that at the time of his criminal activities Salman Butt was captaining his country. Never forget that he was at the pinnacle of his career and at the top of a huge cricket community in a nation of 180 million people. Never forget that cricket is one of the few consolations available to the poor of that nation. Never forget that Pakistan is a troubled country with a fractured history and that cricket is its national game. The scale of the betrayal is numbing.

PETER ROEBUCK'S LAST COLUMN . . .

Peter Roebuck

Australian cricket is lucky that it has a few days of respite between the dumbfounding events at Newlands and its next engagement. The break gives coaches, selectors and captain the breathing space needed to collect their thoughts.

The second Test gives the incumbents an opportunity to redeem themselves and the selectors a chance to study the trends. It's no use ditching players for the sake of it, or in response to public demand. Apart from anything else the replacements might not be any better, or ready.

One change is already inevitable. Shaun Marsh's degenerative back problem flared in Cape Town and he was not able to field or bat properly in the second innings. It is a heavy blow for a fine young batsman and for selectors trying to build a team.

Usman Khawaja will replace Marsh, and deserves the opportunity. It is the fate of the spare batsman on tour to miss a lot of cricket and it won't be easy for him to find his form. Still, he is an impressive player and person, and will bring freshness and calm to the order. Otherwise the batting will stay the same.

Assuming Ryan Harris is fit, and he looked sore as the Proteas neared their target, the only other doubt concerns Mitchell Johnson, the most frustrating cricketer in the country. Johnson bowled without pace or swing at Newlands and batsmen have rumbled him. Not until a handful of runs were required for victory did he attain full speed, 145.8 km/h, or take a wicket as Hashim Amla drove loosely.

Since his inspired bursts in the Ashes Test in Perth he had not taken enough wickets to justify his retention. Nor has he scored enough runs since his blistering 123 in Cape Town 32 months ago to be deemed a handy lower-order batsman. Hopes have been dashed he might lead the attack until the next generation is ready.

John Inverarity and company do not take over duties until after the Johannesburg Test and by then Johnson's fate might have been sealed. Although the existing selectors will be loath to make any important decisions for their last match they cannot duck their duties. Michael Clarke, the captain and a selector, was singing Johnson's praises a fortnight ago but his enthusiasm did not extend to the field of play. Trent Copeland and Patrick Cummins are the alternatives, a medium pacer and a rookie.

In the longer term the new panel has more room for manoeuvre.

The collapses in Cape Town were no flukes. These Australians have been weak against swing because they chase the ball rather than play it under their chin. Some get into poor positions. Phillip Hughes is open-chested on the back foot, Ricky Ponting has been shuffling too far across his crease, making them vulnerable to late movement. Australia failed not once but twice, it's just that Clarke saved them in the first innings.

Apart from technical flaws, the collapses raised even more fundamental issues. How long can Shane Watson continue as a front-line bowler and opening batsman? History provides few instances of a cricketer able to sustain both workloads. The time is ripe to put him in the middle order.

Hughes did his utmost in Newlands only to be removed by two deliveries that cut across him and took the shoulder of the bat. He has become a more compact player but his bat still slides sideways and his shoulders are square.

Ponting has been hitting the ball superbly in practice and has been countering the fastest bowlers with aplomb. In the middle he has been missing straight balls because he is hurried and out of position. He remains convinced that it is a bad trot, not permanent, but evidence to the contrary is piling up. He needs to score heavily at the Wanderers.

Brad Haddin also needs to rethink his batting. His reckless shot was a droppable offence and confirmed his confidence is in his boots. He, too, has a single match to turn around his fortunes. A new broom sweeps clean.

Ironically, Johnson, a bowler, is the most likely player to be dropped. However, the team for the first Test against New Zealand has become harder to predict. Mind you, a lot can happen in a week. It just did.

13 November 2011

STATURE OF AN OUTSIZE LEGEND WILL GROW IN TIME

ARTHUR BEETSON

Roy Masters

Only three nights ago [December 2011], Tommy Raudonikis and myself were telling Arthur Beetson stories to a group of trade unionists at a Canberra social club.

Beetson's death yesterday morning on the Gold Coast at age 66 from a heart attack while riding a bike does not mean the yarns will end.

Rather, they will grow, just as he did. 'If I ate four hamburgers, somebody was soon saying it was eight,' he once lamented.

Yet he was a pioneer in so many unseen and unstoried ways.

Raudonikis pointed out that Beetson's move from the eastern suburbs to Parramatta for $42,000 in 1979 triggered the big pay rises in the then-Sydney competition.

Beetson also fought for the right of players to earn money from the media, both of us successfully taking the NSW Rugby League to court over their order barring coaches from writing newspaper columns. He had an instinctive feel for justice.

When Dick Wilson, one of his teammates at Balmain, was sacked for gambling on a match, Beetson fumed over the hypocrisy of Sydney rugby league officials punting heavily on the racetrack.

He helped create the State of Origin legend by captaining Queensland's first team at Lang Park, after being selected from Parramatta's reserve grade.

The punch he delivered to NSW centre and fellow Eels player Mick Cronin is generally viewed as the flame that lit the annual cauldron, ensuring 'state against state' means more than 'mate against mate'. Yet he felt Queensland used him up, dumping him as a selector when Wayne Bennett returned to coach the Maroons.

Beetson was also moved aside as Australian coach in 1984 in a powerplay in which Queensland chief, Ron McAuliffe—his Maroon ally in the resurgence of Queensland—didn't support him. He will have a wry smile on his face in some heavenly field when the Maroons dedicate next year—and the continuation of their winning streak—to him.

Despite a physical honesty and a mien made for laughter, in the last few years he wore the scowl of a man he was not supposed to be.

It sometimes hung like a dark and wrinkled curtain over his face.

Beetson was furious with the Roosters, whom he led to premierships in 1974 and 1975, for sacking him as talent scout, replacing him with someone who had been involved in the Melbourne Storm salary-cap rorts.

Proud of the honour of being the first indigenous sportsperson to captain a national team, he once told me: 'I'm an Australian first, a Queenslander second and a part-Aboriginal third.'

Yet he was the only living team member not to attend the announcement of the Australian Team of the Century.

He would have sensed the politics that pushed him to the front row, despite spending almost all his stellar, skilful days as a second-rower with explosive feet and quick hands.

But he disappointed many of the internationals with whom he played for not respecting them with his presence.

I suspect he may have reordered his priorities in later life, certainly in terms of the treatment of indigenous people in north Queensland.

Beetson once told me about his first training session as coach of Redcliffe. He ushered the players, almost exclusively white, into the bench seats on the side of the oval in the gathering darkness and spoke of his expectations.

Then, when he ordered the drills to begin, 20 indigenous players who had been sitting listening in the branches of the Moreton Bay fig trees, jumped the fence and joined in.

He related the story in a loving, fatherly way, leaving unsaid the obvious point that the young indigenous players felt confident about trialling only because he was coach.

Yet Beetson did not discriminate when settling scores.

He once fought another giant—of Torres Strait heritage—in a north Queensland town.

The fight was stopped by the police, or mutual friends, but Beetson craved resolution.

He could not sleep that night and climbed out of bed around 5 am, drove to the other man's house, woke him up and resumed the fisticuffs.

Only when they were spent, slumped together exhausted in the early light, was everything settled. They then 'moved on', as the modern expression has it.

Sadly, Beetson died before he resolved some strained relationships and there will be the odd guilty, furtive glance away as beer glasses are lifted to farewell him.

He loved life the most when he was with Raudonikis—captain of NSW in that first State of Origin match—touring the western mining towns of Queensland, telling stories.

'He was the best,' Raudonikis said yesterday, his voice choked with a sadness that he knows will never end.

2 December 2011

T.J. SMITH—MASTER OF HIS CRAFT

Max Presnell

T. J. (Tommy) Smith, a racing legend, the master of Tulloch Lodge, died in St Vincent's Hospital yesterday with family—wife Valerie, daughter Gai [Waterhouse], son-in-law Robbie Waterhouse—and his Girl Friday for 37 years, Pauline Blanche, nearby.

Over the final hours, I figure he had a few flashbacks of the triumphs— Tulloch beating Lord in the Queen's Plate in 1960 at Flemington after a long illness . . . Kingston Town taking his third Cox Plate at Moonee Valley.

Hopefully the famous smile flashed again, the eyes sparkled at the memory of the great days of bone-and-muscle, the result of a preparation generated by the eye, a gift which enabled him to prepare about 50 horses every morning. He even had a few minutes to spare to pick up faults in rivals.

It made him Australia's most successful trainer with more than 5,000 wins.

I knew the name 'T. J. Smith' before my ABCs.

Schooled at Kensington Public alongside Tulloch Lodge, I spent most playlunch breaks shortly after I left kindergarten looking over the fence at colts being gelded.

I still recall a little bloke in a big felt hat, shouting instructions in his shrill voice.

My father, Roy, managed the Doncaster Hotel, down the road in Doncaster Avenue, which proved our university. Patrons included strappers, battling trainers, has-been jockeys, bludgers, urgers, tipsters, standover merchants, SP bookmakers, rafflers and the odd gunman.

Tommy was the best-known graduate and Roy was the champion trainer's greatest admirer.

'Nobody started further behind than Tommy Smith, he was a Tokyo drinker,' he would tell me—a reference to a public bar area where there were 'more nips than in Japan'.

In those days, the champion trainer was known as 'Two-bob Tommy'—a reference to the price of a ticket for a sweep in which he was involved.

'When Tommy started to train a few winners, he came to me and said I should stop the other drinkers from biting him,' Dad said, adding that his reply was that considering the past, this was hardly possible.

'Tommy said if this was the case, he would never come back again and he was true to his word. He never did . . .'

Of course, in those days the popular tip, out of the side of a hundred mouths in the Doncaster, was that Smith would end up in the dung pit.

However, the rebel with a cause went on to change the face of racing and didn't tug a forelock to do it.

In fact, he was described by newspaper tycoon of the time, Ezra Norton, as a 'bloody smart Alec', according to Smith's biographer, Kevin Perkins.

At the time, trainers were mainly stern individuals who made Jack Denham look like Jerry Seinfeld.

To get a correct jockey engagement from them a few days before a race was regarded as a scoop. But it was just a matter of asking Tommy.

His first real horse was Bragger, and Smith took a hint from the name. He sought the headlines others ducked like the plague.

'I look at a big back-page story and see that I've got for nothing what would cost David Jones [the department store] three grand,' he said.

Owners were treated with reverence.

One of the great stories concerning Smith was when he returned from a buying spree in New Zealand. Prospective owners were being told in Tatts Club in Sydney what horses he had bought for them.

One kept on interrupting with the plea: 'What have you got for me, Tommy?'

Smith replied: 'If you don't stop making a pest of yourself, you'll get nothing.'

Watching the master in action at Randwick was a revelation.

He was unique because he could work so many horses, so professionally, shouting instructions like a general on a battlefield.

When it was over, and the typhoon subsided, Tommy would give a press conference.

Over 40 years I knew him as a pressman, Tommy never gave me a bum steer. Possibly he was wrong a few times, tipped a few losers, but if he told you something and there was a change he would pursue you to the end of the earth to set it right.

Tommy was a tough man, and certainly had his critics. You don't get from the 'Two-bob Tommy' to a Rolls-Royce by being a soft touch.

On the other side, he was the much-loved family man, the subject of a poem by his wife, the father who took his daughter to Centennial Park to play with the ducks, a good friend.

Jack Elliott, the Melbourne racing writer who rode shotgun with the trainer through many experiences, maintains Tommy's biggest thrill was not on the racetrack.

'Tears streamed down his face when [vet] Percy Sykes told him that he wouldn't have to put Tulloch down when it was thought he would have to,' Elliott recalled yesterday.

The master of Tulloch Lodge may have been a demanding taskmaster and insisted everybody worked at his pace.

Darcy Christie, his longtime Melbourne foreman, would hear a jet overhead and exclaim: 'Here comes Tommy.'

But ask Pauline Blanche if you have any doubts about his heart.

'He loved to be around women, he said it gave a gathering tone,' she said yesterday about this remarkable man who was regarded as being 'blokey'.

Yesterday afternoon the end of a remarkable life was announced, but it was business as usual for Tulloch Lodge, the empire he founded. Gai Waterhouse had three winners on her birthday at Wyong, maintaining the winning tradition.

The subject of his 'foaling date' and the place of birth weren't subjects Tommy liked to discuss.

Some records say it was on September 2, 1918, at Jindabyne or Goolgowi, and if that's what he wanted, who am I to argue, although some may say he was older.

He was actually born at Jembaicumbene, near Braidwood, but couldn't pronounce it so he went for the easy way out.

While he steered clear of birthdays, Tommy was a stimulating conversationalist.

On jockeys who don't get the opportunities they deserve?

'Bull—, you give me a jockey you can put on five favourites and get five good rides, not necessarily winners, and I'll show you a topliner.'

Those who couldn't didn't last long at Tulloch Lodge.

On three-year-old fillies?

'You don't know whether they will come back after a two-year-old campaign until they show it in a race.'

Overall, though, I'll remember Tommy best for his humour and flashing smile.

How would you thank a man for as many laughs as he trained winners? For the stories and the wit, roughshod perhaps.

Even in times of duress, he never lost his spark. Like when Bart Cummings was getting the glory about 20 years ago and Smith won a good race.

'Just got to pick up the odd crumb off the rich man's plate,' he declared.

Most Fridays, Tom would ring the office for the scandal and a little banter.

Last week he missed me but he caught up at Rosehill races on Saturday.

'Studying the stockmarket yesterday afternoon were you?'

'Well, it wouldn't worry you because all yours is in Switzerland.'—Presnell.

'Not bloody likely. It's at Kenso, Coogee, Randwick and Vaucluse . . .'
—Smith.

'In biscuit tins.'—Presnell.

'You've got to be kidding. I gave that away 50 years ago when I used to keep my money in a cardboard box under the bed. Black money's a joke, you can't do anything with it. I pay tax and put it into property . . .'

I switched the point of attack: 'Any chance of you talking about horses?

'There's a two-year-old by Bluebird. He's pretty good . . .'

The eye was still working, and Tommy, the like of whom I'll never see again, wouldn't tell me wrong.

3 September 1998

LITTLE CLIFFY SHUFFLES INTO OUR HEARTS

CLIFF YOUNG

Peter Stone

Cliffy Young was lying in the Holbrook District Hospital in 1985 and, once again, he told me he was going to quit. He'd said it before, usually lying in a caravan or campervan somewhere with his body, frail by anyone's standards, racked with pain.

'Never again. I've seen the light, mate. I don't want to kill myself,' he said once more, and for a fleeting moment I believed him.

We didn't want him to kill himself either, for the little man in gumboots had given us so much in an increasingly materialistic world in which the doctrine of so many was self-interest, where egos are inflated and wallets correspondingly so.

I thought back then that no longer would it be the loneliness of the long-distance runner for Cliffy Young, no longer the agony which had forced him out of that year's Sydney-to-Melbourne ultra-marathon. He had earned his rest.

I should have known better. Cliffy was born to run and the tragedy was that he didn't discover it earlier. It wasn't until 1983, when Young was aged 61, that he first imposed himself on our consciousness.

Melbourne sports store proprietor John Toleman, a former professional middle-distance runner of quality, had in his employ George Perdon, also a professional distance runner, who was without the publicity machine of Irishman Tony Rafferty who, in the early 1980s, was setting remarkable solo endurance running records.

A race was proposed, with Toleman putting up $10,000 for the winner. Sponsorship was obtained from Westfield shopping centres and entries were invited from other ultra-marathon runners. Young reckoned he could run a bit. He always did, rounding up the cows in his gumboots, and shuffling his way along many a lonely bush track in the harsh Otway Ranges near Colac, west of Melbourne.

Australia unbolted the America's Cup from the New York Yacht Club earlier that year, and then followed the remarkable tale of Cliffy Young. Perdon and Rafferty, along with the other eight runners in the inaugural 875-kilometre hike from Sydney to Melbourne, didn't get a look in as, while others slept on the first night on the road, Young did a runner more than three hours before them and was never sighted again.

Shy, almost embarrassed, he hid briefly before the victory presentation at Doncaster in Melbourne's eastern suburbs. He was so uncomfortable in the public spotlight that when he was presented at many functions afterwards, he would absent himself to the toilet to get away from the fuss.

I wrote on many of Cliff's runs—the old Colac six-day race, attempts on the world 1000 km record around the Colac garden square. The local council wanted to erect a statue of him in that square, but he declined, saying he didn't want birds sitting on his image and doing what comes naturally.

We combined to write his autobiography, commissioned by a small Melbourne publisher, and he was a delight to work with, save for the days taping his yarns in the 100-plus degree temperature at Rock Bottom Farm outside Colac, which he'd purchased a couple of years after his victory.

It was just that, Rock Bottom, where the tomato plants had turned up their toes in the parched earth and the blowflies blew their darndest.

Cliffy wrote stuff down in laborious longhand, with a rich use of language and anecdotes that belied his lack of a formal education past primary school, and needed only a nip and a tuck. His mind was razor-sharp, his humour laconic but mischievous.

Sadly, when the manuscript was completed, the publisher no longer thought it would sell. The words lay dormant for several years until an even smaller publisher, a running enthusiast from Gippsland in Victoria, rescued the project.

I hope Cliffy made a few dollars from it, but I never did ask. My only reward was the friendship of a great character whose spirit was surely that of the early pioneers of this country.

Cliffy is finally at rest. He died on Sunday, aged 81, and his funeral was held at Caloundra on the Sunshine Coast on Wednesday, with a memorial service [to be held] in Colac next Wednesday. Over the past four years, he'd suffered a series of minor strokes and, in his final weeks, could barely walk, using a frame to assist him.

Farewell, Cliffy. You were an original, a bushwise man of simple tastes, yet so rich in the values of life.

8 November 2003

A DARK DAY AS SPORTS COMMUNITY MOURNS ONE OF ITS OWN

ROD ALLEN

Ian Fuge

There has been a lot of talk about dark days in Australian sport recently. And today, as many of us in the sports media industry come to terms with the sudden death of one of our own, we can only ask ourselves what things we should take most seriously, and what things are not so important.

We sports reporters, editors, media managers and others take ourselves way too seriously at times. All that hyperbole, all that end-of-the-world stuff, was put firmly into context when the terrible news began filtering through that Rod 'Rocket' Allen had been found dead after a party at which many of us had been celebrating the birthday of another colleague, Fairfax sports reporter Rupert Guinness.

The awful rumour soon became fact. One stunned phone call followed another among Rod's wide circle of friends. The reaction every time was the same: disbelief. How could this happen? We were with him last night. He'd been the life and soul of the party. Then anger and tears—what a bloody waste.

Then the tributes began coming in—from the Australian Olympic Committee, the Football Federation of Australia, the Australian Turf Club, on Twitter, from journos at News Ltd and Fairfax, who all thought of him as their own.

Rod was found dead, having fallen from a cliff sometime in the small hours after the celebration on Cockatoo Island in Sydney Harbour. He was 45 years old.

His future had seemed rich. He'd been talking all night in that animated way of his about the exciting future of horse racing in this city with the redevelopment of Randwick racecourse. He was still on a high after watching the Western Sydney Wanderers thump Newcastle 3–0 the night before, talking about the amazing success of the new Parramatta-based A-League club and how proud he was to be involved with it. It was typical Rod, really. Opinionated, excited, loud, laughing, optimistic, infectiously enthusiastic.

Those are the words that tell the real story of Rocket, the sort of man he was. But for the record, as Rod would have appreciated, here's the background story.

Rod was brought up in Arcadia in Sydney's hills district, the son of a newspaperman—his dad was a typesetter for News Ltd. From an early age Rod was a Parramatta tragic. A real Parramatta tragic. If you had a couple of spare hours, just mention the P word to Rocket and he would happily fill them for you, whether you liked it or not.

What little time wasn't taken up by rugby league was given over to tennis. He was a talented player as a young man.

Rod's other passion was journalism, a career he pursued with the same determination as he did sport. He joined News Ltd as a cadet in 1986 and went on to work in a variety of reporting roles, most notably as a gun business journalist and also as a political hack in Canberra.

He joined Fairfax in 1998, first as chief of staff on *The Sun-Herald*. Those who worked under him still speak of him in almost reverential tones. Rod, the reporters say, was the best boss they ever had. He went on to become sports editor of *The Sun-Herald* and then, in 2004, took over as managing editor of sport for *The Sydney Morning Herald* and *The Sun-Herald*.

Rod brought with him an absolute commitment to being the best. He had an outstanding news sense and a clear vision of what he wanted his sports coverage to look like. His leadership was consistent: keep fighting for the best story, keep pushing for the best angle, keep chasing the exclusive picture. His four-year tenure as our boss still resonates today and the standards he set are the ones we abide by now.

Rod left Fairfax Media in 2008, taking a redundancy to pursue a career as a media consultant. His services were called upon by a number of sporting bodies, but he chiefly worked for the Football Federation Australia and the Australian Turf Club.

He managed the media for the Socceroos during the 2010 World Cup campaign and was also heavily involved in the FFA's push to win the World Cup hosting rights for Australia. He was shattered when Qatar won the bid. But he stayed involved in football. Having embraced the sport with the enthusiasm of the newly converted, he grew ever more passionate about football.

Rod was also a key figure in horse racing, helping the ATC with much of its media strategy over the past few years. He shared his passion for the sport with his mum, Diane. All of which, of course, is mere detail. It means nothing today. What matters is that Rod's mum and dad have lost their son, his sisters their brother, his wife her husband, and his friends a terrific bloke we were proud to call a mate.

This is indeed a dark day.

1 April 2013